SELLING

PRINCIPLES AND PRACTICE

RAMANUJ MAJUMDAR
Indian Institute of Management Calcutta, Kolkata

TAPOSH GHOSHAL
Central University of Jharkhand, Ranchi

JAICO PUBLISHING HOUSE
Ahmedabad Bangalore Bhopal Bhubaneswar Chennai
Delhi Hyderabad Kolkata Lucknow Mumbai

Published by Jaico Publishing House
A-2 Jash Chambers, 7-A Sir Phirozshah Mehta Road
Fort, Mumbai - 400 001
jaicopub@jaicobooks.com
www.jaicobooks.com

SELLING: PRINCIPLES AND PRACTICE
ISBN 978-81-8495-457-9

First Jaico Impression: 2013

Printed by
Pashupati Printers (P) Ltd.
1/429/16, Gali No.1, Friends Colony, Industrial Area
G.T. Road, Shahdara, Delhi - 110 095

Dedicated to the fond memory of

Late Soumyendra Nath Brahmachary,
Our Spiritual Master & Acharya, Dev Sangha, Deoghar.
Our Parents,
Late Gita & Saroj Kumar Majumdar
& Late Nomita & Hemendra Nath Ghoshal.

Preface

The last mile usually determines the success of any product in the marketplace. Selling skills are that rare set of capabilities that ultimately define the strength of this 'last mile'. The agility of the sales force and its ability to manage the market provides the basis for delivering value to the customers.

This book is aimed at sensitizing the sales professionals with a set of skills that can be learnt. If these concepts are put to use systematically, it would make sales professionals highly effective in a competitive market setting.

Organization of the Book

The book consists of eleven chapters and includes concepts, examples, and case studies. For the sake of simplicity, each chapter is organized as a series of discrete steps, performed in a defined sequence. This will enable sales executives to deal with various issues related to sales management systematically and to perform their role effectively.

The methods, tools and techniques outlined in the book as well as exercises included at the end of each chapter will help the sales manager consider how the same issues can be applied in real life sales management arena. Even if salespersons intuitively follow many of the steps outlined in the book, they can increase their performance level and be successful in this field. In reality, many of these steps may be performed simultaneously. Some of these steps may overlap and interact in various ways. Nevertheless, the purpose is to help salespeople understand the nuances of sales management.

Uniqueness of the Book

Instead of offering a theoretical treatise, the focus of this book is on addressing the challenges being faced by a salesperson in his day-to-day work, and to help resolve many practical problems pertaining to selling. The topic-related short cases and examples, and various topics related to selling are explained in simple language. The precepts, tools and techniques elaborated in this book are intended to enhance the salesperson's selling capabilities in the marketplace. Occasionally, important tips are given that would strengthen the core capabilities of a salesperson.

The book is intended to become a practical handbook or a companion for every sales professional. It would act as a ready reckoner. At times it would provide useful guidance to face many difficult situations.

Ramanuj Majumdar
Taposh Ghoshal

Contents

1 What Do People Buy?

"I buy expensive suits. They just look cheap on me."

–Warren Buffett

CHAPTER OUTLINE

- Understanding consumer behaviour
- The consumer 'black box'
- Spectrum of consumer purchase decisions
- Behind a buying decision
- Triggers to buying behaviour
- Social influences
- The pattern of customer decision making
- Ways to address consumer needs
- Things to remember

OBJECTIVES

After studying this chapter, you will be able to:

- Understand customers and what influences them to buy
- Understand how the consumers' personal characteristics and psychological aspects affecting their buying decisions
- Analyze the consumers' decision process and explain the stages of the buyers' decisions and how they are adopted

Opening Case: A Customer's Agony

Ramesh looked unhappy and fatigued when he returned home that day. He walked through the door, put down his briefcase and went for a bath. His behaviour seemed quite unusual to Nirmala, his wife of nine years. Ramesh was a young energetic man, with a positive approach towards work and life. Born in a middle-class family, he had completed his engineering and ICWA and was working as a cost accountant with a multinational company in Kolkata. He had a taste for good things and liked to have a good quality of life. However, he was not frivolous and looked for value for money in whatever he bought.

As Ramesh came out and sat down with a cup of tea with his wife, Nirmala asked him gently what had happened to him. As soon as she uttered these words, Ramesh suddenly shouted, "What do these people think of themselves? They do not know how to behave with customers? Do they think that people go to their showroom only because things are cheap out there?"

Ramesh went on in this tone, Nirmala calmed him down, gave him a glass of water and asked him what had really happened that made him so angry?

What Ramesh finally came out with was startling! During the day in his office, Ramesh came to know from one his colleagues that Shoeworld had opened a very good showroom near their office, which had a wide variety of shoes at a reasonable price. As the showroom was new, they were also giving discounts. For quite some time Ramesh had wanted to buy a pair of shoes and he immediately decided to go to the showroom on his way back home and buy a pair for himself.

As he approached the store, he got a shock. There was a long queue of customers waiting to enter the store. A security guard with a baton in his hand, was standing at the entrance, regulating the crowd. Somehow, Ramesh was able to enter the store. The place was crowded with no place for customers to sit. Salesmen were just not paying attention to customers nor were they listening to them properly. Their responses to customers' queries were curt to the point of rudeness! Their body language reflected a negative connotation too. Ramesh wondered if he had come to the right place.

As Ramesh was contemplating whether to remain there or go out, a salesman appeared and asked what he wanted? Ramesh told him what was in his mind. To this the salesman immediately pointed his fingers towards the showcase and said, "What are you waiting for? You should go and select the design and tell me the design number so that I can give you the shoe." Ramesh politely asked whether he could show him any other designs. The salesman just shrugged his shoulders. Ramesh started to leave the store. No one paid him any attention nor did anyone try to stop him. The bitter experience left him feeling humiliated and dejected. On his way home he thought to himself – What do people really buy – A product or something else?

Questions

1. What was Ramesh really interested in when he went to buy a pair of shoes?
2. What do customers really look for when they purchase something?

WHAT DO PEOPLE BUY?

Integral Design for Programmed Learning

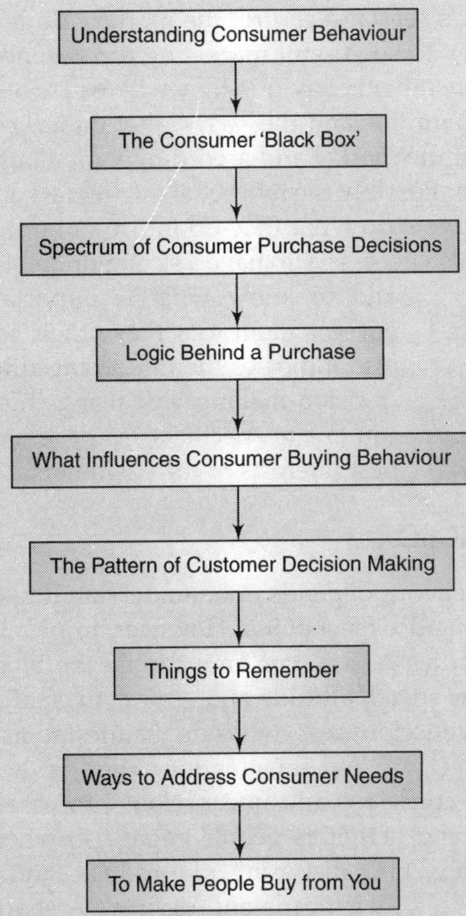

"Consumers can, and often do, spend $88 for a Lacoste polo shirt when one of comparable quality can be garnered for half the price. And consumers can spend in excess of $300 on a Dualit toaster when $30 will produce one of similar, if not equal, functional value to most consumers. That's because power threats are driving consumers to seek perceived status from expensive brands."

Prof. Adam Galinsky
Kellogg School of Management
Northwestern University

UNDERSTANDING CONSUMER BEHAVIOUR

Consumer behaviour is the most unpredictable element in a business. Most of the time a consumer has certain ideas while making a purchase. It is the duty of the marketer to understand the consumer's mind when he or she is taking a buying decision. Today consumers are in the driver's seat and control the market. Understanding why a customer buys what he does is the key to successful marketing today. Once marketers learn how the "why" drives and directs consumer behaviour, they will realize how to get them to buy more products. Marketers need to understand the "why" that underlies consumer psychology, in order to predict the future of the market and accordingly plan out their product, promotion, pricing and selling strategies. Possibly the most challenging task in any marketing deal is the understanding as to why buyers do what they do (or do not do). While such knowledge is critical for salespeople, it is also necessary to have a strong understanding of buyer behaviour and to know what is important to the customer. This enables them to achieve their sales targets successfully. It also indicates the important influences it has on customer decision-making and using this information, salespeople can create specific sales programmes that could be in the best interests of the customers.

> Future marketing success lies in understanding why people buy along with who, what, where, how, how much and how often.

THE CONSUMER 'BLACK BOX'

The success of any sales endeavour depends upon understanding the customers – their likes, dislikes, preferences, hopes and expectations. However, ironically, this is one of the most difficult parts of all sales activities. A customer's mind is like the 'black box' of an aircraft, which records airplane data such as speed, altitude and crew conversations. The customer's mind is made up of intellect and consciousness, which is manifested as combinations of thought, perception, memory, emotion, will and imagination. Mind is the stream of consciousness, it includes all of the brain's conscious and unconscious processes. It is therefore necessary to understand 'the process and activities people engage in when searching for, selecting, purchasing, using, evaluating, and disposing of products and services so as to satisfy their needs and desires'. A sharp salesperson must make an attempt to understand the buyer's decision making process, both individually and in groups. He must also study the characteristics of individual consumers and the behavioural variables in an attempt to understand people's needs and wants.

> Like the black box, the customer's mind, with all its rationality and emotions, has always been a puzzle for salespersons.

The factors affecting how customers make decisions are extremely complex. Buyers' behaviour is deeply rooted in their psychological and sociological background and since every person in the world is different, it is impossible to frame simple rules that explain how buying decisions are made. But experts who have spent many years analyzing customer activity have presented us with useful "guidelines" as to how someone decides whether or not to make a purchase.

SPECTRUM OF CONSUMER PURCHASE DECISIONS

In general, consumers face four types of purchase decisions:

Fig. 1.1 *Purchase Decisions*

New Small Purchases

These purchases are the result of some new needs of customers, which though insignificant in terms of need, money or other factors, are required by the consumer to fulfill his need at that point of time. Such purchases are mostly triggered by emotional needs which could be considered necessary by the customers at that point of time. Examples may include fancy or much publicized, low cost products.

Small Re-purchases

These are mostly regular purchases and often the consumer returns to purchase the same product without giving much thought to other product options (mainly to replenish a stock situation). The product that is "at an arm's length of the customer" succeeds in such situations.

Major New Purchases

> In a competitive sales situation, where every company tries hard to push the product from the counters on to the customers, it is important for salespersons to consider the above stated consumer decisions making and fine-tune the elements of the marketing mix.

These purchases are the most difficult of all purchases because the product being purchased is important to the consumer, is generally high priced, has a long life and the consumer has little or no previous experience regarding these decisions. The consumer's lack of confidence in making this type of decision, often (but not always), requires him to engage in an extensive decision-making process which, might include acquiring knowledge about the product, considering the experiences of existing consumers or getting expert opinion. In such situations, advertising also plays an important role in the decision-making process.

Major Re-purchases

These purchase decisions are also important to the consumer but the consumer feels confident about making these decisions since they have previous experience purchasing the product.

The four '**Ps**' – Product, Price, Promotion and Place – will eventually determine the extent of success of salespersons and decide which product the customers will ultimately buy.

MOTIVES BEHIND A BUYING DECISION

It is important for us to understand why customers or prospects buy products or services. It seems only natural to consider why a company is considering buying from a particular company, and not others! It is often said, "As individuals; people buy for two primal reasons, to seek pleasure or avoid pain". It is also said that people buy something that either relieves them from stress, minimizes their problems, eases their lives and helps to give them happiness.

Fundamentally, the consumer purchase decision can be related to basic human needs and buying behaviour. It is easier to understand a person's beliefs than to understand what motivates him. Motivations can be physical, intellectual and emotional and can be based on needs and wants. They can be triggered by instinct, or learnt after extensive interaction with society and the environment. Other factors that influence beliefs are – knowledge, events, peer pressure, past experiences and perhaps most interestingly enough, the positive or negative thoughts of others.

> People buy essentially for two reasons – to solve problems and to feel good. To solve problems companies come up with innovative products. To make people feel good, one should take care of customers through excellence in service.

TRIGGERS TO BUYING BEHAVIOUR

People buy essentially for two reasons – to solve problems and to feel good. To solve problems, companies come up with innovative products. To make people feel good about themselves, one should take care of customers through excellence in service.

It is believed that people buy with their hearts, no matter how much their brain cells tell them otherwise. However, studying the behavioural pattern, it can be said that consumers' buying behaviour is guided by the factors shown in Figure 1.2.

Psychological Factors

Psychological factors are founded upon Maslow's hierarchy of needs. It is depicted in Figure 1.3 as a pyramid consisting of five levels. This theory states that the physiological needs are met first. Once the lower order needs are met, a human being gradually tries to satisfy the higher order needs.

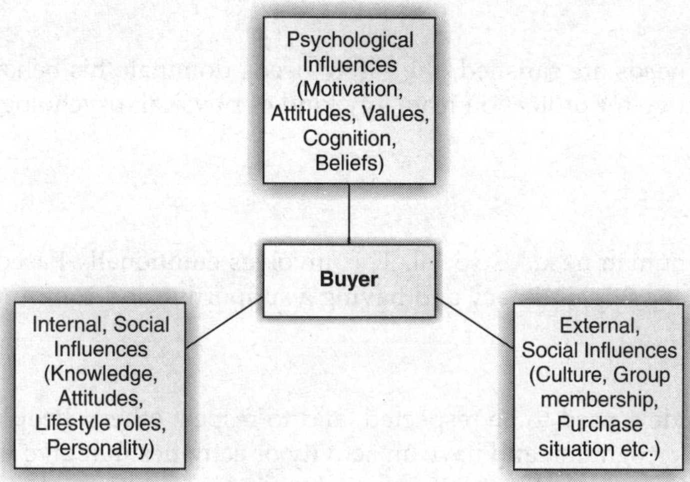

Fig. 1.2 *Factors that Influence Buying Behaviour*

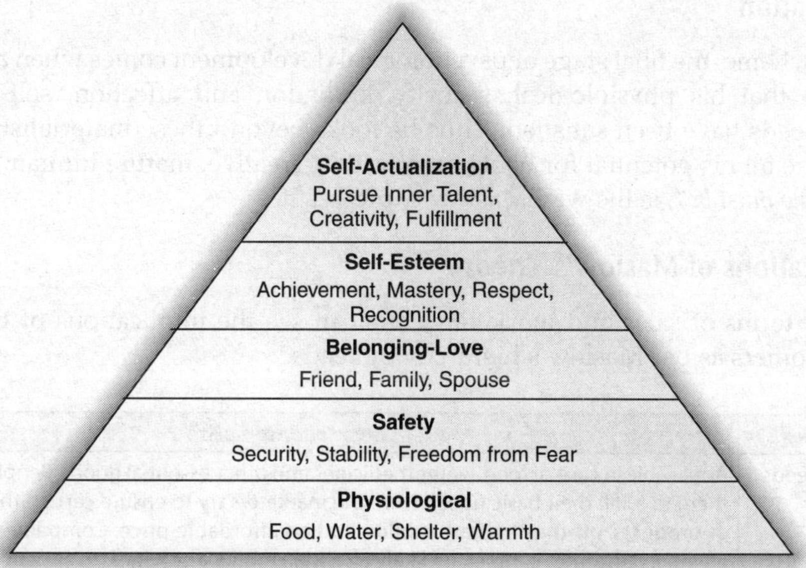

Fig. 1.3 *Maslow's Hierarchy of Needs*

Physiological Needs

These are the basic human needs such as food, warmth, water, and other body related needs. These are also called the primary needs of any human being.

Safety Needs

Once the physical needs are satisfied, the safety needs dominate his behaviour. The safety need includes the urge for protection from any kind of physical, psychological, economic or social insecurity.

Social Needs

The third layer of human needs is social. This involves emotionally-based relationships in general, such as friendship, intimacy and having a supportive and communicative family.

Esteem Needs

Esteem needs include a need to be respected, and to respect others. People need to engage themselves to gain recognition and have an activity or activities that give the person a sense of contribution, to feel accepted and self-valued, be it in a profession or hobby. Imbalances at this level can result in low self-esteem and inferiority complexes.

Self-actualization

In Maslow's scheme, the final stage of psychological development comes when an individual feels assured that his physiological, security, affiliation and affection, self-respect, and recognition needs have been satisfied. Thus he looks beyond these materialistic needs and seeks to realize all his potential for being an effective, creative, mature human being. "*What a man can be, he must be*", is the way Maslow expresses it.

Sales Implications of Maslow's Theory

Translated in terms of sales and marketing, one can see the implications of the following needs of customers as per Maslow's hierarchy of needs.

Hierarchy of needs	*Implication for sales*
Physiological needs	Applicable in case of food, water, medicines and other essential goods. People will consume them to fulfill their basic needs. Here the marketers try to ensure certain threshold quality of products, off-the-shelf availability and an affordable price. Companies who reach or maintain customer contact are likely to obtain more patronage.
Safety needs	Applicable to all products where safety is most important for consumers. Effective communication focusing on safety attributes. Examples are: Aquaguard water purifiers, mineral water, hygienic foods, earthquake resistant steel, etc.
Social needs	These include all products that help people enhance their social interactions, friendships, intimacy and interact with a supportive and communicative family. Examples are: Computers, Internet, telephone/mobile services, event management, etc.
Esteem needs	All products that, people think define their social status. For example: The latest models of television sets, mobile phones, furniture, carpets, crockery, automobiles etc.
Self-actualization	There is little implication of this stage, as here an individual transcends materialistic needs.

SOCIAL INFLUENCES

There are many factors that may affect this process as an individual goes through the process of a purchase decision. These factors may be categorized into three main types: Internal, External and Situational. These influences are not mutually exclusive; rather they are all interconnected and together influence a consumer to arrive at a purchase decision.

Internal Influences

Influences that are intrinsic in nature and emerge out of an inherent need from within fall in this category. Such needs are triggered mainly by knowledge, attitude, personality, lifestyle, roles and motivation of an individual and influence his decision-making process to a great degree.

> Normally a purchase decision is made on the basis of the level of knowledge a person has about the product and its performance. Knowledge is the sum of all information known by a person.

Knowledge

What is knowledge to an individual depends on how an individual's perceptual filter makes sense of the information he is exposed to.

Marketers conduct research to gauge consumers' level of knowledge regarding their product. Thus, aligning the marketing mix to enhance the knowledge level enables the consumers to gather more information and in the process increase their inclination to buy the product.

Attitude

In simple terms attitude refers to what a person feels or believes about something. Attitude may be reflected in how an individual acts based on his or her beliefs. Once formed, attitudes can be very difficult to change. Thus, if a consumer has a negative attitude toward a particular issue it will take considerable effort to change what they believe to be true.

> Sellers facing consumers with a negative predisposition toward their product must identify the key issues shaping a consumer's attitude and then reconfigure the marketing mix to change their predisposition in a positive direction.

For sellers competing against strong rivals to whom loyal consumers exhibit a positive attitude, an important strategy could be to see why consumers feel positive toward the competitor and then try to meet them on these issues. Alternatively, a seller may try to locate customers who feel negatively toward the competitor and then increase awareness among this group.

Personality

In most, but not all, cases the behaviour one projects in a situation is similar to the behaviour a person exhibits in another situation. While one's personality is often interpreted by those salespersons that they interact with, the person has their own vision of their personality, which may or may not be the same as how others view us.

Most of the time consumers make purchase decisions to support their self-concept. An exercise to identify how customers view themselves and how they perceive the product in line with their self-concept may give sellers an insight into products and promotion options that may not be readily apparent.

> An individual's personality may be defined as a set of perceived personal characteristics that are consistently exhibited, especially when one acts in the presence of others.

Lifestyle

Lifestyle is an indicator of one's personality and is often determined by how one spends one's time and money. It relates to the way one lives through the activities and interests he or she expresses. In simple terms it is what everyone values in life.

Products and services are purchased to support consumers' lifestyles. Sellers have tried hard to understand how consumers live their lives since this information is the key to developing products, suggesting promotional strategies and even determining how best to distribute products.

Roles

Roles represent the position one feels he holds or others feel one should hold when dealing in a group environment. These positions carry certain responsibilities, yet it is important to understand that some of these responsibilities may, in fact, be perceived and not spelled out or even accepted by others. In support of their roles, consumers will make product choices that may vary depending on which role they are assuming. As an illustration, a person who is responsible for selecting snack food for an office party which his boss will attend is more likely to choose some higher quality products than he would normally consume for himself or his family.

> Highly motivated consumers will want to get mentally and physically involved in the purchase process. Not all products have a high percentage of highly involved customers (e.g., milk) but marketers who market products and services that may lead to a high level of consumer involvement should prepare options that will be attractive to this group.

Sales promotional campaigns must show how their products benefit consumers as they perform certain roles. Typically the underlying message of such a promotional approach is to suggest that using the advertiser's product will help raise one's status in the eyes of others while using a competitor's product may have a negative effect on status.

Emotions

Motivation relates to our desire to achieve a certain outcome. For instance, when it comes to making purchase decisions, customers' motivation could be affected by such issues as financial position (e.g., *Can I afford the purchase?*), time constraints (e.g., *Do I need to make the purchase quickly?*), overall value (e.g., *Am I getting my money's worth?*), and perceived risk (e.g., *What happens if my choice decision turns out to be bad or inferior?*).

Motivation is also closely tied to the concept of 'involvement', which relates to how much effort the consumer will exert in making a decision.

> Culture represents the behaviour, beliefs and, in many cases, the way people are influenced through interaction or observing other members of society. In this way much of what he does is shared behaviour, passed from one member of society to another.

External Influences

Consumers' purchasing decisions are often affected by factors that are not in their control, but have a direct or indirect impact on how one lives and what he or she consumes.

Culture/Sub-culture

This happens more within smaller community/groups (or sub-cultures) to which they belong to. For instance, sub-cultures exist where groups share similar values in terms of religious beliefs, geographic location, special interests and other factors.

As part of their efforts to convince customers to purchase their products, salespersons often use cultural representations, especially in promotional appeals. The objective is to connect to consumers using cultural references that are easily understood and often embraced by the consumer. By doing so, salespersons hope that consumers will feel more comfortable, as they can relate better to a product that fits in with their cultural values.

> Smart marketers use strong research efforts in an attempt to identify differences in how a sub-culture behaves. These efforts help pave the way for spotting trends within a sub-culture, which can be capitalized on for gaining more control over the market and customers

Other group membership

In addition to cultural influences, consumers belong to many other groups with which they share certain characteristics and which may influence purchase decisions. Often these groups have opinion leaders who have a major influence on what the customer purchases. Some of the basic groups one may belong to include:

- **Social class** – Represents the social standing one has within society based on such factors as income level, education, occupation.
- **Family** – One's family situation can have a strong effect on how purchase decisions are made.
- **Reference groups** – Most consumers simultaneously belong to many other groups with which they associate or, in some cases, feel the need to disassociate from.

> Salespersons can take advantage of decisions made in uncontrollable situations either by using promotional methods to reinforce a specific selection of products or using marketing methods that attempt to convince consumers that a situation is less likely to occur if the marketer's product is used.

Identifying and understanding the groups consumers belong to is a key strategic input for many salespersons. Doing so helps identify target markets, develop new products, and create appealing marketing propositions to which consumers can relate.

Consumption situation

A purchase decision can be strongly affected by the situation in which consumers find themselves. In general, a situation comprises the circumstances a person faces when making a purchase decision, such as presence of guests at home, outdoor or indoor consumption, the nature of the physical environment, the emotional state, or time constraints.

In a nutshell, the various factors influencing purchasing are as depicted in Figure 1.4.

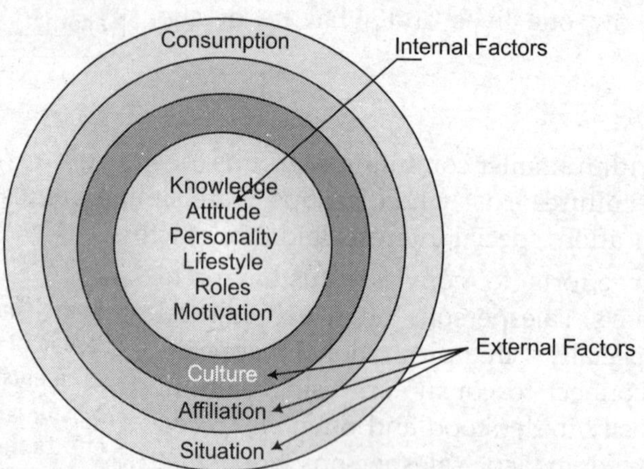

Fig. 1.4 *Factors Influencing Purchasing Decisions*

It should be kept in mind that -

- Consumer behaviour is a process that fulfils different needs or wants.
- Customers could be categorized into different subsets on the basis of their needs.
- Needs or wants can be addressed by appropriately offering a product based on the needs of customers.
- Consumer behaviour includes many activities that lead to fulfilment of a need.
- Consumer behaviour changes with time and complexity.
- Consumer behaviour involves different roles.
- Consumer behaviour is influenced by both internal and external factors.
- Consumer behaviour differs for different people.

THE PATTERN OF CUSTOMER DECISION MAKING

A typical process of customer decision-making is shown in Figure 1.5.

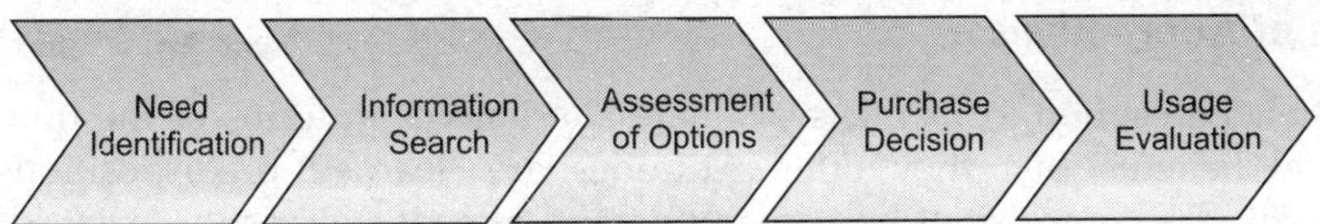

Fig 1.5 *A Typical Customer Decision-Making Process*

As is indicated above, the customer decision-making takes place in five steps:

Stage	*Brief description*	*Relevant internal psychological process*
Identification of needs	The consumer perceives a need and makes effort to meet his needs and wants	Enquiry
Information search	Customer looks for information to validate his perception about the intended purchase	Perception
Alternative evaluation	The consumer compares various brands and products	Attitude formation
Purchase decision	The consumer decides which brand to purchase	Integration
Post-purchase evaluation	The consumer evaluates the purchase decision	Learning

Identification of Needs

Needs may arise from an item that is out of stock, dissatisfaction with a current product or service that the customer is using, new wants and needs that the existing product is unable to satisfy, availability of new, technologically or aesthetically superior products.The consumer perceives a need and makes efforts to solve the problem or meet his needs and wants. The relevant internal psychological process that is associated with problem recognition is motivation.

Search for Information

Belch and Belch (2007) explain that consumers undertake both an internal (memory) and an external search.

> Once the consumers have recognized a problem or a need, they look for information on products and services that can solve that problem.

Sources of information include personal sources, commercial sources, public sources and personal experience. Perception is the most important internal psychological process that guides this process. Perception is defined as 'the process by which an individual receives, selects, organizes, and interprets information to create a meaningful picture of the world'. Selective comprehension enables consumers to interpret messages in line with their beliefs, attitudes, motives and experiences.

Evaluation of Alternatives

Based on their perception, consumers evaluate alternatives in terms of the functional and psychological benefits that they offer. Attitudes are 'learned predispositions' towards an object. Attitudes comprise of both cognitive and affective elements – that is both what you think and how you feel about something. This helps to form an attitude. Here the salespersons need to understand what benefits consumers are seeking, how consumers are evaluating alternatives and making their buying decision and therefore which attributes are most important in terms of making a decision.

Purchase Decisions

Once the alternatives have been evaluated, the consumer is ready to make a purchase decision. Sometimes purchase intention does not result in an actual purchase. The salespersons must facilitate the consumer to act on their purchase intention. The mode of facilitation may differ depending upon the customer's profile and needs. This is the stage when the customer integrates his thoughts to buy a product.

> When consumers purchase high involvement products, for which they exert a greater purchasing effort in terms of time and search, they usually experience some level of discomfort after the purchase.

Post Purchase Evaluation

Consumers always tend to evaluate their purchasing decision by comparing the product's performance with their expectations. If the product does not perform as expected they will experience post purchase dissatisfaction. That is, they experience some doubt that they made the right choice. As a salesperson one should consider the implications of post purchase behaviour and see how the possibility of dissatisfaction can be minimized.

WAYS TO ADDRESS CONSUMER NEEDS

People buy because they want gratification of their physical and emotional drives. Some of these drives are given below.

Peace of mind	Passion	Pleasure
Praise	Prestige	Protection
Convenience	Leisure	Entertainment
Enjoyment	Companionship	Recognition
Respect	Reputation	Happiness
Elegance	Ego satisfaction	Durability
Comfort	Cleanliness	Freedom

People also buy because they want to accomplish, achieve and acquire something that they wish to have. People buy because they want to:

Believe in something	Be part of a group	Do what they really want
Enjoy a certain standard of living	Emulate those they admire	Convey their creativity
Express their individuality	Feel important	Be identified as distinct
Be smart	Be popular	Be liked

Things people do not like:

Criticism	Confusion	Despair
Danger	Death	Deprivation
Dishonesty	Conceit	Irritation
Embarrassment	Failure	Grief
Fragility	Pressures	Tension
Growing old	Hunger	Suffering
Thirst	Illness	Risk
Uncertainty	Delays	Insecurity

For instance, while marketing products such as the ones mentioned below, salespersons should keep in mind what consumers look for.

- **A place of residence** – Comfort, contentment, a good investment and pride in ownership.
- **Computers** – Speed, convenience, ease and accuracy.
- **Airline tickets** – Safe, on time arrival at the destination and make the customer feel pampered.
- **Mineral water** – Safety, health and assurance.
- **Books** – Pleasant hours and self fulfillment by virtue of knowledge.
- **Television** – Entertainment, pride of ownership, happiness and contentment.
- **Clothes** – Elegance, style, status, confidence and attractiveness.
- **Insurance** – Security, safety against uncertainty and a secured future.

In other words, consumers look for ideas, feelings, solutions, hopes, aspirations, safety, health, security and happiness.

THINGS TO REMEMBER

- People buy essentially for two reasons: to solve problems and feel good. To solve problems, one should come up with innovative products and to make people feel good, one should become an expert at influencing human behaviour.
- People buy more with their hearts (emotions), rather than the brain (rational logic). Many buying decisions are based on unconscious needs and wants.
- People buy many products and services that appeal to their own visual, auditory or external influence.

- People buy what is missing in their lives. It leads to newer aspirations and is translated into wants and needs.
- People become interested in buying many products and services if the marketer can demonstrate its value from the consumers' view point. People buy not because it is inexpensive, but because they perceive it to be high value for their money.
- People buy if you understand and promise to deliver their dreams.
- People buy when they know that what has been promised shall be delivered.
- People buy when you do not force them to think too much.

To make people buy from you:

- Try to know your customers' intrinsic needs and wants.
- Listen to what the customers have to say.
- Make the buying process as simple as possible.
- Make the product available within an "arm's length" of the customers.
- Do not push the product to the customer because you have to sell it. Sell it as part of your effort to provide them a solution to a problem that they might really have.
- Be honest in your efforts towards customers.
- Be interested in listening to what they have to say, how they feel, and about the events that are going on in their lives.
- Do not disagree with them even if you do not subscribe to their view points. Try to restate their ideas and help them.
- Show genuine interest in your customers; empathize with them and make honest efforts to fulfil their needs.
- Remember the customers after the sales are over. They will bring more customers than your sales promotions efforts will.

KEY CONCEPTS

- Understanding why a customer buys what he buys is the key to successful marketing today.
- While it is necessary to have complete knowledge about why people buy, it is also important to have a strong understanding of buyers' behaviour.
- It should be understood that consumer behaviour is motivated and needs or wants can be addressed by appropriately offering a product based on the needs of customers, so sellers should ensure that a product must deliver the promise of fulfilling the intrinsic needs of prospects.
- People buy because they want gratification of their physical and emotional needs. People also buy because they want to accomplish, achieve and acquire something that they wish to have. So instead of selling a product, efforts should be made to solve their problems.

- People buy with their hearts, no matter, how much their brain tells them otherwise. So salespersons should aim at touching the hearts of the customers by offering them what they really want.
- People want to have what's missing in their lives. It starts with their aspirations and is translated to their wants and needs. People buy not because a product is inexpensive, but because they perceive it to give a high value for their money.
- People can be interested in buying, but not buy. However, if people believe in something, then the only thing that keeps them from buying – is the opportunity to buy.
- To make people buy from you, know your customers' intrinsic needs and wants, listen to them, make the product available within an "arm's length" and make the buying process as simple as possible.
- Do not push the product to the customer because you have to sell it; instead, take a genuine interest in your customers, empathize with them and make honest efforts to fulfil their needs.
- Remember your customers after the sales are over. They will bring more customers than your sales promotions efforts will.
- Future marketing success lies in understanding why people buy along with who, what, where, how, how much and how often.

Case Study

ENTERTAINMENT TELEVISION COMPANY

Rakesh Tyagi of Entertainment Television Company had just received a telephone call from Krishna Kumar, the purchase manager of Vibgyor, the biggest electronic shop in Agra. Krishna wanted to know how soon he could get 35 television sets as he needed them within three days for a State Training Institute located in the city.

Entertainment Television Company manufactured television sets under the brand name "Spirit". Headquartered in Mumbai, the company manufactured television sets in its factories at Nasik, in Maharashtra and Solan, in Himachal Pradesh. While the Nasik factory catered to the needs of central India, the Solan factory supplied to markets in northern India. Entertainment Television Company was known for the quality and aesthetics of its televisions. Its service was also efficiently handled by a network of service centres that were controlled by its branch sales offices spread across the country.

For years Vibgyor had been the distributor for Electra Televisions Ltd. Krishna had been purchasing all its television sets from them for well over that period, and their prices had remained competitive. Accordingly, Rakesh had never been able to get any business from Vibgyor, even though he was sure that Entertainment Television Company could serve Vibgyor as well as Electra did. Rakesh reasoned that if Krishna gave some business to his company, he would be far less susceptible to the problems inherent in a sole-source arrangement. But Krishna had always been concerned about Entertainment Television's ability to serve him and had decided instead to give all his business to Electra.

In the present case, Krishna had called Electra first, but it was unable to obtain 35 television sets in such a short time. If he did not get the sets within three days he would miss the next order of another 60 sets that the training institute would probably buy in the next month.

The telephone conversation between Rakesh and Krishna was as follows:

Rakesh: Entertainment Television Company. Rakesh Tyagi speaking. Can I help you sir?

Krishna: I certainly hope so! I am Krishna Kumar from Vibgyor. I have a problem and I need help from you.

Rakesh: Oh hello, Mr Kumar, it's been a long time since I met you. How are you?

Krishna: I am fine, thank you. How are you? It's nice to talk to you once again.

Rakesh: Mr Kumar, please tell me your problem. I will certainly help you.

Krishna: Do you recall that the 29 inch FST television sets that I had taken last time for one of my valued customers – the State Training Institute? They were much appreciated. The Training Institute requires 35 more television sets for their hostel annexe. The annexe is going to be inaugurated in four days time. So I need 35 sets of the same type in three days time. You know, if we are able to supply this consignment to them in time, we may get another order next month for 60 more TVs.

Rakesh: Please hold on. Let me check with our godown and see if we have the stock.

After a pause, Rakesh returns.

Rakesh: I checked up on our stock. I think we have the stock, but our finance section says that your last bill has still not been paid and has been due for over 60 days now.

Krishna: Oh yes! Actually payment of that consignment could not be made because of two serious problems – five televisions were found not working and even after a complaint was lodged with your service department, no action has yet been taken. Also, the bill had not adjusted the credit note of Rs. 1,20,000/- that was promised by you on your last visit to us. It has been over three months and the matter is still lying pending. I have blocked over two lakh rupees unnecessarily. Your payment is no problem at all. I am sure you will take care of these two minor issues and when you come in your next visit next week, I will give the payment for your last consignment. You know we have never had any payment problem in the last so many years that we have been dealing. Now I would request you to kindly help me get the consignment so that I can fulfill the order of my customer.

Rakesh: OK. Let me see what best I can do.

Rakesh talked to his finance department who are adamant that as per the company policy, no further bill will be raised or material sent for Vibgyor as their old bill is still lying pending.

Totally disgusted, Krishna Kumar told Rakesh: "You must know why I buy from you. It is because of your good products and more so because of your service. If you don't cooperate with me in my times of need then I would better look for some other alternative. Please do not think that you are the only one who could supply me the TVs that I want so desperately."

Rakesh is on tenterhooks. On one hand he did not want to miss the sales and annoy his big customer and on the other he is unable to persuade his finance department.

Question

1. Please suggest what should Rakesh do to solve this problem?

REFERENCES

1. Arussy, Lior (2010), Customers Don't Buy What You Sell, Searcher, Vol. 18 Issue 1, p. 12.
2. Carter, Tony (2010), The Challenge of Managers Keeping Customers. *International Management Review*, Vol. 6 Issue 2, pp. 20-27.
3. Elberse, Anita, Gourville, John T., Narayandas, Das (2005), Angels and Devils: Best Buy's New Customer Approach (A), *Harvard Business School Cases*, p. 1.
4. Free, Miles (2005), Why Do Customers Buy From Us? *Production Machining*, Vol. 5 Issue 5, p. 19.
5. Goozé, Mitch (2011), Understand What Products Customers are Buying. *Production Machining*, Vol. 11 Issue 1, p. 22.
6. Monat, Jamie P. (2009), Why Customers Buy? *Marketing Research*, Vol. 21 Issue 1, pp. 20-24.
7. Ngobo, Paul Valentin (2004), Drivers of Customers' Cross-buying Intentions. *European Journal of Marketing*, Vol. 38 Issue 9/10, pp. 112-115.
8. O'Grady, Mike (2011), Let Your Customers Buy the Way They Buy, *Air Conditioning Heating & Refrigeration News*, Vol. 242 Issue 4, p. 22.
9. Pookulangara, Sanjukta; Hawley, Jana; Xiao, Ge (2011), Explaining Consumers' Channel-switching Behaviour Using the Theory of Planned Behaviour. *Journal of Retailing & Consumer Services*, Vol. 18 Issue 4, pp. 311-321.
10. Seiders, Kathleen, Voss, Glenn B., Grewal, Dhruv, Godfrey, Andrea L. (2005), Do Satisfied Customers Buy More? Examining Moderating Influences in a Retailing Context. *Journal of Marketing*, Vol. 69 Issue 4, pp. 26-43.
11. Seybold, Patricia B. (2001), Get Inside the Lives of Your Customers, *Harvard Business Review*, Vol. 79 Issue 5, pp. 80-89.
12. Sommer, Lutz (2011), The Theory of Planned Behaviour and the Impact of Past Behaviour, *International Business & Economics Research Journal*, Vol. 10 Issue 1, pp. 91-110.

2 Concepts of Selling

"Everyone lives by selling something."

–Robert Louis Stevenson

CHAPTER OUTLINE

- Selling – a basic human activity
- What is selling?
- Why persuasion?
- What selling is not
- Commonly held beliefs about selling
- Selling: A crucial part of marketing
- The modern concept of selling
- What is salesmanship?
- The effective salesperson
- The nature of a salesperson's work
- Sales as a career

OBJECTIVES

After studying this chapter, you will be able to:

- Define – What is selling and what it is not
- Understand the significance of selling as a crucial activity of marketing
- Understand the commonly held myths in selling
- Know why salespersons fail
- List the key success factors necessary to excel in selling
- Decide whether you want to take up sales as a career

Opening Case: The Best for a Future

Vidyasagar (24) was a Honours graduate in Physics from Bangalore University. Though initially he wanted to pursue a Masters Degree in Electronics, but due to family compulsion he was unable to do so and had to look for a job. He appeared for many entrance examinations conducted by the government, banks, and public sector organizations but did not succeed. He was becoming restless when Mr. Srinivasan, an old friend of his father suggested that he should look for a job in sales function. Vidyasagar liked the idea and started applying for a job in the sales area.

Vidyasagar was very excited when he finally got an offer in the Sales Department from Zenith Electronics Ltd., one of the premier consumer electronics companies in India. He started working enthusiastically and slowly picked up the trade. A very hardworking person,Vidyasagar quickly learnt the nuances of selling and very soon, he was promoted as the sales manager in the company. He used to go to his office at 9 o'clock in the morning and continued till seven in the evening. Often he had to wait for hours to meet and get orders from a big customer. At times he could just grab a bite and rush to be in time for appointments. But he enjoyed it. He worked very hard and intelligently and enjoyed every moment of his job.

The rewards also came his way. He kept on moving up the organizational hierarchy and was given monetary rewards for his superior performance. In the meantime, he joined an one year duration distance learning programme of IIM Calcutta and got a certificate of excellence in Sales & Marketing. In recognition of his performance, he was promoted to the level of General Manager (Sales) in his company. One day he was trying to jot down the different tasks that a Sales Executive should handle. His came up with the following:

1. Prospecting and qualifying prospective customers:
   - Blind prospecting
   - Cold calling or canvassing
   - Sales blitz
   - Lead prospecting
2. Preplanning prior to sales calls:
3. Presenting and demonstrating services:
   - Sales presentation
   - Demonstration
4. Handling objections and questions:
   - Restate the objection
   - "Agree and neutralize" tactic
5. Closing the sale:
   - Verbal closing clues
   - Non-verbal closing clues
6. Following up after closing the sale.

INTEGRAL DESIGN FOR PROGRAMMED LEARNING

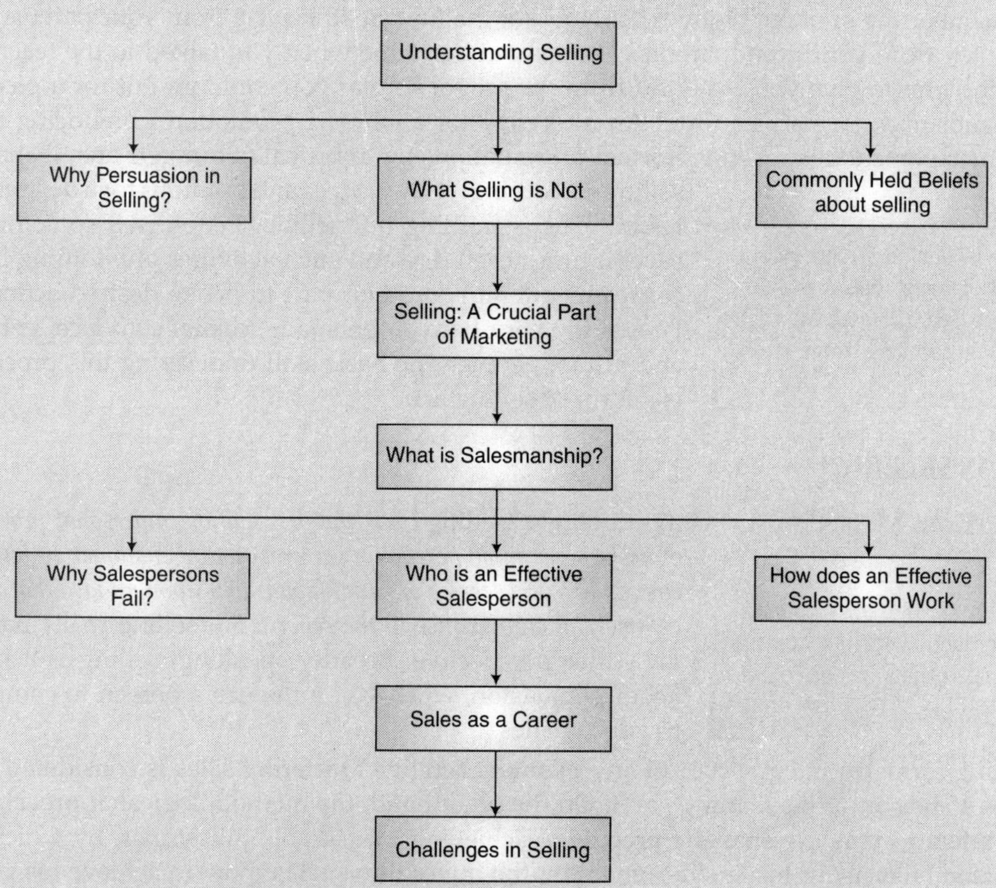

There is no more fascinating business in this world than that of selling. Without salesmen there would be little progress made. Selling is behind every successful enterprise of whatever character. Even a country has to have its salesmen. Character is the salesman's stock in trade. It is he who must first sell himself. The product itself is secondary.... Truthfulness, enthusiasm, and patience are great assets to every salesman. Without them he could not go far. Courage and courtesy are essential equipment. Leave your prospective customer with a smile and he will welcome you on your next visit. Bear in mind to be always a salesMAN!"

–George Matthew Adams

SELLING – A BASIC HUMAN ACTIVITY

Selling is a basic human activity; more than business, it is an integral part of our life. Do you remember the moment of joy when you got the first small bicycle from your parents or a lovely toy from your grandparents? How about that time when you talked to the teacher requesting him to give you a day off from the school so that you could go out for a picnic with friends and have a nice time? An interview for a job or a promotion, convincing the senior management in a meeting, formal presentations for approval of budgets are all about selling something – views, ideas and opinions for a desirable result. This is nothing but selling. People sell something several times each day and such activities are nothing but conscious attempts on their part to evoke desired actions. People try very hard to persuade, cajole, convince, entice and attract people. The basic skill underlying this process is a form of selling art.

> Success in business, and in life, depends largely upon people's ability to sell themselves, their firm, their services, their ideas, to others.

WHAT IS SELLING?

The American Marketing Association defines "selling" as *"the personal or impersonal process of assisting and/or persuading a prospective customer to buy a commodity or a service or to act favourably upon an idea that has commercial significance to the seller."* But selling really has a far wider perspective. Broadly speaking, selling is a fine act of persuasion, when you influence a person to comply to your wishes.

> Selling is the fine art of persuasion through which a person influences others to do something...

Selling forms an integral part of any business activity. Mastering sales is considered by many as some sort of persuading "art". On the other hand, the methodological approach of selling refers to it as a systematic process of achieving measurable milestones, by which a salesperson talks about his 'goods,' enabling the buyer to visualize how to achieve his goal in a profitable manner. Selling is a practical implementation of marketing and one of the most crucial ones. It is the culmination of the entire business processes; the ultimate test of success of any company.

The right questions to successfully understand a customer's goal, and the creation of a valuable solution by communicating the necessary information that encourages a buyer to achieve his goal at an economic cost is the responsibility of the sales person.

From a marketing point of view, selling is one of the methods of promotion used by marketers. Other promotional techniques include advertising, sales promotion, publicity, and public relations.

> The primary function of professional sales is to generate and close leads, educate prospects, fill needs and satisfy the wants of consumers appropriately, and therefore turn prospective customers into actual ones.

WHY PERSUASION?

In a buyers' market, customers have innumerable options available to them. It depends upon the seller to carve out a space in their minds by conveying the distinct attributes of their offerings (product quality, price, durability, availability, services etc.) and creating a desire to buy that product. Persuasion is the art or influencing the mind of the prospective buyer favourably by reasoning. In selling, the ability to persuade determines achievement of sales targets. The four important parts of persuasion include Attention, Interest, Desire and Action (AIDA). Strong (1925) originally described these as the critical tools to create effective advertising, but they are equally applicable for achieving productive sales.

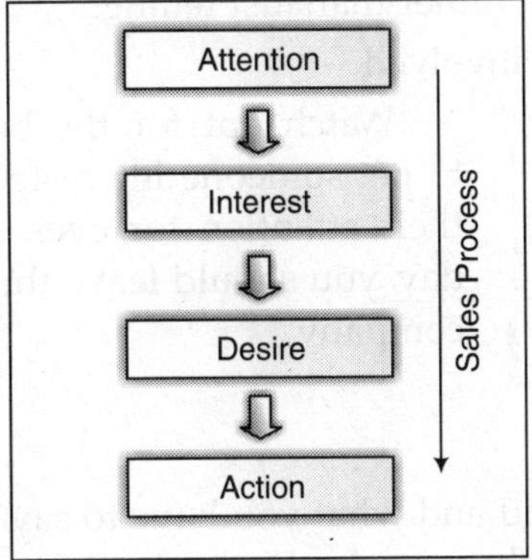

Fig. 2.1 *The AIDA Model (Strong, E.K.)*

Attention

First a marketer tries to get a customer's attention. Without attention, one can hardly persuade customers about anything. People can get attention in many ways – a good way is to surprise them. When salespersons are talking to them, the first few seconds are critical as people will listen most then and gradually decide whether it is worth giving any further attention. It is generally better to open with something that pulls them towards you rather than something that scares them (as this may push them away).

> Good salespersons do not waste these precious moments and attract the other person's attention instantaneously.

Good openers address their problems and begin with statements such as:

- Have you ever...?
- Have you noticed...?
- Can you see...?

Bad openers give customers something to object to, demonstrate their disrespect, or just bore them to tears, and may begin with statements such as:

- I've got just the thing you want...
- I just dropped by so that I might...
- I was wondering whether you could...

Interest

Once you have a person's attention, it must be sustained by getting the other person interested. This can be done by:

- Listening to them or talking about their problems.
- Telling them things that concern their problems.
- Demonstrating things, rather than just telling.
- Getting them actively involved.

> Customers can recognize that they have a need, but this is not desire. Desire is a motivation to act and leads towards the next stage.

Watch out for the boredom factor. You may be able to get someone interested, but you cannot expect to keep their attention for ever. If you want to come back some day, you should leave them wanting more, at least of your company.

Desire

Once they are interested in you and what you have to say, the next step is to create a desire in them for what one wants them to do. Desire is like a fire, and can be stoked by many methods, such as:

- Telling them how the desirable item will not be available for long (Scarcity principle).
- Telling them how other people approve of the item and have acquired it for themselves.
- Showing them how what you have to offer will solve some of their problems.

Action

This is the magic stage when they act on their desires and actually buy the product or agree to your proposals.

The critical point is when one can ask for the sale or ask them whether they actually agree fully with you.

> The idea is that spark before one gets to a final purchase action, a cognitive state of understanding of the value is needed that matches the emotional state of desire.

One must be aware of the signals they are sending. Are they asking you when you can deliver or what after-sales support you can give?

You can summarize the problems you are solving for them and how what you are proposing solves these problems.

You must also use an appropriate closing technique, such as alternatives ('Do you want the red or the blue?) or presupposition ('What time can I meet you next week?').

And...

Many new aspects have been added to this classical AIDA model over time to make it more self-explanatory. One school of thought has added a 'C' i.e. Conviction. This sometimes appears before Desire (AICDA) and sometimes after (AIDCA), perhaps indicating two different approaches: one which starts with getting a logical agreement and then moving to emotional desire, as opposed to creating desire first and then reaching the state when the purchase also makes logical sense.

Others have added the letter 'S' for Satisfaction, indicating the fact that happy customers will buy more (whilst unhappy customers will tell their friends not to). Though this could be true in some cases, it may not be so in all cases and may depend on the sales methods (which can be highly emotion-based), the person (who may prefer emotional assessment), and the context (for example selling clothes can be very emotionally based).

> Persuasion has to be logical and based on rationality or else it will fail to appeal to the prospect. This will require thorough homework; gathering, collating and synthesizing information about the products, market, customers, and competitors.

It is necessary to identify unique, distinguishing attributes of the product and present them effectively to evoke a favourable response from the buyers. This also involves the ability to handle people and includes a pleasing personality, positive behaviour, nice mannerisms, empathy and good communication skills.

It is therefore necessary not only to have a product that the customers really want, but also be able to communicate some of the distinguishing attributes effectively. Communication, if supported by effective persuasion, ensures a desirable response from the customer towards buying the product.

WHAT SELLING IS NOT

Most of us have an ideal image of salespersons in our minds. This image of an ideal salesperson is of a person with a nice physique, dressed to 'impress', carrying an expensive leather briefcase, smart, talking impressively and having their way despite all odds. We often see such people and it reinforces our impression of what a salesperson should be.

At the same time, there are some unpleasant experiences too. Often, who has not opened the door after hearing the bell to find a salesperson on the doorstep? Talking in a typical manner, with artificial manner, and at times irritating body language, he/she tries to persuade you to buy the products. On other occasions, you must have seen salespersons trying to sell products to shopkeepers when you have gone to buy something from a shop. These salespersons are sometimes impressive, but

> Selling needs creativity, imagination, intellect, hard work and 'lots of inspiration and perspiration' correction

more often than not, create an unfavourable impression on the target group, by their posture, gesticulation and gestures.

From these experiences you can form some perceptions of selling and what it is like. However, such perceptions are often misleading and incorrect. So what is the real nature of selling? One must try to understand this and try to see what selling is all about.

COMMONLY HELD BELIEFS ABOUT SELLING

Selling is a function that deals with many variables – the market, customers, their needs and expectations all vary and selling success depends a lot upon the available options *vis-à-vis* the offering made by the salesperson. Many notions about selling have done the profession more harm than good. Some of these beliefs relate to the core nature of sales as a profession, salespersons, the selling style, predisposition and their approach to customers. Some of these presumptions are as follows:

Salespersons are Born; they Cannot be Made

The first commonly held idea about sales is that salespeople are born and not made. Such a thought often leads salespersons to believe that they must have the qualities of fluent persuasive talking, street smartness and the ability to 'outsmart others'.

> Selling is an intricate art, which requires immense sensitivity, intelligence and experience through exposure to real life situations. It requires thorough homework before going into the field for sales.

In order to be an ace salesman, some people feel that all a person needs to do is wear smart clothes, carry a good bag and talk fluently to charm prospective dealers/distributors/customers. People with such presumptions are in for a shock when they find that what a customer needs is a person who is able to understand their needs, provide a product, extend excellent services and empathize with them in times of problems and resolve them effectively. Selling is an intricate art, which requires immense sensitivity, intelligence and experience through exposure to real life situations, and of course thorough homework before actually going into the field.

This is not to undermine the fact that as in any other profession, a good salesman must have some inherent traits. These traits are given in the box alongside. Above all salespersons must realize that they may have to spend years studying and practicing this complex art before they can be considered proficient. There is really no "born" seller, who can give the product a quick once over and sell it right away. Such an attitude gets neophytes into trouble quickly. They have to learn the hard way that they must study and practice their art just as other practitioners must before they gain competence.

> Good communication skills, a keen eye for observation, honesty, determination, self-motivation etc. are necessary prerequisite for any salesperson to succeed in the market.

It is established that the principles of salesmanship can be taught and learned just as those of engineering, medicine or aeronautics. As in all these vocations, the learner is not a skilled practitioner until enough practical experience has been gained. But a student will become a skilled salesperson much more quickly by imbibing the tenets and by not learning completely by trial and error.

> Individuals have the capability of becoming good salespeople if they are willing to put forth their best efforts.

It is well recognized that the environment has much more influence on human beings than heredity. It is believed that it is possible to even change behaviour by training; some opine that a conducive atmosphere and good instruction can improve human capabilities appreciably. It is well-known that nearly everything essential to selling success can be learnt. The adage that "salespersons are born and not made" is really not true. Vincent Riggio, formerly President of the American Tobacco Company and known as one of the country's finest salesmen, said, *"Salesmen are made, rarely are they born; and generally when the so-called 'born salesman' gets into rough going, he fails."*

It has been confirmed over and over again that a trained salesperson can far outsell an untrained one.

In India corporate houses like Hindustan Unilever Ltd., Proctor & Gamble, GSK Pharmaceuticals etc. invest in expensive sales-training on their sales force as they get results from training their sales persons through the intricacies of selling. "Johnson & Johnson increased the sales of its products in chain and independent drug stores by as much as 300 percent through training courses for retail salespeople." Many companies prefer bright young people who have had no selling experience as they feel that they can be taught to sell correctly more easily if they do not have fixed ideas and notions about selling.

> Another compelling answer to the beliefs of people who have conviction on the genetic basis of selling skills, can be found in the understanding of hundreds of highly successful business organizations which have for many years trained or taught their salespeople proven skills, tools and techniques.

The "get-rich-quick" advertisements for sales jobs have also reinforced people's wrong beliefs about selling. These beliefs have often led people to rush into the field without any proper education or training in the profession. By the time they realize the stark realities of the market, they have suffered a humiliating failure for which they were not prepared.

Good Salespeople are Good Talkers

This is a trap that most people venturing into the sales profession fall into. A good talker has to be proficient in articulating his or her thoughts effectively. This again requires careful preparation about what to say, how it is to be presented, how questions are to be handled and how to deal with the situation if the receiver has rigid views. Good salespeople are good listeners. Selling is the art of asking the right questions – questions that lead the prospect to think that the sales proposition will solve their problem. When a salesperson talks before the customer

> While fluency in talking is a desired trait, too much talking may put off prospective customers. Selling is the fine art of communicating effectively for a favourable action on the part of the receiver.

talks he may offer a proposition that may not be interesting to the prospect. If the salesperson talks too much it has the following disadvantages:

- It may show your thoughts and ideas before knowing the mind of the customer.
- It exposes your cards before knowing what the customer wants.
- You may talk about things that are not really relevant to the customer, which may lead to the customer getting irritated or bored, as it is a waste of his or her time.
- You may reveal weaknesses which the customer can take advantage of.
- Reveal the limits of the product leading to being pressurized by the customer.
- It gives a feeling of self importance.
- You will not learn anything that will help you make a sale.

When the customer talks, there are several advantages:

- One learns what the customer really wants.
- One learns the viewpoints of the customer about the product, the company, alternative products etc.
- One learns what the customer is like.
- One has time to think about the sale and devise ways of satisfying the customer's expectations.
- The customer feels happy that the salesperson is really concerned about him and is trying to understand his problems and respond to them with specific recommendations.
- The customer feels important.

So salespersons must develop the ability to listen and get the customer to talk.

The Good Salesperson can Sell Anything to Anyone

People have a notion that a good salesperson can sell anything. This may not be true all the time. A salesperson, highly successful in retail selling may not succeed as much in industrial selling and *vice versa* unless he has complete knowledge of the product, management of its distribution channel and unique characteristics of the particular business. Also, to be successful in selling, a salesperson, besides requiring all the traits of a good salesman, must have a good product.

> Good salesmanship cannot substitute for an inferior product or inefficient management of other accessories like product promotion, distribution and improper product positioning.

A good salesperson does not even try to sell to everyone. Good professional salespeople spend their time with good prospects – people or companies that need their products and can afford to pay for them. The salesperson who insists on trying to push the product to someone who does not need it, eventually loses a customer and also his own credibility.

Selling Means only Entertaining and Merriment

It is widely believed that selling is a profession that is full of fun, partying and high spirits. Of course, salespersons stay in good hotels and have the luxury of dining in the best of restaurants; but there is another side that includes hard work from dawn to late nights, having food at odd hours and at times sleepless nights in small towns where there are neither good hotels nor good eateries. As most of the consumer product companies are expanding to rural markets, these are some of the difficulties that salespersons have to live with. However, these could be termed as job hazards that are eclipsed by the immense thrill and sense of achievement that a salesperson gets once he achieves the given targets.

> Do not feel you have failed when someone refuses to buy your wares. That also should not de-energize us; successful salespersons consider it as a challenge and attack the market with a carefully drawn up strategy.

Salespersons Never Fail

It is often believed that salespersons must not fail, that every sales call should and must result in sales. However, the fact remains that while there are good times, there also are bad days for even the finest salespersons. People might turn your proposition down, and there can be days when every sales call might fail to end up in productive orders. A good salesperson considers this a challenge and can often turn it into success beyond expectations!

The Locker Room Syndrome

Many people think that the successful industrial salesman does most of his business on the golf course, at ball games, or around the poker table. The image of the hard-drinking, sports-loving, golf or billiard playing male chauvinist has permeated the sales world for years. And it is largely out of place. Many sell goods by simply calling on the right people in prospective companies and selling their goods on their merits. Moreover, many more call on people in their offices and sell their products on the basis of their merits and use to the customer.

People Do not Want to Buy

Many sales managers are guilty of conveying the idea to their salespeople that people do not want to buy, therefore, you, as the salesperson, must coerce them to make a sale. This is completely untrue.

Most goods and services are bought, not sold. There are all sorts of people and firms who need all sorts of things and have the money to buy them. Salespersons do not sell their wares because of their selling talents but rather because the market wants what they are selling.

> To a large extent, your job is to locate such people and sell them what they want. If people didn't want to buy, most of the people who are passing themselves off as salespeople would starve to death.

The Profession of a Salesperson makes you Rich Overnight

Some people do make a lot of money quickly in selling. But it does not always pay. More often, money will come to you after you learn your trade and your territory. Do not expect to be an immediate success in sales. If you are, it is to your credit. But if you are not, do not be discouraged. Give yourself time to develop your selling skills.

SELLING: A CRUCIAL PART OF MARKETING

Selling is an active element of marketing. It is an inseparable part, on which depends the ultimate success of marketing. It is the initiation of a 'domino effect' that concludes in the satisfaction of a buyer's need, having pursued a route that inevitably embraces the creation, maintenance and expansion of business. In other words, the company mechanism cannot operate until the products produced by it are sold profitably in the market. It is a positive agent for change, innovation and new ideas that ignites organizational growth. Selling is a bridge between the manufacturer and the user; it is a justification and outlet for the product of a business enterprise in its ability to persuade potential consumers to try, buy and use it. To describe it merely as a transfer of goods, services and ideas from one party to another in exchange for money is a serious understatement.

> Selling is the process on which the health, growth and survival of a commercial business ultimately depends. It is the sustaining force of a free enterprise.

Selling is the point of culmination of all marketing activities and determines their success in a dynamically changing environment. It provides that litmus test, which indicates the competitiveness of the marketing arm of the company in terms of its strategies, systems, structure, policies and orientation of the company towards markets and customers. It tests the extent to which products and services are liked by its customers and decides the inherent strength of the company in the market.

THE MODERN CONCEPT OF SELLING

The modern concept of selling lays much more emphasis on the finer aspects of the sales process rather than on the flamboyance of a personality, a blatant line of sales talk, and a liberal use of high-pressure tactics to get the order. Prospects have seen so many salespersons of this sort that they recognize the type, regard them as nuisances, and give them a short hearing, if any.

With this elevation in the level of awareness of consumers, the art of selling has assumed a modern form. This is possible only with a better knowledge of the product, awareness about competition, knowledge about the needs and wants of the markets and customers, a high degree of sensitivity and responsiveness, commitment and

> Selling is perhaps the only job where there is hardly any supervision; salespersons move in the market on their own, contact their prospects, discuss deals and close the sales successfully – all by themselves, far from the watchful eyes of their supervisors.

dedication and an unflinching desire to accomplish the given targets. It also requires total honesty and high moral rectitude.

> Salespersons are today looked upon not only as salesmen but as friends, philosophers and guides who would advise and provide the right guidance with respect to the product, maintenance and service for consumer products and also to tell ways and means for growth and sustenance of the business of the prospect.

The very term "salesman" or "saleswoman" is thus being redefined. Today, a Professional Sales Representative (PSR) is an expert in the medical field, who knows the finer details of the latest medicines available for a disease and confidently briefs the doctors and the pharmacists on the merits and efficacies of a particular drug or a pharmaceutical therapy. Similarly, the life insurance agent has assumed the role of an insurance advisor or consultant who not only suggests the best plan for the prospect, but also advises him how to get maximum returns on investment on the plans besides life coverage. The salespersons involved in selling engineering products are now sales/service engineers, who often hold formal engineering degrees, besides having a high level of selling skills. This enables them to discuss the technical aspects of the products as per the consumers' needs. Thus, a sales representative is now regarded as an expert, a person professionally trained, who is competent to render a highly valuable service.

Customers also expect a high level of ethics from salespeople. It is not uncommon for a salesperson to advise the prospect against buying, even though a sale might easily be made. An automobile sales representative once told a potential customer that he did not yet need a light commercial van now, and that it would be more appropriate for him to buy one when his business attained a certain stage. The prospect waited till his business had grown, and then asked the sales representative to recommend the kind of van needed. No competition was invited by the buyer, for he had confidence in the representative. What emerges from this discussion is an essential element of selling that makes or mars a selling career and that is the ethics and morality of the salesperson because selling is an outcome that besides resting upon a good product and service, depends fundamentally upon the honesty of purpose, sincerity, earnestness and genuineness of the salesperson. It builds up his credibility and establishes him as a person who is dependable, trustworthy and responsible.

WHAT IS SALESMANSHIP?

The short version of the definition of true, professional salesmanship is simply *"the ability to reach an agreement with a customer in the shortest amount of time possible, using the least number of words."* However, this definition is not as simple as it sounds. Being able to reach an agreement with your customers in the shortest amount of time possible means you have a planned procedure that includes methods to:

> Salesmanship is that unique quality of a salesperson that enables him to accomplish preconceived sales objectives. It is a fine blend of attributes that are essential for anyone to succeed in selling.

- Determine customers' needs, wants, and reasons.
- Establish credibility and rapport.

- Explain the features and benefits of the products, as well as the benefits of doing business with the company.
- Close the sale in a dignified, professional manner, without over-pressuring customers to make a decision; without being at a loss for words; and without overstaying your welcome.

Salesmanship is thus a unique competency that helps a person sell a service or product. It is fundamentally a fine art of persuasion. It is an ability to get the prospect to trust you and look upon you as a friend, philosopher and guide. He must consider you as his well-wisher who will help him in the growth of his business by sound professional advice and guidance. A customer's faith and trust in you comes through sustained efforts over a long period of time and proven hard work.

It is noteworthy that salespersons are often keenly observed by customers while they are at work and it is the degree of their sincere efforts and hard work that helps them to create credibility: this credibility creates respect and helps a salesperson to strike up a relationship with the customers that is the essence of business. Successful salesmanship is therefore a phenomenon that must lead to a win-win situation – both for the salesman as well as for the customer.

> There is no better way to win the confidence of customers than by proving that their interests are supreme.

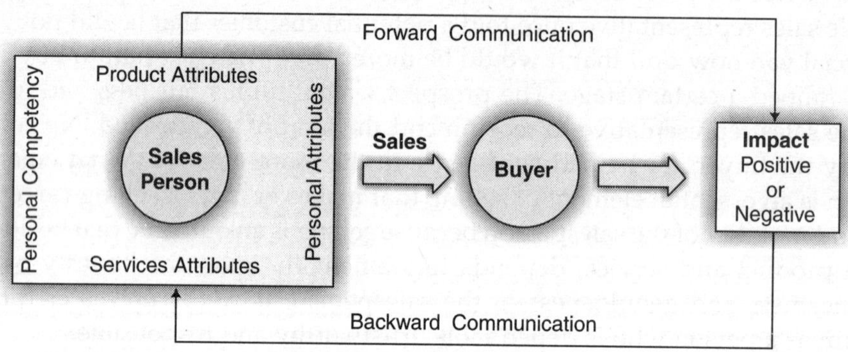

Fig. 2.2 *The Sales Process*

THE EFFECTIVE SALESPERSON

What qualities should a salesperson have? This is a question that is asked in different divisions of companies. Interestingly, salespersons are the people whose achievements are always measured. On one hand while they are always under pressure to perform, their targets – sales, collections, new product development, dealer development call reporting system etc. are always under the scanner. It is therefore very important for them

> Salespersons must have those human qualities that energize them in times of gloom and re-inforce their strengths in times of success.

to keep their minds in a state of dynamic equilibrium; Professionals in the field state that salespersons must have the following characteristics:

- Possess the basic ability to sell
- Consciously select selling as a profession they are proud of
- Have high ethical standards in their working and personal life
- Have a thorough knowledge of the product, customers and competition
- Are true to their words
- Are honest in their profession
- Are hard working
- Maintain self-discipline
- Knows that 'to sell is to serve'

The various traits that salespersons must possess fall into three categories:

- Psychological traits
- Social traits
- Physical traits

> Salespersons should be optimists – who never accept defeat. Even when they fail, they take it up as a challenge and through careful planning and hard work continue their efforts until they are successful.

PSYCHOLOGICAL TRAITS

The following psychological characteristics are said to be very important in selling.

Optimism – Optimism that success is inevitable. It follows hard work, dedication and honesty of purpose.

Enthusiasm – Enthusiasm is a blend of interest and belief, of energy and activity. Enthusiasm leads a salesperson to become courageous in facing challenges and overcoming them. It reflects the degree of confidence a salesperson has in his company, products and services and inspires prospects to buy.

Confidence – Confidence is a result of knowledge and experience and must be nurtured. To a salesperson, confidence is a belief in ones' own self, a respect for his own capabilities and his competence to sell. It is a motivation that enables him to sell even in spite of objections.

Sincerity – Nothing is so vital in selling as the sincerity of a salesperson. Prospects usually have little trouble in detecting sincerity in salespersons and are influenced easily in the face of stiff competition. Salespersons cannot hope to make other people believe that which they themselves know to be untrue.

Determination – Determination is the will to succeed. Successful salespersons are those who are determined to go ahead. This determination makes them industrious individuals who are willing to work very hard even under discouraging situations. Determination also leads to

> A salesperson has to be a dreamer. He must imagine the big picture of sales and by harnessing his resources, move ahead to achieve them.

aggressiveness, competitive spirit and pride in wanting to be the best person in the sales force.

Dependability – This is another vital trait of successful salespersons. A customer does not have interaction with many people in the company; he is in touch with only the salesperson who visits him regularly. The customer depends upon the salesperson, to fulfil his needs, solve his problems and satisfy his expectations. If a salesperson is not dependable he loses credibility and also loses business.

Initiative – A salesperson with initiative is a self starter who undertakes new tasks and challenges willingly and accomplishes them. Salespersons with initiative, learn to rely on themselves, chart the growth of their own business and follow those plans religiously.

Imagination – A salesperson has to be a dreamer. He must see the big picture of sales and by harnessing his resources, move ahead to achieve them.

SOCIAL TRAITS

Equally important are the social characteristics necessary for a salesperson to succeed in the market. These social characteristics are as follows:

Friendly nature – A permanent sales relationship between the salesperson and the customer is grounded on the former's genuine interest in the latter and an accompanying desire to help him. A salesperson should be responsive, sociable and affable in his approach to customers. He must be a friend to his customers and eager to help customers expand their business.

Social graces – A salesperson should be courteous, sober and positive. Courtesy must be exhibited from the moment of entering the prospect's office until it is time to go. Courtesy should not only be extended to the customer but also to his staff, including the junior staff and all other personnel contacted in the prospect's place of business.

Conversational ability – To be a good conversationalist, a salesperson should be concerned with five basic things: Assume the "You" point of view and talk from that position. This requires a sympathetic understanding of the customer and his needs and problems.

- Prospects are generally interested only in business. Talk beyond business only when asked to.
- Make the prospect feel important: Compliments given in this respect must be genuine and should not look artificial.
- Control the conversation with finesse by exercising a subtle control over the subject and the direction of the conversation, a salesperson can channelize the discussion towards a fruitful conclusion.
- Guard against the overuse of certain words or expressions. This practice restricts the salesperson's ability to express a precise meaning. Excess repetition leads to monotony and even irritation.

> Nothing is more essential to a salesperson's personality than self-confidence and that confidence permits poise. Poise is a characteristic that permits people to be in effective command of themselves – physically, mentally and emotionally. Poise reflects emotional stability.

Poise – Poise is a characteristic that permits people to be in effective command of themselves – physically, mentally and emotionally. It reflects emotional stability.

PHYSICAL TRAITS

The physical image of a salesperson is the first thing that makes an impression on the prospect. Appearance is an important factor in personality and influences selling significantly. The salesperson must appear to be decent, dependable, trustworthy and respectable. He must therefore look into the following aspects carefully.

Personality – It is very difficult to define personality. A person can be tall or short, dark or fair, slim or fat, but the way he is able to carry himself, will determine his ability to impress the prospect; personal hygiene, cleanliness and grooming play a large role in this. Clothes are also important to a salesperson's personality. Neat and clean clothes bear silent but powerful testimony to the attention and care they receive. Moreover, gestures, body language, choice of words, communication skills and voice, all add up to the personality and influence prospects.

Mannerisms – Many salespersons acquire habits of which they are not conscious. Scratching the head, biting one's nails, tapping a pencil, cracking of knuckles, chewing gum or even talking with food in the mouth are considered undesirable mannerisms. Such mannerisms distract the attention of the prospect from the core issues of sales and create a bad impression.

Good health – The sales job is exacting and exhausting. The daily grind of selling makes heavy demands on a salesperson, causing expenditure of much physical effort and depletion of energy reserves. Moreover, eating at odd hours or even missing a meal is quite frequent for a salesperson. Thus, good health is a necessary pre-requisite for a salesperson.

Ten Secrets of Highly Successful Salespersons

Successful Salespersons -

1. Are true to their commitments
2. Have empathy
3. Create relationships with customers and maintain them
4. Take pains to resolve customers' problems
5. Acquire, manage and use information for the good of customers
6. Are naturally curious
7. Love their profession and enjoy doing what they do
8. Do the unexpected and more for their customers
9. Are creative and care for their customers
10. Have passion and fire to achieve the impossible

THE NATURE OF A SALESPERSON'S WORK

Certain misconceptions exist concerning the job of a salesperson. Many people think of the sales representative as a person who travels extensively, has an unlimited expense account on which to live an exciting life, is seldom home, tells a lot of jokes, and ends up defeated. Such is the way of myths; they seldom touch reality. So let us ignore stereotypes and examine various aspects of a sales career.

> Today, the sales representative may be a woman, may travel little, may have no expense account, and may live a long, and rewarding life with a lot of satisfaction.

Traveling – It is true that there are sales jobs which require the person to be away from home for several days at a time. However, these jobs are far from typical. Salespeople for retail outlets, wholesale houses, and industrial firms selling to a wide assortment of customers usually have small territories, which allow them to return home every night. A PSR of a pharmaceutical company will have a relatively small territory to cover because of the density of potential prospects – doctors, drug stores, and hospitals. It is this *customer density* factor that determines the size of the sales territory. Also, firms are attempting to cover each sales area more thoroughly. This results in small territories.

Expense accounts – Again, this aspect of selling is overemphasized. Many salespeople have no expense accounts at all, but must pay their own expenses. Intelligent people who are paying their own expenses do not spend excessively. Those employees who are on expense accounts are usually under careful instructions as to how the company's money should be spent. And their expense accounts are strictly audited at headquarters.

> Warm and enduring friendships with customers can be among the most rewarding aspects of sales work.

Selling jobs differ widely in this aspect. It is true that some salespeople are expected to do considerable entertaining; but many actually do none at all.

Customer contact – It is a myth that is always open season on salespersons, that they are fair game to bait. One advantage for women in selling may be that the traditional code of social conduct towards them provides considerable protection from most rude, inconsiderate prospects.

SALES AS A CAREER

A few things are very important to any person in his or her life – professional esteem, self respect, self-fulfilment, happiness, and of course money. Indeed your path to achievement of these goals depends to a large extent upon how well your job is able to fulfil your goals in life. While a career in selling has many things to offer, there is a lot of ignorance and misinformation about it.

> Like other professions, sales as a career offers bright opportunities to pursue life goals. However, this is not an attempt to influence anyone to go into selling. Only an effort to bring to the fore the real picture of what sales as a career offers to one who aspire for it.

A sales career possesses some distinctive characteristics which sets it apart from most other professions. Interestingly, selling is not a homogenous activity. A salesperson faces dissimilar situations every day, each one being unique, which have to be resolved to the satisfaction of the prospects. There are many differences in sales as a profession, which make it almost impossible to generalize the activities. Thus there is no "sales type" of individual who will succeed in any line of selling. The person who is an outstanding success in one field of selling may fail miserably and be extremely unhappy in another sales field. Keeping this in mind there are some common characteristics.

Good Remuneration

The average earning of sales people usually higher than that of personnel at the same level in other departments, so it is not at all uncommon to find sales people refusing promotions into the managerial cadre as they will lose the various incentives and commissions that they usually earn in many industries..

It takes time for salespersons to gain the experience, learn about the territory and the product line, and develop sales acumen or know-how. But, once they master these arts, sales peoples' earning levels rise with experience and are usually proportional to their productivity, while the incomes of most other people in the same company will be according to the going market wage rates for their rank and position. Larger earnings are mostly accounted for by compensation plans with attractive incentives.

> Studies of business incomes indicate that selling is one of the better paid professions.

The Ability to be Quickly Recognized

In many professions it requires considerable time to prove one's caliber or promotions tend to be based on seniority. This is not so in selling! The salesperson need not wait for many years to earn recognition and a larger income. On the other hand, if a person lacks talent or is lazy, there is no place for him or her to hide. Sales tell the story.

This does not mean that success in selling automatically comes quickly. Most salesmen and saleswomen must learn the trade through hard work. Many sales situations are so critical to a company's success that the company simply cannot let inexperienced people deal with its customers – a company's most valuable asset.

> This is one career where output is measured in quantifiable terms and if you can sell, you can prove it quickly and clearly.

Freedom of Action

While the majority of business personnel spend most of their time in the office, salespeople spend most of their time in the field. They are relatively free to get their jobs done in their own way, as long as they show satisfactory results. In a sense, salespeople usually organize their time as they desire.

This aspect of selling appeals to people who value their freedom, and like to operate in the way they want to. However, this freedom carries with it tremendous responsibilities for the person to manage time wisely. You must be able to manage yourself.

As an example of this aspect of the sales job, one of the authors met a salesman of Reliance Retail working in western India. While he was able to arrange his time so that he could pursue his hobbies, at times he still had to wake up at 5.30 am and travel over a hundred kilometers to see some good prospects, who would not wait (and finally he got the orders). He used to go to the office after scheduled office hours to catch up on paper work. The point is that a good salesperson will get the work done, but has some control over when to do it.

Mobility

Salespeople enjoy almost unparalleled mobility. This high degree of job mobility is one of the factors underlying their relatively high earnings. If you can deliver results, you will grow faster than others. Also, there is a growing tendency among this profession to change jobs for the sake of taking up new challenges in a different domain/industry. Salespeople, in general, are found to be less at the mercy of managerial whims than other employees.

Sales – Necessary Experience for Top Management

Surveys have shown that today, the top management of many companies feels that time spent in the sales function is an important part of managerial training. Moreover, a large number of these top managers began their climb up the corporate ladder from a successful sales career.

> It would be easy for a salespersons to ascend to the top level of consumer goods companies like HUL, Procter & Gamble because these firms are basically marketing organizations.

The key to look for in judging the type of background that will be prized in promoting people is the basic element underlying the concern's success.

Challenge

Intelligent people do not like to engage in routine jobs; if sufficient challenge is not provided by their work they soon tire of it. Most selling jobs are anything but boring, and this is especially true of the better paying ones. Each customer or prospect presents different problems. Conditions in the market are continually changing, and the salesperson must make adjustments to allow for such changes. The thrill of matching wits with a clever prospect adds zest to sales work.

Experts have extolled the advantages of "security" as opposed to jobs offering the challenge of greater opportunities, so it is not unusual for people think of a future in which they will perform routine tasks for what they hope will be a steady income, even though it may not be as large as they wish. To such people a career in selling seems hazardous and uncertain; people who have no wish to confront unknown situations, which they have never coped with, may find it difficult to enjoy this profession, but for people who love thrill in their lives, selling is perhaps the most enjoyable profession.

This reluctance of many people to tackle a job like selling plays right into the hands of the person who aspires to a selling career. The latter will encounter less competition and garner more personal satisfaction because of this timidity on the part of others.

KEY CONCEPTS

- Selling is a basic human activity and is an integral part of our lives; knowingly or unknowingly, we all are salesmen selling something or the other all through our lives
- Selling is an integral part of marketing and is the culmination of all business activities.
- Selling is an inter-personal persuasive process designed to influence another person's decision. It is a critical part of marketing.
- Selling is an art; selling is more than just common sense; it is a professional discipline that can be learnt and developed.
- Selling is an active element of marketing and is inseparable from it. The ultimate success of marketing depends upon it.
- The primary function of a professional salesperson is to generate and close leads, educate prospects, fulfill needs and satisfy the wants of consumers appropriately, and therefore turn prospective customers into actual ones.
- Successful selling involves four basic steps called AIDA – Attention, Interest, Desire and Action.
- There are far too many myths about selling that often undermine its image as an important business function to be pursued seriously
- The modern concept of selling lays much more emphasis on the finer aspects of the process of sales rather than only on the flamboyance of personality, a blatant line of sales talk, and liberal use of high-pressure tactics to get the order.
- Salespersons fail because of lack of knowledge, skills or attitude.
- Selling is an outcome that besides resting upon a good product and service, depends fundamentally upon the honesty of purpose, sincerity, earnestness and genuineness of the sales person. It builds up his credibility and establishes him as a person who is dependable, trustworthy and responsible.
- To be effective, a salesperson must have certain psychological, social and physical traits and nurture them.
- Selling as a career is promising, rewarding in terms of money, status, adventure, thrill and gives a sense of fulfilment. However, it requires, as any other job, hard work, honesty, foresight, commonsense and other such attributes that make a person successful anywhere in any place.

CASE STUDY

COURAGE TO SELL

After five years of working for a large appliance manufacturer, in charge of the godown, Manjit Singh yearned for a more challenging job "somewhere in marketing," as he put it.

Manjit had graduated from a reputed college in Jalandhar with an outstanding record with Economics major and had been working in the sales office of the Delhi branch of the company since five years. Over the years, he had earned the reputation of an intelligent and hard working man in the company. While he was highly attentive in his job of dispatching goods to different dealers in the territory that the Delhi branch was serving, he took utmost care of the dealers who came to the branch to personally take goods that they urgently required. Mr. R.K. Chauhan, the branch manager of the Delhi branch took note of his high degree of customer orientation and asked him if he would like to be a part of his sales team.

Manjit could not have hoped for a better opportunity He readily agreed and joined the sales team of the branch – a group of five, bright, energetic boys, all in their mid twenties. Soon Manjit's ambition was to become the best of them and started learning the essentials of his new profession. He went to his old friend Surjit Bakshi who had been an ace sales manager with Johnson & Johnson and whom he considered as his mentor. Sharing his happiness with Manjit, Surjit said, "Manjit, you are a very old friend of mine so I will tell you a couple of things that you have to always remember in your new assignment." He said: "Be humble, be polite and try to understand the customers and their needs; take care of them! Try to see their difficulty, make an attempt to appreciate their problems and help them to the extent that you can. But always remember you are the representative of your company and always strive to protect its interests in the marketplace. Promise within the framework of company rules. Remember that customers are the most important part of any business. You are there because of your customers. The more you help them to do their business, the more they will be associated with your company and sell your product. So serve them sincerely."

With these valuable tips from Surjit, Manjit started the second innings of his career; and he did it splendidly! He tried his best to take care of his market and customers, promised what he could deliver and delivered what he promised. In a short span of time, he earned a good name for himself and was regarded as Mr. Dependable. His sales went up, demand expanded and dealers were contented.

Manjit has spent 27 years, selling his company's products. He is now the all India sales manager. As he goes down memory lane, he has realized that the cues to success lay in nothing but intelligence, sincerity, empathy, dedication and hard work. A man who started his career dispatching consignments to dealers of the company is an example to all young sales professionals who aspire to make selling their career.

Questions

1. How do you interpret the mind of Manjit Singh?
2. What aspects are worth learning from Manjit Singh's example?

REFERENCES

1. Boe, John, Senior (2011), What are you Selling?, *Market Advisor*, Vol. 12 Issue 4, p. 48.
2. Chonko, Lawrence B. and Jones, Eli (2005), The Need For Speed: Agility Selling, *Journal of Personal Selling & Sales Management*, Vol. 25 Issue 4, pp. 371-382.
3. Dwyer, Robert F. and Tanner, John F. Jr (2005), *Business Marketing: Connecting Strategy, Relationships, and Learning*, 3rd Edition, Burr Bridge, IL, McGraw Hill.
4. Hopkins, Tom (2001), People Skills, *Executive Excellence*, Vol. 18 Issue 11, p. 17.
5. Johnston, Mark W., Hair Jr., Joseph F., Boles, James, Kurtz, David L. (1989), Why Do Salespeople Fail? *Journal of Personal Selling & Sales Management*, Vol. 9 Issue 3, p. 53.
6. Schiffres, Manuel (2008), He Buys What Everyone Else Is Selling, *Kiplinger's Personal Finance*, Vol. 62 Issue 8, pp. 30-33.
7. Schwantz, Randy (2005), The Wedge Sales Call, *Sales & Service Excellence*, Vol. 5 Issue 9, p. 15-15
8. Shane, Ken (1994), The Selling Continuum, *American Salesman* Vol. 39 Issue 2, p. 7.
9. Szymanski, David M. (1988), Determinants of Selling Effectiveness: The Importance of Declarative Knowledge to the Personal Selling Concept, *Journal of Marketing*, Vol. 52 Issue 1, pp. 64-77.
10. Tanner J.F., Honneycut Jr E.D. and Erffmeyer R.C. (2009), *Sales Management: Shaping Future Sales Leaders*, Pearson Education, New Delhi.
11. Tanner, John Jr and George W. Dudley (2003), International Differences: Examining Two Assumptions About Selling in *Advances in Marketing*, William J. Kehoe and Linda K. Witten eds, Society for Marketing Advances.
12. Tasso, Kim (2006), What is Selling? *Dynamic Practice Development*, Viva Books, New Delhi, pp. 46-54.
13. Ziyal, Leyla (1995), Why the Best Salesperson is Not the Best Sales Manager, *Journal of Managerial Psychology*.

REFERENCES

3 Selling: Traits and Tasks

"Keep away from people who try to belittle your ambitions. Small people always do that, but the really great ones make you feel that you too, can become great."

–Mark Twain

CHAPTER OUTLINE

- ✦ Why salespeople fail
- ✦ About effective selling
- ✦ Sales psychology: Behavioural leadership managerial grid model
- ✦ Key result areas for sales professional
- ✦ The three pillars of success
- ✦ Traits of highly effective salespeople
- ✦ Secrets of super successful sales professionals
- ✦ Encouragement for success
- ✦ Service and sales

OBJECTIVES

After studying this chapter, you will be able to:

- ✦ Understand the foundation of effective selling and how salespersons can be effective in their profession
- ✦ Know the key result areas for sales professional
- ✦ Realize why salespeople fail
- ✦ Understand how salespersons work and imbibe the desired traits necessary for success
- ✦ Learn the top secrets of the super successful sales from experts professional

Opening Case: Healthy Life Pharmaceuticals Ltd.

Healthy Life Pharmaceuticals Ltd. was in the business of manufacturing and sales of pharmaceutical drugs. Most of these drugs were Schedule H prescription drugs which meant that they were sold only on doctor's prescription. So the Professional Sales Representatives (PSRs) of Healthy Life Pharmaceuticals regularly called on physicians in their territories to appraise them about their company's products. Sales took place if the doctors prescribed their medicines for their patients. The PSRs also visited their C&F Agents, distributors, wholesalers and retailers and ensured availability of their products at all times.

Arun Chandok has been working as a PSR in Healthy Life Pharmaceuticals for last five years. He looked after the Central UP and his territory covered the districts of Lucknow, Allahabad, Varanasi and Gorakhpur. During last year, Chandok led his region in sales and was placed quite high in the All India Ranking in sales as related to potential.

Quite naturally, S B Singh, the Regional Manager of Central UP of Healthy Life Pharmaceuticals was very proud of Mr. Chandok. However, he recently discovered that Chandok spent only two days in a week in the market. On other days he used to spend with distributors and wholesalers. Mr. Singh also learnt that Chandok had joined some evening classes to study MBA. Spot checking a few of the physicians in Chandok's territory he discovered that Mr. Chandok was not regular in seeing the doctors though the distributor and stockists spoke highly of him as a salesperson – very helpful, prompt and with a lot of positive attitude.

As part of its expansion plan, this year Healthy Life Pharmaceuticals decided to be much more aggressive in the market. It has planned to achieve a sales growth rate of 40% over last year. While the company decided to add few new products to augment the sales growth, it expected the sales team to give their best to achieve the new target.

On talking about the new targets, Chandok reassured Mr. Singh that it would be achieved, but Mr. Singh was not sure about his claims.

Questions

1. What are the fundamental issues and challenges being faced by Mr. Singh in Healthy Life Pharmaceuticals?
2. Please explain what steps should Mr. Singh take now to be sure of achieving the new challenge of steep sales growth?

SELLING: TRAITS AND TASKS

Integral Design for Programmed Learning

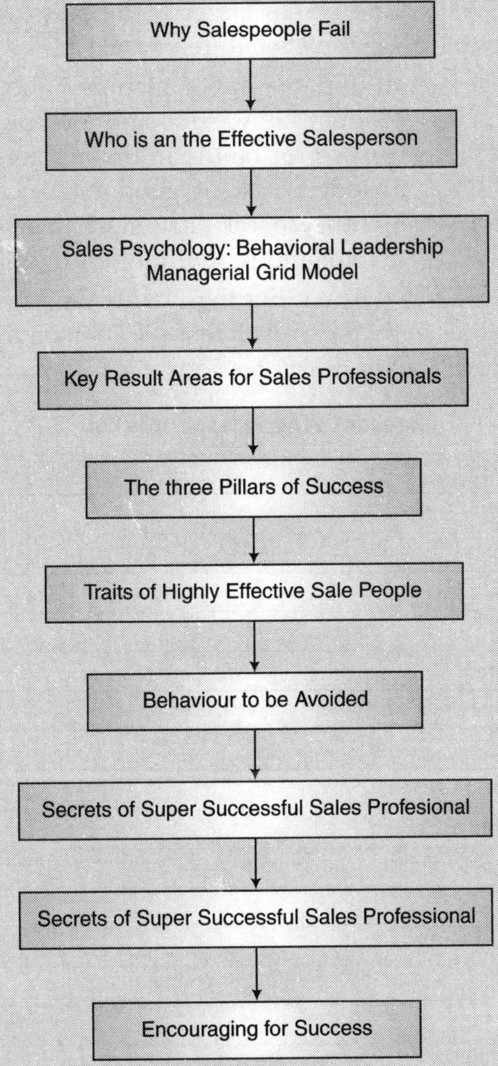

"Outstanding sales professionals are "word merchants" and "picture painters".

–Zig Ziglar

WHY SALESPEOPLE FAIL

In spite of having professional skills, salespeople sometimes fail to procure orders, are not appreciated by their customers for their services and do not win accolades of their colleagues for achieving marvels in the market. In a survey conducted by Kirpatrik CA and Russ FA (1981), sales personnel of 500 of the USA's largest companies were asked what, in their experience, were the causes of salespeople's failure on the job.

What emerged was that lack of initiative, poor planning and organization; inadequate product knowledge and lack of enthusiasm are the main reasons for failure in the market. Other important reasons included lack of good inter-personal relationships, lack of concern for customers, inadequate knowledge of the market and lack of interest in self-development.

Lack of initiative, poor planning and organization; inadequate product knowledge and lack of enthusiasm are the main reasons for failure in the market.

Their findings, with the percent mentioned for each cause, as given below explain clearly the traits that a salesperson must have to be effective in the market place and be successful in his profession.

Reasons Why Salespeople Fail

Cause of failure	*Percent*
Lack of initiative	55
Poor planning and organization	39
Inadequate product knowledge	37
Lack of enthusiasm	31
Salesperson not customer oriented	30
Lack of proper training	23
Inability to get along with buyers	21
Lack of personal goals	20
Inadequate knowledge of market	19
Lack of knowledge of the company	16
Lack of job satisfaction	15
Unsuited for sales career	14
Lack of adequate background	13
Insufficient self-discipline	12
Salesperson not company oriented	12
No interest in self-development	11
Failure to follow instruction	11
Lack of self-confidence	11
Improper supervision	9
Inability to improvise	8

Lack of imagination	7
Personal problems	6
Difficulties in communicating	6
Dishonesty	5
Unfortunate appearance	5
Improper attitude	5
Failure to ask buyers to buy	3
Lack of tact and courtesy	2
Gambling and drinking	2

Source: Kirpatrik CA and Russ FA (1981), Effective Selling, South-Western Publishing Co. Cincinnati, p-24.

ABOUT EFFECTIVE SELLING

It is often asked – Who is an effective salesperson? Perhaps, there is no one answer to this question. Is he a personality who knows all, does all and achieves all? Should he be flamboyant, smart, and a glib talker, one who can mesmerize his customers with his very presence and can achieve his targets somehow or the other? Or should he be a person who has a low profile, but works very hard, is sensitive, maintains a good relationship with his customers and works hard to create and increase sales on a continuously?

It is said that there is no such thing as a single ideal sales personality. However, it can be said without doubt that an effective salesman is one who has the ability to achieve his targets and at the same time is able to resolve the problems of his customers. It is certain therefore, that to be successful in a sales career, a salesperson should have certain personality traits and attitudes that are admired by others and at the same time help him to achieve his targets successfully. The real test of a true salesperson is his ability to drive the sales discussion with logic and close the deal with a pleasant emotional impression that helps him to get additional sales whenever he visits the territory again.

> An effective salesman is one who is loved and trusted by his customers, enjoys their confidence and is respected by them as their well-wisher.

SALES PSYCHOLOGY: BEHAVIORAL LEADERSHIP MANAGERIAL GRID MODEL

A good way to understand the underlying psychological make-up of different types of salespersons is by adapting the behavioural leadership Managerial Grid Model (1964) developed by Robert Blake and Jane Mouton to describe the behavioural pattern of salespeople. The adapted model identifies five different selling styles based on the concern for customers and the concern for sales. A graphical representation of the sales grid is depicted in Figure 3.1.

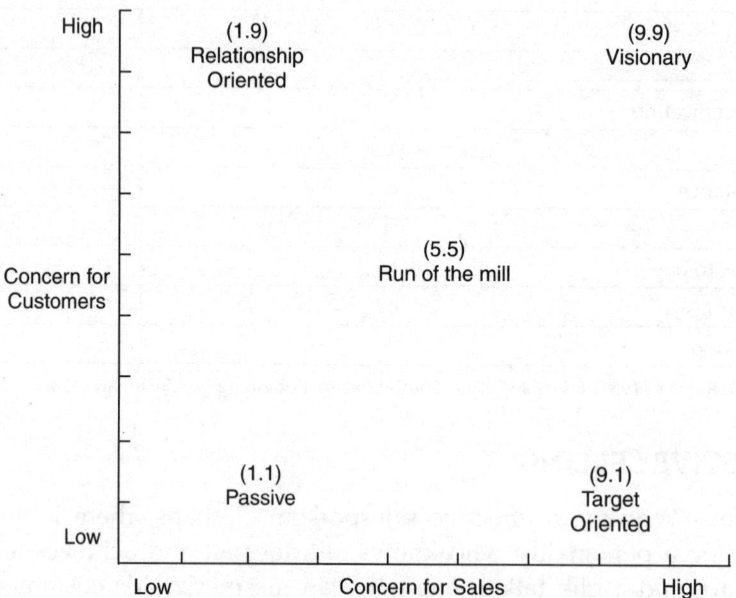

Fig. 3.1 *A Graphical Representation of the Sales Grid*

As shown in the figure, the model is represented as a grid with *concern for sales* as the x-axis and *concern for customers* as the y-axis; each axis ranges from 1 (Low) to 9 (High). The five resulting sales styles are as follows:

Passive (1,1)

In this style, salespersons have *low* concern for both customers as well as sales. Salespersons of this kind are neither able to stretch themselves nor are they able to take innovative decisions. The underlying psychological make-up of such salespersons is not really suited for a sales profession.

Relationship Oriented (1,9)

This style has a *high* concern for customers and a *low* concern for sales. Salespersons using this style are very concerned about their customers' interests often at the cost of sales and in the hope that this will increase performance. The resulting atmosphere is usually friendly, but not necessarily that productive.

Target Oriented (9,1)

With a *high* concern for sales, and a *low* concern for customers, such salespersons feel that customers as people are unimportant; they look upon them only as order booking entities; they try all ways and means to achieve their targets. Sales professionals using this style also pressurize their employees, using rules and penalties to achieve sales targets, without really leading them to achieve their goals. This dictatorial style is based on Theory X of Douglas McGregor, and is commonly applied by salespeople on the edge of real or perceived failure.

Run of the Mill (5,5)

Managers using this style try to achieve a balance between company goals and workers' needs. By showing concern for both people and production, managers who use this style hope to achieve a good performance.

Visionary (9,9)

In this style, a lot of attention is paid both to people and production. As suggested by the propositions of Theory Y, managers choosing to use this style encourage teamwork and commitment among employees. This method relies heavily on making employees feel a constructive part of the company.

KEY RESULT AREAS FOR SALES PROFESSIONALS

Any salesperson has certain duties and responsibilities to carry out in his territory. There should not be more than 7-8. These Key Result Areas (KRAs) which should make up nearly 85% of the workload are listed below.

1. Service current customers and develop new customers to meet sales and collection targets and minimize outstanding receivables.
2. To explore and secure new business to ensure continual growth for the company products, in accordance with set new business targets.
3. To review productivity of the territory regularly by reviewing its profitability.
4. To provide effective, efficient, professional service and advice to ensure client satisfaction of the highest level.
5. Monitor competitive activity and report significant developments to the management.
6. Remain informed and up to date with regard to industry related news, market activity, product knowledge and continuously strive to develop one's own skills and knowledge in order to perform optimally.
7. Contribute to annual sales and to nurturing important customers.
8. Establish and maintain a high level of customer satisfaction. Communicate to and work with the other departments as necessary to resolve unique customer issues/ concerns.

These key result areas are commonly known to all salespersons but, it is not uncommon to see salespeople failing to perform in the market. Since the results in this field are always in black and white, performance whether laudable or otherwise is immediately clear. As salespeople address this issue, certain facts emerge.

THE THREE PILLARS OF SUCCESS

Customers buy from salespeople whom they like. They trust and believe in such persons. Colleagues admire such salespersons and seek help and mentoring from them. Senior managers trust and rely on effective salespeople to get the job done, come what may. Effective salespeople always look for new ways to help customers. Such salespeople enhance business relationships with their customers and hence sales volume.

> Customers buy from salespeople whom they like.

What then makes an effective salesperson? It is believed that to be an effective salesperson requires an exceptional blend of knowledge, skills and attitude. These qualities are explained below.

Attitude

The most important quality of a good sales professional is his attitude. A positive attitude comprises an inherent sense of responsibility and indomitable courage to achieve targets assigned to him. Successful salespeople find a way to succeed despite fluctuations of fortunes in the market. They have a determined attitude to achieve results.

> Being a successful salesperson means being disciplined, so that over-promising and under-delivering are avoided.

Working alone is not an option for a salesperson. They rely on individuals and teams within their own organization and within the customer's organization to be successful. They work in and build teams, inspiring others to excel so that they might achieve their desired sales results.

Further, self development and learning is the norm. For example, they learn about their customer's industry and business as a matter of course. If they have supervisory responsibilities they address performance issues directly and fairly.

Successful salespeople find ways of improving their customers' business by making it more efficient or effective. They are prepared to try out new approaches and take well balanced risks.

Skills

The skills of building relationships are vital to success in selling. Salespeople must value and work at developing interpersonal relationships in all the interactions they have in the customer's organization, as well as their own. For example, the importance of a good relationship with the personal assistant of the general manager is no more evident than when trying to access the general manager at a busy time.

Negotiating to achieve outcomes considered valuable to customers and to their organization is necessary for building profitable relationships. Likewise, ensuring the supply chain fulfils the needs of the contract or agreement often requires subtle negotiating skills.

> Salespeople must value and work at developing interpersonal relationships in all interactions they have across the customer's organization, as well as their own.

Managing the financial aspects of the contract is very important. Salespeople must be able to ensure that bills are paid on time.

Successful salespeople raise the capability of the sales organization through the development of others. They will coach and train those who need it to deliver a better overall outcome for the organization.

Identifying the critical issues or opportunities using all relevant and available information is crucial to sales success. Successful salespeople determine the causes and possible solutions of problems in a manner that enhances customer relationships.

Knowledge

Knowledge is the foundation of effectiveness. It is as true for salespeople as it is for other professions. To be effective, salespeople must:

1. Have good knowledge about the company, the product, services and logistics, as they are the basis of the knowledge that successful salespeople use to help solve customers' problems.
2. Understand the customer's operations, services and products and their value chain. This is also essential, as it is the knowledge that successful salespeople use to define customers' problems.
3. Have a deep understanding of the customers' business structure and process. This is the knowledge by which successful salespeople determine the most pressing customer problem to solve and for whom to solve it.
4. Plan sales calls. This is critical to success, because to be efficient and effective salesmanship requires detailed knowledge of the geographical areas where customers and prospects reside as well as their daily schedules.

A successful salesperson is a professional. It is difficult to find all the behavioural attributes, knowledge and skills required to be a successful salesperson in one person. This is why successful salespeople stand out.

TRAITS OF HIGHLY EFFECTIVE SALESPEOPLE

> In the selling profession, a salesperson has to be his own master, he has to be a complete individual who can take command of any situation that comes to him.

A salesperson's job is quite different from other professions. A salesperson works twenty-four hours, is almost always on tour, alone, away from his family and friends, often facing adverse weather conditions, and always exposed to uncertainties – uncertainty about getting orders, payments and achieving targets; uncertainty about meeting prospects, and also uncertainty in his personal comforts while away from home. He faces adversity, encounters difficulties and comes across hard times quite often. And he has no one to guide him at that point in time; no one to support him, nor anyone to take care of him. A complete salesperson has to be a leader, a follower, a friend, a guide, a thinker and a doer. What traits, then, should a salesperson have?

Given below are some of the important traits that all salespeople should have to be successful in their profession.

Psychological Traits

First and foremost, effective salespersons should have a very strong mental make-up. This strength enables them to weather all storms that are inherent in their profession. Accordingly, a salesperson should have the following psychological traits.

Courage

The will to win is the most important trait that a salesperson should possess. Courage fires the will to succeed. Successful people are those who have the courage to step ahead, face uncertainty with determination and emerge victorious. Their strong urge to achieve and driving ambition to get what they want make them different from others. Courage gives confidence, instils a competitive spirit, leads to aggressiveness, and helps them to win.

> Successful people are those who have the courage to step ahead, face uncertainty with determination and emerge victorious.

Passion

Passion is an intense emotion of compelling feeling, enthusiasm, or desire for anything and often requiring action. Salespeople, who have a passion for selling, excel at selling. It all starts with passion. Selling is about transferring the passion you have for your product or service to a prospective customer. If you are not successful in sales, you should look at your passion.

Optimism

Optimism is a matter of attitude. It is the tendency to expect the best possible outcome or dwell on the most hopeful aspects of a situation. Optimism is a characteristic of a success-minded person – one who does not admit to failing to attain his goals. Successful salespeople are optimistic about themselves, their product, their company and their market and customers. Optimism is a critical component for salespeople as it gives them that vital ray of hope that leads to results.

Confidence

Confidence is all about knowing that what you know is the right thing and standing up for it no matter what; holding your head high even if others make fun of you; simply being who you are and not letting anyone deter you from that, no matter who they are. Confidence rests on the firm belief in oneself and one's own abilities. To a salesperson, confidence is a belief in oneself, a reassurance of one's own capabilities. It is the motivation that propels the salesperson to face adverse situations boldly and achieve success.

> A confident salesperson inspires confidence in the customers that enable him to take a favourable buying decision.

Sincerity

Nothing is so vital to selling as sincerity. Sincerity is the quality or condition of being genuine, honest, and denotes freedom from duplicity. To a salesperson, a sincere effort in solving the problems of customers and working for their well-being is the best way to show them that you care. Sincerity in making sales calls and truthfulness in making promises makes a salesperson win in the market.

Dependability

Dependability is a value showing the reliability of a person to others because of his/her integrity, truthfulness, and trustworthiness; traits that can encourage people to depend on them. On the other hand, undependable salespeople are most disliked. In fact, a salesperson, who customers know to be undependable, has no chance of achieving anything in the market.

> Salespeople who are dependable are welcome in the market

Initiative

By initiative is meant the power or ability to begin or to follow through a plan or task; enterprise and determination. It is the eagerness to come forward and take on new assignments, whatever the difficulty. A salesperson with initiative is essentially a person with ambition, one who is industrious and is continuously working on his own to achieve his goals, irrespective of whether there is any supervision. He is a person who takes risks, explores unknown territories, develops new markets and customers and brings new business all the time. He is a person who is most liked and is the pride of any company.

Creativity

Creativity is the urge to generate or recognize ideas, alternatives, or possibilities that may be useful in solving problems, communicating with others, and entertaining oneself and others. Effectiveness in selling also means, among other things, the ability to generate new possibilities or new alternatives. The ability to generate alternatives or to see things uniquely does not occur by chance; it is linked to other, more fundamental qualities of thinking, such as flexibility, tolerance of ambiguities or unpredictability, and the enjoyment of things previously unknown.

> Salespeople who are successful have the ability to view things in new ways or from a different perspective.

Persuasiveness

Selling is a fine art of persuasion and an effective salesperson is one who has mastered this art of persuasion. It is an important psychological attribute that is reflected in their personal conviction in what they are selling and belief and passion for their position.

The sixth sense

Salespeople must be able to "read and relate" to the prospect. Experiencing the feelings, thoughts and attitudes of others permits the salesperson to form their presentation and responses in a way that will foster true communication. A prospect's motivations and a salesperson's responses to the prospect's verbal and non-verbal language (body language) represent the basis of all sales efforts.

Sense of urgency

The function of sales is like fighting a war. It is a function where speed, accuracy and focus are of prime importance. It is therefore necessary that salespeople must have a "sense of urgency." Their work requires total commitment, involvement and persistence to achieve the targets – in time and as per schedule.

> Effective salespersons are those who work as if there is no tomorrow.

Learning from failure

Salespeople must always be able to achieve "accomplishment from adversity." Such people are proud of their accomplishments and they will usually value the lessons learned and skills developed from a particularly challenging obstacle. They may even be proud of their failures because of their ability to rebound and refine themselves. These people win, even when they lose.

Social Traits

One of the very important characteristics of a salesperson is his amicable nature. A salesperson's long-term success depends to a great extent on his social inclination and a basic liking for people. Some of the traits necessary for a salesperson to be successful are as follows:

Mannerisms

A salesperson's visit should be eagerly awaited by his customers. Not because they have problems, but because of his pleasant mannerisms, his courtesy, his smile and his respect for others.

> A salesperson with good manners tries to make every call a happy experience for his customers. His courtesy, etiquette and behaviour are long remembered after the sale is closed.

Conversational ability

A good conversation can win over a customer and overcome adverse situations. An effective salesperson must have the following four characteristics to be a good conversationalist.

1. Customers will listen only if the subject matter is of any interest to them. So a salesperson must take the "you" approach and talk from that stand point all through the interaction. This requires a stance where the salesperson has to put himself in the customers' shoes and try to understand their problems so that he can resolve them effectively.
2. The salesperson must make the prospect feel important and this can be done only by a genuine understanding and appreciation of customer's point of view. A salesperson must also take the customer's views and guidance and involve him in discussions as to how the sales of that particular territory can be further improved. This will make the customer feel important and at the same time will give the salesperson valuable insights about the territory and its dynamics.
3. The salesperson must ensure that he exercises a subtle control over the subject matter through the entire course of the conversation and see that the dialogue moves in the desired direction. Of course, to make this happen, the salesperson must enter the market fully prepared.
4. He should also be very articulate in his conversation and guard against overusing certain words or expressions. He must ensure that he is precise, focused and accurate in his conversation with customers all the time.

Poise

Poise is that attribute which enables people to be in good command of themselves – physically, mentally and emotionally. It is a vital element of a salesperson's personality that makes his customers respect him. Poise comes from self-confidence and self-confidence comes from knowledge about the company, its systems and procedures, the products, market, customers, competition, and other related facets of sales. To be effective, a salesperson must nurture this trait over a period of time as it helps tremendously in accomplishing sales tasks.

Physical traits

Whenever people think of a salesperson, they think of a smart, good-looking, well-dressed, nice-mannered gentleman who is courteous, polite and has a pleasant personality. People are impressed by him and are attracted towards him instantaneously. This gives us some idea as to what should be the physical characteristics of an effective salesperson. Given below are some of the important physical traits that he must possess.

Personality

The physical appearance of a human being is not entirely in his hands but he can definitely groom himself in such a manner so that he looks attractive. What then makes a person attractive?

> A salesperson should exude energy, should be vibrant and radiate authority and command.

A salesperson should groom his hair decently, cut his nails, brush his teeth and use a pleasant, soothing fragrance on his body. He should wear smart clothes, as neat, clean and well fitting clothes are a testimony to his being meticulous in whatever he does. Shoes should be polished and if he is wearing a belt it should look good.

A salesperson should avoid having messy hair, a beard, and wearing jazzy clothes and belts with big, odd looking buckles. The clothes must be buttoned properly. He must also avoid smoking, and chewing gum, tobacco or beetle nut (so prevalent in India).

Posture and bearing can also influence a salesperson's personality. Because posture and bearing (body language) are revealing, salesperson should see that they emanate positive, rather than negative energy.

Mannerisms

Mannerisms distinguish one salesperson from another. It creates a first impression that lingers in the minds of a customer and tells his subconscious mind whether or not to deal with the salesperson. Mannerisms are unconscious gestures that often become a habit, made unknowingly but which can create an unfavourable impression and often even irritate the prospects. At times some people speak very loudly, laugh loudly, or wear a sullen expression. These mannerisms irritate others and must be stopped. Every salesperson must be aware of such mannerisms and exercise conscious control to get rid of them.

> Scratching one's head, playing with a pen while talking, cracking the knuckles, chewing gum, belching, reading a newspaper when the prospect is talking are some of the undesirable mannerisms that create a negative impact to the listeners.

Language

A person's sense of hearing ranks second, after his sense of sight. So what a customer hears from the salesperson is important for him to register an impressing about the salesperson. For the customer to have a good impression, the salesperson's voice should be pleasing, i.e. clear and modulated, his body language warm and gestures friendly. He should be courteous and respectful. His voice should be convincing but polite, emphatic and firm, but congenial.

A dull presentation is as lifeless and boring and is unlikely to persuade the prospects to buy anything. Since effective expression of thoughts is very important to get sales, salespeople should work hard to refine their language and ability to articulate in a very precise manner.

Behaviour to be Avoided

Often, salespeople, in their eagerness to achieve the targets, fall into behavioural traps, often unknowingly and by the time they realize the ill effects, the damage has been done. The damages might include loss of face, credibility, reputation, mistrust, and destruction of sales and personal image.

> Undesirable behaviour is like an itch; it is an irritant, which though seemingly small, may mar success and spell disaster for the whole process of selling.

Listed below are some of the traits that are disliked most by customers. These include:

1. Dishonesty	2. Sarcasm
3. Cheating	4. Untruthfulness
5. Criticism	6. Negativity
4. Begging	8. Complaining
9. Prejudice	10. Intolerance
11. Over-familiarity	12. Aggressiveness
13. Arrogance	14 Pretentiousness
15. Discourtesy	16. Indifference
17. Complacency	18. Narcissism
19. Superiority-complex	20. Egotism
21. Double-dealing	22. Cynicism
23. Conceit	24. Unresponsiveness
25. Dull presentation	26. Uninspiring manner
27. Authoritarian behaviour	28. Unfairness
29. Subjective attitude	30. Deceit

There are salespersons that loathe hard work, and have no patience to nurture the fundamental qualities necessary to bring in better sales. They want quick results, even if they are through unethical means. They may even entice the customers through sponsorships, and trade through unscrupulous means. The impact of such unethical promotions is:

- The cost of obtaining business is very high.
- The organization's as well as the salesperson's image is spoilt in the whole process.
- Salespeople who indulge in such activities generally work less in the field, as their business is fixed. Therefore, they may be out of touch with the ground reality.
- Such supplies, if not supported by corresponding increase in prescriptions, may find their way out to other territories/areas as well.
- Such bad habits may be picked up by other salespeople too.
- Salespeople who indulge in such practices tend to become more of traders and less of marketers.
- They may put themselves at the mercy of customers and traders.
- If a salesman is unable to offer anything more beyond a certain point, the deal may get broken, and the sales fall drastically.
- If such unethical practices are brought to the knowledge of organizations, they may take action against the concerned salesmen, which might often be unpleasant.

People who live with such ideas often forget that such short cuts do not lead to good results. Such activities are exposed very soon and once they are out in the open, they spell disaster. Salespeople must remember that customers/dealers/distributors are also human beings with emotions, hopes and aspirations, likes and dislikes, happiness and sorrow, love and hate, and the "moments of truths" they experience during the entire process of

> Experience shows that long after sales is over, the salesperson and the product that he has sold, is remembered.

sales, leaves an indelible impression in their minds, about the product, the company and above all the salesperson. And this impression guides their decision making in all subsequent purchases and also influences others in their purchases too. The words "moments of truths" were coined by none other than the well known personality, Jan Carlzon, who turned around Scandinavian Airlines, from disaster. Carlzon had said that during the entire process of sales, the customers interact with the company and their salespersons many times. He called these interactions "Moments of Truths" and said that it is the experiences that they gather at each such interaction end up forming an impression of the customer about the company, its products and services and its people.

Organizations also need to extend their support to the salespeople. These are the fundamentals for any salesperson to succeed. However, it requires passion for the job, perseverance, hard work and efforts in the field, and therefore, takes its time to yield results. Once a salesperson has imbibed these fundamentals, the improvement in sales that he will bring to the organization may be sustainable and might last longer. It is highly unlikely that such a salesman will fail the organization with a string of poor sales performance, in the normal circumstances.

This is the trait that organizations should encourage and develop in every salesman. Ultimately, improved sales performance by salesperson, which contributes greatly to the bottom line, is the result of building up of strong fundamentals. Any sales result, achieved in the absence of strong fundamentals in a salesman, may not last long.

> Salespeople who believe in developing good fundamentals for better sales ethically last longer in any organization, they are rewarded, have career growth and are taken care of well.

It is also observed that salespersons who do business ethically have greater chances of staying with a company for a long time. As opposed to this, salespeople who believe in doing business unethically, and are in a hurry to show results quickly, generally do not last long in any organization.

SECRETS OF SUPER SUCCESSFUL SALES PROFESSIONALS

1. **A passion for people, products or services**
   Super sales professionals care for people and help them to solve their problems/ get their buying needs met. The buyer feels his true concern. It is not an act; it is a calling.
2. **Attitude to help customers to feel**
   Super sales professionals do not just look at giving free samples or gifts as a way of getting the person to buy. Instead, they create possibilities that genuinely excite the buyer.

3. **Selling to buyer's buying strategy instead of using selling techniques**
   Every buyer has his preferred way of purchasing. A good salesperson should get to know these preferences that customers have in making purchases.
4. **An ability to discern who is going to be a buyer and who is not**
   Super sales professionals have a sixth sense that helps them to distinguish between real buyers and those who are just passing time. This sixth sense can be developed, and saves a lot of time and frustration when mastered.
5. **Match the exact features/benefits of the product with the customers' spoken or unspoken needs or wants.**
6. **Sell the sizzle, not just the steak**
   No buyer cares about all the features and benefits; they usually only care about 1 or 2 of them. Your mission should be to sense, feel or discover the key benefits that turn this discussion into a sale, quickly.
7. **Do not rush to make a sale**
   Do not appear too hungry. Hungry salespeople scare away the customer.
8. **Show how effective and valuable your product/service really is**
   Facts inspire confidence. Get to know the real facts about how effectively your product or service performs and pleases customers. This will make you a formidable sales professional.
9. **Add value to the lives of everyone you interact with**
   Be a resource to potential customers.
10. **Be humane, and genuine with everyone**
    Do not be artificial in your approach. Do not put up a façade. Customers can quickly sense if you are only there for 'as long as you think there is a chance that the customer will buy something from you.'
11. **Listen with your heart and soul**
    Listening is more important than talking, as it tells us what to speak. As salesmen, you must listen actively and then respond.
12. **Be genuinely interested in your customers**
    Try to be one with your customers and have a good personal rapport with them. If your existing customers do not enter your office with a smile on their faces and if they do not establish instant eye contact, it is time to introspect!
13. **Work with full enthusiasm**
    Working at high energy not only leads to results but also makes the environment vibrant and improves the productivity of your entire team.
14. **Never criticize**
    Whining and complaining about the system, or co-workers or circumstances will rob you of energy. Good salespersons never criticize the competitors or the circumstances

as it only damages their credibility. You should be excited about the product and customers and work hard to make things even better.

15. **Smile with your heart**

    A smile seldom goes to waste. If you smile with your heart, you are bound to get a smile in return. If you are happy about seeing someone, let your whole self smile. Salespeople attribute their success to how often they smile during work.

16. **Tell customers what is in it for them**

    People are generally self centred. So tell them what they will get instead or how they will get it. As a salesperson, tell your prospects what they will get in terms of profits.

17. **Appeal more to the emotional mind rather than the logical mind**

    Give customers an emotional reason to take your advice. Everyone has two minds – emotional and logical. The emotional mind is stronger. A jeans' salesman should explain how one will look and how well the pair will fit him rather than describing the fabric used to make the jeans. A car salesman should tell the prospect how a premium car will increase his prestige in society. Show customers the happiness, health and prosperity a product will give them rather than its technical details.

18. **Always follow up**

    Excellent salespeople always keep in touch with their existing and former clients. They ensure that they get repeated business and referrals from existing customers. So, you could send them birthday cards and new year wishes, remind them of their appointments with you, call them over for a cup tea and give them information. The idea is to keep in touch with them.

19. **Take pride in your personal performance**

    Like pilots in the air force or soldiers in the armed core of the infantry of an army, salespeople are always in the front line and the fortunes of the company always depend heavily upon them. Sales is more than a job. You must be proud to say that you are in the sales division of the company.

20. **See the big picture**

    Look beyond tomorrow, share the growth curve of your company with your customers, build a future plan with them and discuss how their performance will impact their business, their clients' lives and their own lives.

21. **Adopt a positive attitude with action towards selling**

    A positive attitude is the spark that propels a salesperson to attain success. It strengthens him to take on adversity, fight competition and sell to customers with conviction. So adopt a positive attitude with action towards selling.

22. **Take ownership**

    A successful salesperson is one who takes charge of his territory well, feels responsibility towards his customers and believes in his actions. He is committed to fulfilling all promises made to his customers and feels accountable for anything that goes wrong. Such salespeople are self-empowered to perform and they always are respected by their customers, admired by their colleagues and feared by their competitors.

ENCOURAGEMENT FOR SUCCESS

To be successful in this highly competitive market scenario, organizations must also support and compliment salesmen who develop and nurture good fundamental qualities so that sales improve and are sustained in the long run.

Organizations should support the field force in the ways given below.

- Proper induction, training and development to all personnel in the field.
- Salaries, other perks/allowances, incentive payments, samples, promotional inputs should be paid on time.
- Line managers must act as guides and on the job trainers and nurture salespersons to give better performances.
- Line managers should go through the reports received from their salespersons, carefully and give suggestions for better performance/improvement, wherever necessary, to the concerned team member.
- Responding to all communications received from salesmen promptly.
- Ensuring career growth within the organization for consistently performing salespersons.
- Set appropriate targets to salesmen, which should be ambitious, but achievable with sincere efforts.
- Inculcating good fundamentals in all salesperson, and complimenting their efforts, is the most potent weapon to combat severe competition in the market, and also leads to a better and sustainable sales performance.

An effective sales offering should be customized to suit the needs of the customers. For example in the case of a motor vehicle:

1. Competitively priced products made by factory trained technicians.
2. Factory parts designed specifically for the customer's vehicle.
3. State-of-the-art equipment.
4. Maintenance service with no surprises.
5. Maintenance packages that cost less than individual services priced separately.
6. Less risk of having their vehicle break down if maintenance schedules are kept to.
7. Credibility that customers can "see in writing" what services are needed.

It is interesting to know why Toyota sells more vehicles every year. The *J.D. Power Customer Retention Study*, published in 2007, gives the reasons for Toyota's success. *"Toyota maintains its high retention rates by providing high-quality vehicles and service to its existing customers, which in turn generates favourable word-of-mouth recommendations that attract new customers."* The report

> The service you provide should be so special, so valuable to your customers, and so important to their needs, that your dealership becomes their only real choice.

shows that 64% of Toyota's customers stated that they are staying with the company. If Toyota were to rewrite Chevrolet Malibu's *"The car you can't ignore"* advertising headline, it might go something like – *"The car you're glad you bought."*

History is replete with examples where good, efficient service has pulled up the sales in spite of stiff competition and has made the company front runners! Sales and service are like the two wings of a bird; both are needed for the bird to fly!

It is said that to be an effective salesperson, one needs to know what has been taught to him in his kindergarten school. This learning – honesty, purity, dedication, truthfulness, commitment, love, friendliness etc. – is what he essentially requires to be an effective salesperson. Selling the idea of a healthy, happy and prosperous life is the essence of the job of a salesperson. Your success depends upon how many customers are happy after 'buying' your product.

KEY CONCEPTS

- Selling is about solving customers' problems. The successful salespeople are those who identify pressing customer problems, spot a customer's priorities, and help them find a solution in the most convenient, cost effective, innovative and timely way.
- Determining the problems that a customer wants to solve the most, which you are distinctively competent to solve, is a winning combination.
- The key to success is know how to market your problem-solving abilities so people know what you can do for them and how they can benefit by using your solutions.
- Customers trust salespersons that empathize with them and this realization has done wonders to increase sales for salespeople.
- Your self image will determine whether your prospect develops a positive image of you.
- Selling is knowing your product and your company well; it gives you a competitive advantage
- People do not buy what you wish to sell. They buy what they need.
- Selling does not take place when you are talking. Selling takes place when your prospect is talking. Great salespeople are great listeners. So listen! It will help you to sell well.
- Selling is not about what you think is right, it is about whether you're right for your prospects.
- The litmus test of a true salesperson is his ability to drive the sales discussion with logic and close the deal with an pleasant emotional impression that helps him to get further sales whenever he visits the territory again.

- Successful salespeople are those who find a way to succeed despite fluctuations of fortunes in the market. They have a determined attitude to achieving results.
- Being a successful sales person means being disciplined, so that over-promising and under-delivering are the rare occurrences.
- Successful salespeople find ways of improving the business by making their customer's business more efficient or effective. So you should be prepared to try out new approaches and take well balanced risks.
- Successful salespeople determine the causes and possible solutions of problems in a manner that enhances customer relationships.
- Good knowledge about the company, the product, services and logistics is necessary, as they are the base of knowledge that successful salespeople use to help solve customers' problems.
- Sell to buyer's buying strategy instead of using selling techniques.

BOND SUNGLASSES: SELLING AT THE CROSSROADS

For over 27 years, Bond Sunglasses has been one of the most popular companies making high-end sunglasses. The range included spectacles manufactured at its various factories situated in India and abroad. The company also had a collaboration with Orion Optics, one of the most reputed makers of sunglasses in the world.

Ramesh Babu was a sales executive from Bond Sunglasses, who was considered as one of the best in the world by customers. Ramesh was young, enthusiastic and vibrant. He was confident about his market and dealers. As Bond Sunglasses were in high demand, Ramesh was assured of his sales, though often this led to complacent behaviour on his part, while interacting in the market. His performance reinforced his contentions. He was one of the best salespersons of the company, His collections always exceeded the targets and his dealers were eager to sell the products of his company.

As part of a sales visit, Ramesh, along with his area sales manager, D.K. Dutta, went to visit the dealers of Bangalore. At 11 a.m., they started the day by visiting the first dealer, New Wave Opticals in Plaza Street in Bangalore. Pratap, the owner of the shop greeted them and requested them to wait for a while as he was busy dealing with two customers. Dutta said, 'No problem Mr. Pratap, please carry on with your customers, we will wait till you are free'. As Pratap continued attending to his customers, Dutta went around the showroom, saw the display, checked the competitors' products lying on the shelf and re-arranged the Point-of-Purchase material use in the store. All this while Ramesh was engrossed in reading the newspaper that he had found lying on Pratap's table. Dutta and Ramesh had to wait for nearly half an hour.

As his customers left, Pratap apologized once again for keeping them waiting and started the discussion. Pratap seemed a little perturbed at the insensitive approach of the company towards handling his complaints. He took out his files and pointed out the different claims that had been unattended since the last 7-8 months. Some defective goods sent for replacement had also not been sent back. A few credit notes also lay unadjusted. Dutta seemed visibly upset at the state of affairs. Later on when Mr. Dutta asked Ramesh the reasons he could not obtain any satisfactory reply. Dutta wondered what was wrong with Ramesh. Were his products in demand because of the brand pull or was it the contribution of his sales team?

Questions

1. How do you perceive the behaviour of Ramesh in the store?
2. What could he have done to utilize the time as he waited for Pratap to become available?
3. What should have been the activities of Pratap and his team in a market where his products are in high demand?

REFERENCES

1. Brooks, Bill (2006), Aggressiveness and Sales Success…How Do You Measure Up? *American Salesman*, Vol. 51 Issue 5, pp. 21-24.
2. Cronin, Bernard M. (1999), The ABCs of Success in Sales, *American Salesman*, Vol. 44 Issue 11, p. 3.
3. Decker, Charles (Jul 2004), The 5 Paths to Persuasion, *Fast Company*, Issue 84, p. 92.
4. Getting More Out of Life, *American Salesman*, May 2005, Vol. 50 Issue 5, pp. 21-24.
5. Gitomer, Jeffrey (2001), Who Made the First Sale? *Warsaw Business Journal*, Vol. 7 Issue 48, p. 9.
6. Graham, John R. (May 2006), Producing Positive Results, *American Salesman*, May 2006, Vol. 51 Issue 5, pp. 3-9.
7. Johnson, Paul (2009), The Top Five Traits of a Successful Salesperson, *American Salesman*, Vol. 54 Issue 9, pp. 24-27.
8. Kahle, Dave (2008), Characteristics of Successful Salespeople, *American Salesman*, Vol. 53 Issue 4, pp. 3-6.
9. Kahle, Dave (2009), Learning from Failure, *American Salesman*, Vol. 54 Issue 2, pp. 3-6.
10. Kahn, George N., Shuchman, Abraham (1961), Specialize Your Salesmen! *Harvard Business Review*, Vol. 39 Issue 1, pp. 90-98.
11. Mayer, David, Greenberg, Herbert M. (2006), What Makes a Good Salesman, *Harvard Business Review*, Vol. 84 Issue 7/8, pp. 164-171.
12. Milord, James T., Perry, Raymond P. (1977), Traits and Performance of Automobile Salesmen, *Journal of Social Psychology*, Vol. 103 Issue 1, p. 163.

13. Moine, Donald J. (1984), Going for the Gold in the Selling Game, *Psychology Today*, Vol. 18 Issue 3, pp. 37-44.
14. Schiffman, Stephan (1988), Successful Salespeople Know How to Lead, *American Salesman*, Vol. 43 Issue 2, p. 28.
15. Weiss, W.H. (2006), How Creative Are You? *American Salesman*, Vol. 51 Issue 2, pp. 6-12.

4 Planning for Sales

"Sales people don't plan to fail...
Many simply fail to plan."

–Harvey MacKay

CHAPTER OUTLINE

- Everyone needs planning
- What is sales planning?
- Preparing for planning sales
- Sales planning and SWOT analysis
- Sales forecast
- Conducting a competitive analysis
- Preparing a winning sales plan

OBJECTIVES

After studying this chapter, you will be able to:

- Define what is meant by planning
- Preparing for planning sales
- Conduct a competitive market analysis
- Prepare a winning sales plan
- Harness resources to make a sales plan effective
- Implement the sales plan to achieve your targets successfully

Opening Case: Kanpur Industrial Supply Company

Kanpur Industrial Supply Company (KISC) based in Kanpur, Uttar Pradesh was a full time distributor of industrial supplies. Its products included drills, saws, lubricants, abrasives and grinding wheels. Nearly all its customers were small to medium size machine shops. Kanpur Industrial Supply Company was a growing firm with a good demand for its products in the northern parts of the country.

Ravi Prakash, a sales representative for the Kanpur Industrial Supply Company had a problem. One of his clients – Om Machine Tools was a prospective good customer with immense potential. Om Machine Tools was a medium size machine shop situated in the industrial area of Kanpur and was in the business of producing high-end machine tools. KISC, though a progressive company, was not able to develop its sales potential to the fullest extent. The best Ravi Prakash was able to do was to get a fraction of Om's business, and that too by offering lower prices and more credit facilities than he usually offered to others. Om Machine Tools employed around 225 employees and its business had been improving steadily. Ravi had known its owner Mr D K Agarwal for several years, but he had never used his acquaintance to influence his dealings with Navin Mittal who was the purchase head of this company.

Ravi considered Navin a pleasing, although not very competent, person. He often talked about how he was in charge of keeping Om Machine Tool's inventories at their conventionally low levels, though the lack of certain machine tools like drills, saws, lubricants, abrasives and grinding wheels affected production. Ravi was in a fix and wanted to do something to improve his sales to Om Machine Tools.

Ravi decided to work out a plan to enhance his sales with Om and analyzed the data available with him. He reviewed the quantity of off take in the last five years, analyzed the price sensitivity of demand, seasonality of demand, purchases by Om and their correlation with payments and of course the financial capability of Om, its off take from KISC's competitors, and its own share of the total off take by Om. He also studied the growth plans of Om and its plans for expansion.

Ravi concluded that Navin's actions were solely for the purpose of putting more pressure to decrease the prices and getting more time to make payments. Ravi took an appointment and met Navin. He explained the rationale behind optimizing purchases and elicited the benefits of procuring from KISC. Ravi was well prepared and said that if Om Machine Tools entered into an MoU with KISC, the latter would give the following offer:

- Assured supply on a priority basis
- Fixed price to be reviewed every six months
- Guaranteed supply within 7 days
- Payment after 45 days from the date of billing
- Settlement of all complaints – quality and finance related within 7 days
- Supply of customized products to be developed in collaboration with Om, and
- Any other aspect that would be mutually beneficial to both firms.

In return, Ravi requested an order for a guaranteed quantity every month, to which Navin readily agreed.

Question

1. Would Ravi's offer increase his sales or would it be detrimental to his company on a long-term basis?

PLANNING FOR SALES

Integral Design for Programmed Learning

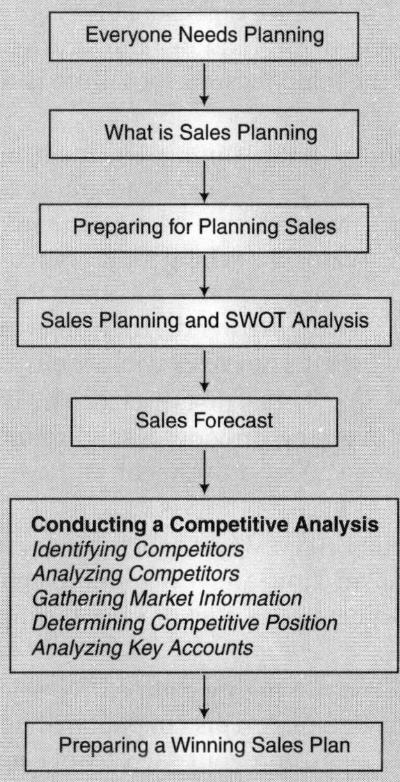

"If you want to succeed, you must create and write a multi-year business plan. A three-to-five year plan is typical. I always use three years. It's almost impossible to plan intelligently beyond that. If you are a dreamer - with no written goals - it's necessary to change your thinking now."

–John Alquist

EVERY SALES EXECUTIVE NEEDS PLANNING

A planning exercise prior to a sales call is such a common occurrence, that every salesperson admits to it. However, it is often seen that in spite of planning, salespeople still fail to achieve their targets. What are the reasons for this? More often than not, one tries to externalize the reasons for failure, attributing it to unreasonably high targets, recessionary market conditions, high prices, low level of promotions and unfriendly company policies. While this may be partly true, one of the main reasons for failure is the lack of proper planning on the part of the salespersons.

Most salespeople enjoy selling – not planning. For them, account and territory planning are a tedious, academic exercise for the benefit of the management. Many of them think that it is waste of their valuable selling time. Since salespeople are in-charge of their territories and they think they know the market and changing trends, they invariably assume that they can plan their sales reasonably well.

> A sales or sales territory plan is more than having the sales force plan for product pricing, distribution, collection, market movement and coverage of distributors/dealers/customers.

Let us first discuss why it is necessary to plan sales and state its benefits, describe how planning provides a solid foundation for all sales, provides a simple, yet powerful, time management assessment and describe smart goals as effective tools for achieving sales goals.

In sales, the goal is revenue-driven. How much money do you want to make? How much profit do you want to make? How are you going to achieve your targets? Accurately forecasting your sales and building a sales plan or sales territory plan can help you to avoid unforeseen cash flow problems.

In order to be successful in today's highly competitive sales world, a sales manager and individual salesperson must have a plan. This chapter will help you define both your own individual, territory, or regional plan, and your sales team's approach.

WHY SALES PLANNING?

Just as a road map guides us on a journey, a sales plan guides salespersons in reaching their goals. Moreover sales planning helps to establish, direct and coordinate various sales efforts. Preparing a sales plan makes you to assess what is going on in the marketplace and how it is likely to affect your business. It also provides a benchmark to gauge your sales. Often, while embarking on the process of preparing a sales plan you develop a meaningful sales strategy.

> Sales planning is the process of preparing for effective sales and service interactions with customers. It requires thinking about activities and interactions in a systematic way, and it helps to bridge the gap between current staff ability and desired staff ability.

WHAT IS SALES PLANNING

Sales planning is the process of preparing for effective sales and service interactions with customers. It requires thinking about activities and interactions in a systematic way, and it helps to bridge the gap between current staff ability and desired staff ability. It involves setting specific goals, keeping work areas organized, and managing time in a way that leads to greater efficiency and effectiveness. It is a managerial tool to predict market fluctuations in sales and formulate strategies for achieving targets or end results.

A sales plan describes all the marketing activities you will carry out during a specified time period. It takes into account all the background information and past results to decide specific deliverables. Finally, you will have to document the costs associated with such planned marketing activities as well as the yardsticks you will apply to judge your performance.

PREPARING FOR SALES PLANNING

You need to have a thorough understanding of the following points when you try to develop a sales plan:

- Your products or services and their features and benefits
- The problem, need or desire your product or service solves or meets for your customer
- Your target market and its characteristics and buying habits
- Current and potential competing products or services

> A sales plan should contain information about your company and its products, sales objectives and strategies, as well as how you will measure the success of your marketing activities.

The five steps given below are followed when one prepares any sales plan for a particular territory.

Step I - Analyze Your Territory

Understanding the territory is most important for all sales planning. The analysis must include an understanding of the following:

- Economic and social profile of the customers.
- Nature and number of different industries located there.
- Level of awareness amongst consumers about your product.
- Strength of your marketing channel i.e. how big are your distributors, dealers and retailers, what is their credibility and reputation in the market, their economic strength and their influence in the market.
- Nature and intensity of competition prevailing in that territory.
- Your comparative market share, level of product promotion and advertisements.
- Comparative pricing including sales schemes.
- Growth potential of the market.

Step II - Analyze and Set Objectives for Top Outlets

It is often necessary to segment the market into some homogeneous categories, – big medium and small outlets.

- Big companies are always eager to sell through the big dealers and offer them many special benefits, such as longer payment terms, replacement guarantee as per the wishes of the dealers.
- These big outlets are manned either by the owner himself or else by their salesmen. In the first case, the owner is tough at the negotiation table and looks to get the most in view of his dominant position in the market. In the second instance, the salesmen decide which product that has a demand to stock while the owner is just the financer and is concerned about the return on investment.

> One must remember that 20 percent of the dealers account for 80 percent of the sales. Hence efforts must be made to scrutinize the top 20 percent of the dealers in terms of their ability to sell, payment history and proactivity.

Both these situations are to be handled carefully. Handling the owner in the first case and the salesmen in the second requires continuous interaction. While owners are concerned about their profits and look for attractive margins, their ego must also be taken care of. Salesmen, on the other hand, need periodical positive motivation in terms of gifts, non-monetary incentives and of course respect. They are to be handled very intelligently as they can make or mar a product in the market.

Step III - Prepare a Comprehensive Offer

This is a vital step that could be a deciding factor in the success of your product in the market. The package to be offered to the dealer or distributor will depend upon the following aspects.

- The core product (physical product), which can vary from soap to television sets, including the packaging.
- The net delivery price that includes the discounts/schemes offered.
- Payment terms – credit period, cash/advance payment discount etc.
- Delivery terms – free delivery or paid delivery.
- Local advertisements and sales promotion plan.
- Performance guarantee including service facilities, promise of repairs/ replacements.

Step IV - Getting a Commitment from Your Dealer/distributor

A frequently asked question is what kind of commitment you should expect from your dealers. While you should offer an attractive package to them you should expect them to:

- Set a sales target for your products and sell them.

- Send payments as per the commitment.
- Promote your products and ensure a desirable growth rate.
- Give prominent shelf space to your products.
- Do in-shop promotion of your products.
- Actively participate in different schemes.

> While it is necessary for you to have an attractive proposal that offers something more to the customers than what the competitors are offering, it is essential to also get the commitment of dealers/distributors to promote your business in their areas.

This can happen only if your company and your products are strong in the market, customers ask for them and you have a very strong relationship with the dealers/ distributors. You must understand that the channel members would be interested in your products and your company only if customers ask for your product or they are getting a larger margin than what competitors are offering.

Step V - Take Action and Measure Territory Results

Planning for sales is not complete until the steps taken to promote sales are successful. To see that the plan is carried out in detail, there should be a system of continuously monitoring the actions taken and measuring the results against the targeted objectives. The conclusions help in fine-tuning the plan for the subsequent period.

> The crucial part of the sales plan is to consider the unique strength of yourself and those of competitors, variable factors like the market conditions and what unique value you can offer that would give you a competitive differentiation advantage.

You should review your plan on a regular basis and update it accordingly. Past strategy may not work given this year's market conditions, though it may give you an idea where to start. Competitive advantage is created by using resources and capabilities to achieve either a lower cost structure or a differentiated product. A company positions itself in the industry through its choice of low cost or differentiation. This decision is a central component of the firm's competitive strategy.

SALES PLANNING AND SWOT ANALYSIS

SWOT is the acronym for Strengths, Weaknesses, Opportunities and Threats. It is a simple, much-used technique, which can be used to prepare plans, as well as in problem solving and decision-making. It is customary for the analysis to take into account the various internal resources and capabilities (strengths and weaknesses) and identify factors external to the organization (in the form of opportunities and threats).

> SWOT analysis involves the generation and recording of the strengths, weaknesses, opportunities, and threats in relation to a particular task or objective.

Benefits

SWOT analysis provides:

- A framework for identifying and analyzing strengths, weaknesses, opportunities and threats;

- An impetus to analyze a situation and develop suitable strategies and tactics;
- A basis for assessing core capabilities and competences.

Action Checklist for Conducting SWOT Analysis

1. Establish the objectives

The first key step is to be clear on what you are doing and why. The SWOT analysis helps to set your objectives.

2. List the strengths

A list of possible strengths *vis à vis* the key competitors in different aspects of the market (such as distribution channels, access to supply chain etc.), and consumers' perceptions about you and your products/services. Your capabilities as an effective salesperson play an important role in this respect. "People" elements would include the skills, capabilities and knowledge of participants. Other people strengths include:

- Friendly, cooperative and supportive channel members;
- Appropriate levels of involvement driven by trust

3. List the weaknesses

This step should not merely focus on the negative aspects, instead it should be an honest appraisal of the way things are. Key questions include:

- What obstacles may prevent progress?
- Which elements need strengthening?
- Are there any real weak links in the chain?

There are many "people" related problems in the area of sales. For instance, you may suffer from poor communication, inadequate leadership, lack of motivation, inadequate number of sales personnel, too little delegation, no trust etc. These feature among the major weaknesses.

4. List the opportunities

This step is designed to assess the socio-economic, environmental and demographic factors, among others, to evaluate the benefits they may bring through your sales. Examples include:

- Development of new markets.
- Development of new customers.
- Development of new products.
- Development of improved products.

It must also be remembered just how long opportunities might last and how you can get the best advantage from them.

5. List the threats

These are the opposite of opportunities – which may, with a shift of emphasis or perception, have an adverse impact.

Weighing threats against opportunities is not a reason to indulge in pessimism; it is rather a question of considering how possible negative experiences could be limited or eliminated. The same factors may emerge as both a threat and an opportunity.

6. Evaluate the situation against the objectives

Once the above information is compiled, the ideas should be sorted and grouped in relation to the objectives. It may be necessary to choose the five most important items from the list in order to gain a wider view. Clarity of objectives is the key to this process, as evaluation and elimination will be necessary to pinpoint your focus. Although some aspects may require further understanding, a clear picture should, at this stage, emerge in response to the objectives.

Do's and Don'ts for a SWOT Analysis

Do

- Be analytical and specific.
- Record all thoughts and ideas in a sequential manner.
- Be selective in the final evaluation. Choose the right people for the exercise.
- Choose a suitable SWOT leader or facilitator.

Do not

- Try to disguise weaknesses
- Merely list past errors and mistakes
- Lose sight of external influences and trends
- Use SWOT to make a blame game
- Ignore the outcomes at later stages of the planning process

SALES TARGET

Forecast the level of sales you expect to achieve. Armed with this information you can spot problems and opportunities – and do something about them. With a well-defined sales target or territory plan, you can devote more time developing your business plan rather than attending to day-to-day problems of sales and marketing.

Seven Questions That Will Help You to Achieve Your Sales Targets

1. What are your current average sales in monetary terms?
2. What is your targeted sales revenue?
3. What is your dealer-wise and unit-wise sale?

4. What is the potential of your existing network?
5. What are the extra network and product units you would require to achieve your sales target?
6. What is and should be the pricing strategy?
7. What support will you need in terms of advertising and sales promotion?

MAKE A COMPETITIVE ANALYSIS

An in-depth analysis of your competition helps you to know your competitors' strengths and weaknesses in the market. It enables you to choose effective sales strategies and it will ultimately improve your competitive standing.

Identifying Competitors

An example of direct competition is branded products like television sets which offer similar features and price ranges. Firms offering dissimilar or substitute products in relation to your product or service are indirect competitors. Good examples of indirect competitors are manufacturers of air-conditioners vs. manufacturers of desert coolers; manufacturers of fruit juices vs. those of cold drinks and manufacturers of eyeglasses vs. contact lens manufacturers.

Simply stated, indirect competition will satisfy the customer's need with a particular product or service, although the product or service used may be different. If a firm has similar products and distribution channels, but has chosen to operate in different market segments, they are not at this time your direct competitor. However, it is important to keep an eye on the sales activities of such firms because they may decide to move into your market and vice-versa (i.e. you may decide to move into their territory). Thus, you may identify your direct and indirect competitors.

> Any company marketing similar or substitute products in the same geographic area and offering similar value as your product is your direct competitor.

Assessing Competitors

To assess your competitors you should follow the steps given below:

- Scan the market
- Identify sources for competitive information
- Analyze competitive information
- Determine your own competitive position

There are situations where it is easy to name all competitors. These are industries where only a handful of companies operate. In India the steel and automobile industries are typical examples of this type of competitive markets.

However, when you operate in a market with many competitors, your task of assessing competitive intensity becomes difficult. Since it is often difficult to collect and maintain information about all players in the market, one usually applies the famous 80/20 rule. That is, in a fragmented market with many players, it is found that 80% of the total market is captured by 20% of the competition. It is this 20% that you should examine most closely.

For instance, in the personal computer industry, today there exist hundreds of clone manufacturers. However, it is found that the majority of the market is captured by a handful of companies such as Compaq, Dell, IBM, and Apple.

> Market segmentation, is a process of breaking down larger heterogeneous markets into smaller ones. It is an effective tool to limit and know your specific competitors.

Gathering Market Information

A salesperson is the best person to report on the nature of the competition faced in his/her territory. Another way to assess the intensity of competition is to talk to the channel members (distributors/wholesalers/dealers/retailers). Much valuable information you may require to know your competitors is often readily available with all these people.

Questions to be asked to channel members to determine market information

- Who are my top three competitors?
- What is the range of products and services they offer?
- Are their products or services aimed at satisfying similar target markets?
- Are my competitors making a profit?
- How long have they been in business?
- What are their positive attributes in the eyes of customers?
- What are their negative attributes in the eyes of customers?
- How do current customers view us compared to the competition?
- What is their marketing strategy?
- What is their promotional strategy?
- What are their pricing structures?
- Do they operate in the same geographic area?
- Have there been any changes in their targeted market segments?
- What is their size?
- What are their revenues?
- What is their percentage of the market share?
- What is their total sales volume?
- What is their growth rate?
- How do they rate on:
  - Customer service?
  - Quality of product/service?
  - Operations?
  - Pricing, incentives?
  - Employees?
  - Resources?
- Do they have a competitive advantage; if so, what is it?

- How do current customers rate the following features of my company compared to the competition.
- How do I compare with the competitors in terms of:
    - Price
    - Quality
    - Durability
    - Image/Style
    - Value
    - Name recognition
    - Customer service
    - Customer relations
    - Location
    - Convenience
- On what aspects (please collect specific information from the market) is your company superior to the competition?
- Is the level of competition expanding or contracting/scaling down?
- How can I distinguish my company from my competitors' companies?

A comparative statement should be made to show how your product differs from others and what unique features and benefits you are offering to your customers. For instance, the competitive position of Sony (in the television industry) can be assessed against their key competitors, such as LG, Samsung, Onida and Videocon on a range of factors.

The most crucial part of sales planning is to analyze the information received about the competitors.

Factors	*Sony*	*LG*	*SAMSUNG*	*Onida*	*Videocon*
Product	*Wide range*	*Wide range*	*Medium range*	*Limited range*	*Low Priced range*
Perceived quality					
Service					
Unique offerings					
Sales strategy					
Pricing structure					
List price/Discount					
Promotional strategy					
Targeted market segments					
Distribution pattern					
Growth rate					
Image					
Additional benefits (instalments/credit/ free AMC etc.)					

Determine the Competitors' Position

Based on a comparative analysis of your position and your competitors' position it is easy to ascertain your competitive position. The important factors on which analysis is made can include:

- Product range and uniqueness of product
- Price, including the schemes and discounts
- Commercial benefits like facilities given in terms of delivery and post sales service
- Delivery lead-time
- Brand image
- Quality of your distributors/dealers/retailers
- Intensity of your advertising back-up including local advertisements
- Sales promotion schemes

Analyzing key Accounts

Nowadays, the practice of key account management is a common practice to retain customers and achieve a distinct competitive advantage. Preserving those customer relationships is of strategic importance to a firm's future financial wellbeing.

Key account management provides the processes and tools to equip you to engage with your important customers and nurture them to build a more mutually-profitable and sustainable relationship. The templates below will help you to deliver "win-win" business solutions against these high-potential accounts and produce actionable tools to implement a Key Account Management (KAM) plan in your organization.

The accruing benefits of key account management are as follows:

- Understand what is important to customers
- Develop customized solutions
- Build long term partnerships
- Develop loyal, satisfied customers
- Retain and service current customers
- Acquire and develop new customers
- Increase your business
- Exceed your sales objectives
- Experience success
- Receive recognition and rewards

Criteria for defining key accounts

- Profitable customers
- Large sales potential
- Influential thought leaders

PREPARING A SALES PLAN

The five steps given below can be followed to prepare a sales plan in a territory.

5 Steps to creating a sales plan in a territory

Step I	Analyze the territory
Step II	Analyze and set objectives for top accounts
Step III	Identify 2 key accounts that require individual key account plans (Use template)
Step IV	Set territory objectives, strategies and action plans
Step V	Take action and measure territory results

- Identify "opportunity" (high potential/low performance) territories and develop improvement plans.
- Identify those territories that are under performing and/or unexplored and have a large potential for growth of market share and sales. You may also utilize this format to identify the middle performers (grow the business) and high performing territories (customer retention).
- Establish quarterly business plan objectives. For each product, select 1-2 key performance factors to measure on a quarterly basis. Examples: Sales in Rupees, sales volume, market share switch, new customers.

Key performance factors	*Q1*	*Q2*	*Q3*	*Q4*	*Full Year*
Product #1					
Product #2					
Product #3					

Carry out a monthly/quarterly sales planning for different types of customers as per the following format.

Customers	*Jan*	*Feb*	*Mar*	*Q1*	*Apr*	*May*	*June*	*Q2*	*July*	*Aug*	*Sept*	*Q3*	*Oct*	*Nov*	*Dec*	*Q4*	*Total*
Existing																	
New																	
Switched																	
Lost																	
Total																	

Identify Sales Strategies and Tactics for each Customer Segment

Example: Customize to meet your individual requirements

Segment	*Strategies for segment*	*Sales tactics/Action plans for each segment*
Priority	Develop strong, vocal customer advocates for your product as the first line supply	o Increase call frequency month o Send representatives to training program
	o	o o
	o	o o
	o	o o
	o	o o
	o	o o

Step I: Analyze Territory

Summarize the following territory information in 2-3 concise paragraphs:

Sales potential
Demographics
Geography/Size of territory
Number of accounts by segment
Account analysis: Retained, new, lost, recaptured
Reimbursement/Pay or information
Treatment protocols used in territory
Overall company product usage and perceptions
Market & competitive information

Record the territory sales history for the last year

Sales results	*Quarter 1*	*Quarter 2*	*Quarter 3*	*Quarter 4*	*Total*
Sales goal					
Actual results					
% Goal attainment					

Step II: Analyze and Set Objectives for Key Accounts that Represent 70-80% of Sales (most profitable) or have high Sales Potential

Account name	*Potential sales/qtr*	*Competitive share*	*Company share*	*Quarterly sales goal*	*% Sales*	*Segment current/ goal*	*Current call frequency*	*Call frequency goal*
1.								
2.								
3.								
4.								
5.								
6.								
7.								
8.								

Step III: Identify the 2 Highest Sales/Potential Key Accounts that Require Full Key Account Plans

Key Account # 1:______________________________

Sales Potential:______________________________

Company Share:______________________________

Competitive Share:____________________________

% Territory Sales Contribution:____________________

Sales Goal for 2012 :___________________________

Segment- Current/Goal:__________________________

Call Frequency Goal for 2012_______________________

Key account # 2: ___________________________

Sales potential: ___________________________

Company share: ___________________________

Competitive share: ___________________________

% Territory sales contribution: ___________________________

Sales goal for 2012: ___________________________

Current segment goal: ___________________________

Call frequency goal for 2012: ___________________________

Step IV: Set Territory Objectives

- Establish monthly sales/market share objectives for territory for the year 2012
- Measure actual results on a monthly and quarterly basis

2012	*Month 1*	*Month 2*	*Month 3*	*Month 4*	*Quarter*
Sales goal					
Actual results					
% Goal attainment					

Develop a call plan by customer segment and measure actual results vs. goals

Sample call plan:

Note: The sales representative calculates available calls to make sure the call plan is realistic.

Total available calls = Days available × daily call average: __________

Example: 20 working days in the month × call average of 4 = 80 available calls. The sales representative will need to increase their call average to make their total targeted call plan realistic.

It is recommended that the sales representative develop a call plan for each account they plan on visiting at the beginning of each month. The majority of time should be spent with the high volume or high potential accounts.

Customer segment	Number	Target call frequency	Total targeted calls/month	Actual calls Month 1	Actual calls Month 2	Actual calls Month 3
Priority	1	8/x month	8			
1	2	5x/month	10			
2	4	4x/month	16			
3	7	3x/month	21			
4	10	3x/month	30			
Total	14	10/x month	85			

Each sales representative develops a key account plan for their top 2 key accounts

The sales manager makes the final decision as to how many key account plans the sales representative is responsible for.

Preparing a Sales Plan in an Industrial Setting

Industrial sales refers to the sales of goods or services to organizations. Industrial sales involve a number of key differences from selling to consumers. These include a smaller customer base with higher value or larger unit purchases, more technically complex or specialized products, professionally qualified purchasers, closer buyer-seller relationships, and possible group-purchasing decision making.

Since the goods and services purchased by industries are usually input material aimed at producing goods for their own set of buyers, the focus of industrial buyers is primarily to understand the needs of their target market and accordingly procure goods and services that help them to produce goods to satisfy those needs more successfully than their competitors.

Generally, industrial organizations tend to be technically oriented and more interested in products that possess high efficiency. Accordingly, technical values tend to dominate the decision-making. It is thus important for salespersons to understand the complexity of the problems industrial buyers face and resolve them appropriately.

Characteristics of Industrial Selling

Buyers of industrial products are usually technically trained and buy for their business institutions. They are technically highly qualified and specialized and generally buy on a rational basis with their three major buying motives being quality, price, and service. In most cases, the product or service must be customized to meet the buyer's exact requirements. Consequently, the buyer's needs and problems must be carefully understood by the salesperson and specific selling programs should be prepared in advance of making the call.

In industrial sales, the sales orders are generally large, are for a specified period of time, and usually decided upon by several key persons such as the purchase manager, the chief engineer, the plant engineer/manager, the president, the director of production, and others. Negotiations for buying are often extended over long periods of time and are usually in accordance with predetermined specifications, which frequently involve competitive bidding.

In view of the above, the manufacturers of industrial products generally have fewer sales personnel than organizations in the business of consumer products. This is due to the fact that industrial products are more selectively distributed as compared to consumer products, which are marketed to a large consumer base. Industrial salespersons generally have fewer but larger accounts. Their interactions are more rational, relationship oriented and often more technology oriented.

Industrial selling thus requires a personal approach to sales. The salesperson needs to deal with one or more functions/departments like purchase, finance, projects and even operations – all at the same time to procure orders and sustain his presence with the customer. Such salespeople demand less advertising and promotional efforts as compared to salespersons in consumer products. As a result it requires more stress on personal selling rather than general advertising. As a result of these differences, the industrial salesperson has more specific accountability for selling. Due to topographical constraints, the industrial salesperson is usually the only contact that the buyer has with the company he represents, and almost exclusively deals with the buyers. As a result, it is essential for the salesperson to know more about the company, the products, profile of buyers and their policies. The industrial salesperson is thus a "consultant" to industrial buyers, who takes the sales through from their inception to the end.

The industrial salesperson has a shorter distribution channel to manage and selling is generally direct from the manufacturer to the user. The basic role of a distribution channel is to explore possibilities of new business, follow-up potential orders and expedite payments. The salespersons are also responsible for maintenance of industrial products sold to the buyers in their area. Industrial demand is also a derived demand. What this market purchases is dependent upon what happens in end markets. For example, the amount of ore a steel plant buys is largely determined by the end market demand for automobiles, appliances, and other products made of steel.

Another characteristic of industrial selling is that occasionally reciprocity is a crucial factor in the sale. Reciprocity is the practice of buying from a particular company because it buys from you. If the product is comparable or better than competitive products in terms of quality, service, and price, such a practice poses no problem. However, problems occur when there is pressure to buy an inferior product reciprocally. The purchasing departments, being professional and technically sound, base their purchase decision-making on the basis of the merits of the case rather than undesirable reciprocity. As the quality and price of input material is critical to ensure the competitiveness of their products in the marketplace, their job is to buy the best product at the lowest price, and in the majority of cases, this policy is followed.

Industrial Buying Practices

The involvement of top management in buying decisions is quite common, particularly with large purchases and in smaller organizations. The purchasing department handles purchase orders and has considerable authority in the purchase of some items and less with others. Others are also often involved in the decision. For instance, in the case of selling steel, the industrial salesperson must work with and secure the approval of the designing engineers, the research department, the purchasing agent, production engineer, the sales manager, and others. Or in selling packaging material, he must clear the decision with the product planning department, the sales department, advertising, production, purchasing, the customer service department, shipping, and even the legal department. Hence, the industrial salesperson must understand many different operations within the company. He is usually selling to a "management team" with varying backgrounds and interest. He may also face the problem of constant changes that occur in the company. Frequently, people are promoted or transferred, titles and duties change, and it is not uncommon for fewer than 50 percent of those involved in buying decisions to remain in the same job throughout the year.

As mentioned, the major buying motives of the purchasing agent are quality, price, and service. Quality refers to the suitability of the product or service. It must fulfil specific requirements if it is to be successfully marketed. For example, steel must have a certain hardness to be used in tools. Consequently, a product not meeting the required degree of hardness would not be acceptable. This is why industrial buying is geared to predetermined specifications, and any product falling below requirements is automatically rejected. Quality can also refer to how the buyer regards the salesperson and the company he or she represents. Some salespeople and companies have a "quality" image while others do not.

Price is an important consideration in industrial selling, for the cost at which the material is bought will greatly influence the monetary value of sales in the end market, as well as profits that will be made. The purchasing agent naturally attempts to buy the best and most for the least amount of money. However, if the agent forces the seller to sell at an unprofitably price, it can often work against the company's best interest. In such cases, the seller may be forced to "cut corners" by decreasing the quality or service normally offered. Or the salesperson may simply stop selling to the purchasing agent and make it necessary to find a new source of supply. The old adage that "you get exactly what you pay for" certainly applies to industrial buying, and the purchasing agent must therefore weigh the importance of price in relation to the quality and service it buys.

The Industrial Sales Plan

Considering the unique nature of industrial buyers and their needs, an industrial sales plan requires a totally different and distinct treatment. The sales plan should involve the following steps:

- Mapping the market and ascertaining the potential of the territory
- Understanding the targeted organization – its structure, systems, policies, culture and people
- Learning the different operational processes involved in production
- Identifying and meeting officials involved in purchase
- Following up the tenders floated by the purchase
- Participating in bids (this involves a lot of spadework with respect to justifying the technical and commercial competiveness of its offering vis-à-vis competition)
- Making presentations before the purchase and also the user departments
- Pursuing the bid to close the deal

The industrial salesperson, accordingly, has to prepare his plan meticulously for he might have to spend more time with his target customers, plan the frequency of his visits and always try to differentiate his offering against that of the competition. His sales plan must also include building up strong relationships based on trust. This in turn demands building up high credibility for himself and his organization.

Thus an industrial salesperson has to be a visionary, a planner, and an efficient executor who will serve more as a "consulting specialist" as compared to other types of salespeople. Work in this area, therefore, requires a person who has technical expertise, good analytical abilities, and one who can creatively approach different problems in the field.

To be a successful industrial salesperson requires considerable domain knowledge, skill and training. Purchasing agents not only buy from him, but they also rely on him for information on new products, improvements, and new applications or uses. He is also a source of information on what other companies are doing. The purchasing department expects the industrial salesperson to help them to solve their problems. They do not want him to take up their valuable time with idle conversation or unnecessary visits. Therefore, he must carefully plan each call and design it to serve the buyer in some specific way.

KEY CONCEPTS

- In order to be successful in today's highly competitive sales world, a salesperson must have a plan.
- Sales planning is the process of preparing for effective sales and service interactions with members. It requires thinking about activities and interactions in a systematic way, and it helps bridge the gap between current staff ability and desired staff ability.
- Sales planning helps to establish, direct and coordinate your sales efforts.
- Preparing a sales plan enables you to assess what is going on in your marketplace and how it affects your business. It also provides a benchmark for later measurement. Often, simply embarking on the process of preparing a marketing plan guides you in developing a successful sales strategy.

- Sales planning involves setting specific goals, keeping work areas organized, and managing time in a way that leads to greater efficiency and effectiveness.
- A sales or sales territory plan is more than having the sales force to plan for product pricing, distribution, collection, market movement and coverage of the distributors/dealers/customers. It is a managerial tool to predict the market fluctuations in sales and formulate strategies for achieving targeted results.
- A sales plan should contain information about your company and its products, sales objectives and strategies, as well as how you will measure the success of your marketing activities.
- To prepare a good sales plan, you must have a thorough understanding of your products or services; the problem, need or desire your product or service addresses; your target market and its characteristics and buying habits and current and potential competing products or services.
- Ideally, a sales plan should be analytical and specific and should be made looking into the strengths and weaknesses of the company, competitors and the market.
- A well-constructed sales or sales territory plan, combined with accurate sales forecasting should be able to develop the business rather than responding to day-to-day developments in sales and marketing.
- A salesperson is the best person to evaluate the level of competition in his territory. The information provided by him about the intensity of competition helps a lot in formulating the sales plan.
- A strong sales plan, together with its efficient execution is sure to give companies a definite competitive advantage in the marketplace. Salespersons have a critical role to play in this context.
- A sales plan is dynamic in nature and must be reviewed vis-à-vis achievements on a regular basis. This helps in making online corrections quickly and enables it to respond to the changes in the market more successfully and professionally.

CASE I: AVON CORPORATION

The Avon Corporation supplied items of luggage and vanity cases under the company's brand name – Sinclair to a chain of dealers in northern India. By 2005 the company had captured a 32 percent share in its served market through a series of acquisitions of regional competitors having long-term supply contracts. The largest competitor, with 28 percent of the market, had decided to diversify into other product categories. The remaining competitors, holding 40 percent, comprised many local players with low cost, medium quality products with lenient commercial terms.

Avon Corporation was very proud because they had been the market leader for more than two decades. Of late its management had spent a considerable amount of time in discussing various problems related to distribution.. This deflected their attention from the ongoing management of existing operations, and began to take its toll in an apparent decline in customer relations, and threats on the quality and sales of dealers though numbers were increasing. There was strong emphasis by the sales personnel on maintaining volume and little or no emphasis on development of dealers and markets or innovative marketing programs in the retail markets. The management team could not agree on the advantages they had in the eyes of their dealers and retail customers. Surprisingly little was known about the competitor's capabilities, cost structure, marketing strategies and tactics. Quality was treated as a matter of adherence to standards for physical product quality, and not of superior performance on attributes that customers value.

The result was lower market spread, and a lesser number of dealers who started dictating their terms of business. Sales outstanding was increasing and the sales team was facing a tough time meeting targets as the dealers were not very keen to lift material. They felt that consignments were being dumped. It was evident that the sales function was not a priority for the company at all.

In this situation one of the biggest dealers declared that he was fed up with the nonchalant attitude of the company and its salespersons. So his company sent a notice to terminate their trade agreement with the company wef the next financial year.

The Vice-President (marketing) pacified the dealer and assured him that the problem would be resolved soon. To determine the seriousness of these problems of the market, a survey was undertaken with 17 dealers accounting for 55 percent of total sales. The objective was to learn how these dealers perceived the company, and how the salespersons were dealing with them.

The results were quite shocking. While the dealers generally agreed that the company was performing very well on the five key attributes of delivery dependability, price, product quality, product representation, and product promotion & merchandising, they were not at all happy with the handling of sales by their salespeople. They complained that the salespersons were not regular in their market visits, were not covering the market fully, made commitments that they did not fulfil and were not settling claims. They also said that the approach of salespersons was casual and in order to meet their targets, they were pushing material without orders. The feedback received from the market can be summarized as below.

Market feedback					
	Poor	*Unsatisfactory*	*Satisfactory*	*Good*	*Excellent*
Product quality	0	5	12	0	0
Price	0	2	13	2	0
Product promotion	1	9	7	0	0
Sales visits	4	9	5	0	1
Market coverage	3	8	6	0	0
Behaviour	2	10	5	0	0
Fulfilling promises	4	11	2	0	0
Claim settlement	5	8	4	0	0

It was also perceived that efforts should be put in with dealers who buy in bulk irrespective of whether the material is sold in the retail market or is offered to traders for trading purposes. Considering the tough competition in the market, it appeared that the sales function would have to be geared up again.

Questions

1. Suggest steps that need to be taken to put the sales function on the right track.
2. What kind of sales planning do you suggest for Sinclair?

CASE II: GREEN GARDENING STORE

Vijay Kumar was working with his father in a small firm in the business of gardening equipment in Lucknow for nearly two decades. When his father died five years ago, Vijay reorganized the business under the name of The Green Gardening Company. He had a small factory where he manufactured equipment and marketed it through a string of stores. He added two new stores to the existing eight stores and had plans to add three more.

Green Gardening Company, over the past five years, had been a great success in the garden stores but faced a steady decline in gardening services. Each of the garden stores had averaged an annual growth in sales of about 20 percent. The stores were known for their indoor plants, ornamental shrubs, and bonsai trees. Planning and planting indoor arrangements for office buildings was a popular service.

Vijay dreamt of expanding his operations by increasing the number of stores, but the problem, as Vijay saw it, was that his firm was not able to add enough new customers. Making a number of cold calls to homeowners, he found they did not believe that his service was any better than the one they were using at present. Though his quoted price for the monthly service charge was lower than that of their present service, customers were suspicious of his claims for better service.

His father used to take care of sceptical customer's lawn for a month, and if the customer was not satisfied he did not have to pay for the month's service. This was successful for his father, but times had changed and Vijay could not continue this practice any longer. He was at a loss as what to do. He knew, from his experience in making cold calls, that words were not going to do the trick and he could not demonstrate his services on customers' lawns. He also sought a way to tie his stores with the gardening service.

Question

1. Suggest how Vijay should plan his sales so that he can fulfil his dream.

REFERENCES

1. Bower, Patrick (2005), 12 Most Common Threats to Sales and Operations Planning Process, *Journal of Business Forecasting*, Vol. 24 Issue 3, pp. 4-14.
2. Buell, Victor P. (1956), Organizing for Marketing Planning, *Journal of Marketing*, Vol. 21 Issue 1, pp. 68-71.
3. Dubinsky, Alan J., Ingram, Thomas N. (1983), Important First-line Sales Management Qualifications: What Sales Executives Think, *Journal of Personal Selling & Sales Management*, Vol. 3 Issue 1, p. 18.
4. Else, Robert A. (1973), Sales Planning by Objectives at General Electric, *Management Review*, Vol. 62 Issue 8, p. 47.
5. Grimson, J. Andrew, Pyke, David F. (2007), Sales and Operations Planning: An Exploratory Study and Framework, *International Journal of Logistics Management*, Vol. 18 Issue 3, pp. 322-346.
6. Harwell, Jack (2006), Sales & Operations Planning in the Retail Industry, *Journal of Business Forecasting*, Vol. 25 Issue 3, pp. 4-10.
7. Holzgrefe, David (2009), Prepare your Business for Sale, *Charter*, Vol. 80 Issue 8, pp. 50-51.
8. Jones Jr, George S. (1943), Salesmanship's Responsibility for the Future, *Journal of Marketing*, Vol. 8 Issue 1, pp. 75-78.
9. Keen, Mike, Evans, Carl (2010), Maximize Your Chances of Success, *Management Services*, Winter 2010, Vol. 54 Issue 4, pp. 30-32.
10. Leslie, Mark, Holloway, Charles A. (2006), The Sales Learning Curve, *Harvard Business Review*, Vol. 84 Issue 7/8, pp. 115-123.
11. Rayney, Peter (2009), If You're Looking For a Way Out, *Accountancy*, Vol. 143 Issue 1390, pp. 74-77.
12. Robillard, Eugene (1975), On the Planning of Sales Planning, *Industrial Marketing Management*, Vol. 4 Issue 4, pp. 213-216.
13. Slone, Reuben E., Mentzer, John T., Dittmann, Paul J.,(2007), Are You the Weakest Link in Your Company's Supply Chain? *Harvard Business Review*, Vol. 85 Issue 9, pp. 116-127.
14. The Power of Inertia, *Journal of Advertising Research* (2011), Vol. 51 Issue 2, pp. 356-372.
15. Tinham, Brian (2009), *Works Management*, Vol. 62 Issue 8, pp. 23-27.
16. Wallace, Tom (2010), Executive Sales and Operations Planning: Cost and Benefit Analysis, *Journal of Business Forecasting*, Vol. 29 Issue 3, pp. 13-17.

5 Making the Sales Call

Don't Sell, Solve!

–Anonymous

CHAPTER OUTLINE

- Introduction
- Activities in the selling process
- The sales meeting
- Handling buyers' resistance
- Reasons why customers raise objections
- Overcoming resistance
- Closing the sale
- Maintaining accounts
- Things to remember
- From 'no' to 'yes'
- All about referrals

OBJECTIVES

After studying this chapter, you will be able to:

- Understand the activities involved in the selling process
- Know how to deal with buyers' resistance
- Know the assumptions in sales
- Learn the art of questioning
- Be able to use referrals as potent instruments for sales

Opening Case: The First Sales Call

Ajith Menon was about to enter the office of Prof. N. Srinivasan; a professor in marketing in a leading management institute in Bangalore. After graduating from Madras University in Chennai and doing an MBA course in NIIT Trichi in 2011, Menon got an offer of a sales executive in Woodhead Publishers Ltd., a leading publishing house in India. He was given a two month orientation programme at Woodhead Publishers Ltd. (WPL) headquarters in Mumbai, and then he was posted in Bangalore.

This is his maiden sales call on behalf of the company.

The discussion that took place between Menon & Prof. Srinivasan was as follows:

Menon: Good morning, Professor I am Ajith Menon from Woodhead Publishers Ltd. India. Is this a convenient time to talk to you, sir?

Srinivasan: Yes, it is, (Prof. Srinivasan looks at his wrist watch) however, please keep in mind that I have my next class at 4 o'clock. You look very young. How old are you, Menon? When did you join Woodhead Publishers?

Menon: Sir, I am about to complete 24 years. I joined WPL in July last year after completing my MBA from NIIT Trichi. I was posted in Bangalore only a month back. In fact, you are the first academic person I am calling on, sir.

Srinivasan: Oh, that is interesting! Well, tell me, have WPL come up with any new books in marketing where I could find lots of Indian examples and case studies?

Menon: That's why I am here, Professor. We are going to publish an exciting book entitled 'Product Management in India'. It will be in the market within the next two months. Here is the write-up on it (handing him a sheet of paper from the bag). What do you think about such a title for your students?

Srinivasan: Well, the author – Prof. B.K. Mukherjee is a renowned name in the academic world in India. I still use his books on marketing research & strategic brand management in my compulsory marketing management course. Though your company has popularised Chatterjee's Marketing Management book in India, but in today's context we need books with Indian examples. What do you think?

Menon: That is true sir, here the focus of the book is on realities of the Indian market and how a variety of fast moving consumer goods (fmcgs) and durable products are managed in India and this will enable your students to gather many practical insights of Indian market.

Srinivasan: Oh, I see. What is your company's plan on its pricing? Because you know in our business school, unlike the IIMs which have a huge grant for their libraries, the students buy the textbooks. So the price is a big issue for us to adopt any textbook.

Menon: Sir, we are aware of this problem. Our company always tries to keep the cost of educational material as low as possible for the students. We have decided to keep its price at Rs. 350/.

Srinivasan: I think the price set by your company seems very reasonable. Moreover, there is an absolute paucity of good books on product management in the market. It is a good decision on the part of WPL to persuade Prof. B.K. Mukherjee to write such a text book for our Indian market.

Menon: Yes sir, our managing director, Sri Ashok Mukherjee, has known Prof. Mukherjee for more than three decades. Regarding the pricing issue, I must admit that our company's management wanted to keep the price at Rs. 300. But, as you know sir, the printing costs have gone up tremendously in the last year. I also think our initial volume of printing will be about 5000 copies. In the near future when the book is widely adopted, then we shall be in a position to take the advantage of scale of printing.

Srinivasan: Well, Menon, you do not have to give me a complimentary copy. Let me know as soon as the book comes to the market and I shall buy it.

Menon: Thank you, Professor.

Questions

1. Explain whether Mr. Menon was effective in his communication with Prof. Srinivasan or not.
2. Was he too informal in his approach to explain the new offers?

MAKING THE SALES CALL

Integral Design for Programmed Learning

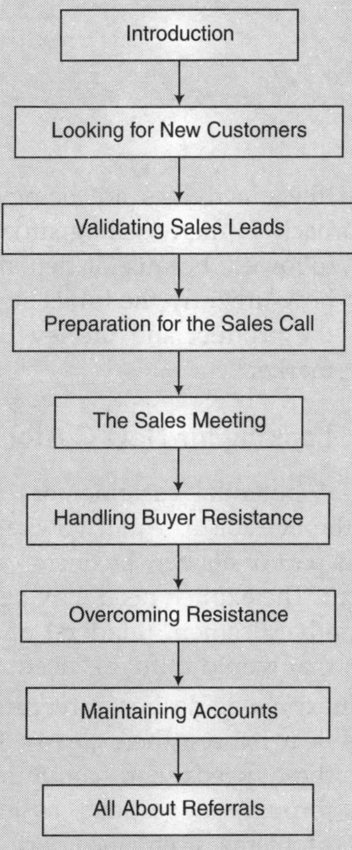

"Better service for the customer is for the good of the public, and this is the true purpose of enterprise."

–Konosuke Matsushita

INTRODUCTION

Most of what is covered in this chapter concerns the various activities undertaken during the selling process, though the ultimate objective of any sales call is to secure orders. However, the chapter also discusses how to handle customers' resistance and the role of referrals in sales.

> The selling process is a set of activities undertaken to successfully obtain an order, supply it as per the requirement of the customers and build up long-term customer relations.

THE SELLING PROCESS

The selling process is a set of activities undertaken to successfully obtain an order, supply it as per the requirement of the customers and build up long-term customer relations. The selling activities undertaken by professional salespeople include:

1. Looking for new customers
2. Validating sales leads
3. Preparation for sales calls
4. The sales meeting
5. Handling buyer resistance
6. Closing the sale
7. Account maintenance

It may be noted that while these activities are being presented in an order that is suggestive of a step-by-step approach, in many selling situations this sequence may not be followed, because it depends upon many factors such as how urgently the buyer needs the product, availability of the product and the level of competition existing in the market.

> It is necessary that the professional salespeople with the basic occupation involving selling products (i.e., goods and services) are well-trained and ethically responsible.

Looking for New Customers

A potential customer or "prospect" is one who is either buying a similar product from the market to whom you can sell or one who has not used previously, but requires it now as part of his new business ventures. Such needs of potential customers can be explicit or latent. The explicit need may be reflected as a formal invitation by the buyer in the form of an advertisement (tenders) or as structured discussions with potential suppliers for a product that would fulfill his need.

Latent needs are a form of unexpressed desires or requirements that the customer either is not aware of himself or is not able to express them clearly. A salesperson has to understand these needs and communicate to potential customers, through suggestions, as to how his product can resolve problems or enhance performance of the latter's business. The sales leads can come from many sources:

> Latent needs are difficult to gauge as often they are not expressed by potential customers.

- **Prospect initiated** – Includes leads obtained when prospects initiate contact through advertisements, trade shows, a personal approach or any other means.
- **Market scanning** – Uses market research tools, such as company profiles and other published information to locate leads that may help to sell the company's products.
- **Market observation** – Through this method leads are obtained by observing media outlets, such as news articles, Internet forums and corporate press releases.
- **Cold-calls** – Here leads are gathered by cold-calling, i.e. contacting someone without pre-notification personally, by telephone, through email or any other means.
- **Data mining** – This technique uses sophisticated software to evaluate information (e.g. in a corporate database) previously gathered by a company in hopes of locating prospects.
- **Referrals** – A very common mode for identifying sales leads uses referrals. Such referrals may come at no cost to the salesperson or, to encourage referrals, sales people may offer payment for referrals. Non-paying methods include asking acquaintances (e.g. friends, business associates) and networking (e.g. joining local or professional groups and associations). Paid methods may include payment to others like organized groups and companies who keep a market watch.
- **Sales promotions** – The method involves the use of free gifts to encourage potential customers to provide contact information or attend a sales meeting. This is seen more in the case of multi-level sales companies engaged in selling consumer products.

Validating Sales Leads

Not all sales leads have the potential to become sales prospects. There are many reasons for this, such as:

- **Difficulty of reaching customers** – Some potential customers (e.g. high-level executives) may be good prospects but finding a good time to meet them may be very difficult.
- **Order already placed** – Prospects may have already purchased a similar product offered by a competitor and, thus, may not require the same products.
- **Lack of financial strength** – Just because someone has a need for a product does not mean they can afford it. Lack of financial capability is a major factor why all potential customers do not become prospects.
- **May not be a key decision maker** – Prospects may lack the authority to take a decision in favour of the purchase.
- **May not meet requirements to purchase** – Prospects may not meet the requirements for purchasing the product (e.g. they may lack other products needed for the seller's product to work properly).

In order to evaluate the potential of a prospective customer, it is necessary to "qualify" the lead. Through use of research reports, evaluation of a company's financial position and feedback of his market credibility, it is possible to get a basic idea about the prospective customer. The assessment of a potential customer has to be through personal evaluation. To ensure a long-term, stable, transactional relationship, a personal review with the prospect is necessary. With a lead, a personal meeting to re-confirm the authenticity of the buyer becomes an obvious necessity.

Preparation for the Sales Call

What is often overlooked is the preparation required before a sales call is made. Such an approach damages the quality of interaction with the prospect during the sales call. Salespersons must therefore put in their maximum efforts to gather information about the prospect and analyze it while preparing for the sales call.

> More often than not, many salespersons are either too confident about themselves and their information base about their prospects or are complacent in their preparatory activities.

Learn More about the Customer

During the processes of lead generation and qualifying the selling process a seller may gain a great deal of knowledge about a customer. Invariably however, there is much more to know that can be helpful once an actual sales call is made. The salesperson can use their investigative skills to learn about such issues as:

- Who is the key decision maker?
- What is the customer's organizational structure?
- What products are currently being purchased and from whom?
- How are purchase decisions made?
- What are the customers' main concerns, likes and dislikes in business?

Salespeople may gather this information from the market from outlets selling similar products, salespeople of other companies who have dealt with the prospect, and by asking questions to the customers themselves. Collecting this information help immensely in preparing the salesperson for the sales presentation. For example, if the salesperson learns which competitor currently supplies the prospect then the salesperson can tailor promotional material in a way that compares the seller's products against products being purchased by the prospect.

> Having more information about a prospect allows the salesperson to be more confident in his/her presentation and, consequently, come across as more knowledgeable when meeting with the prospect.

With some information about the prospect in-hand, the salesperson must then move to make initial contact. In some cases a salesperson may be fortunate enough to have the prospect contact her/him but in most cases salespeople will need to initiate contact. In many ways arranging a contact requires as much effort as selling a product.

Contacts can be made in either of the following two ways:

- **Cold calling for presentation** – A good way to contact a prospect is to attempt to conduct a sales meeting through a straight cold call. In this approach the intention is not only to contact the prospect but also to make a sales presentation during this first contact period. This approach can be difficult since the prospect may be irritated by having unannounced salespeople interrupting them and will not give time out of their busy work schedule for a sales presentation meeting.
- **Cold calling for an appointment** – A better approach for most salespeople is to contact a prospect to set up an appointment in advance of the sales meeting. The additional advantage of making prior appointments is that it gives the salesperson time to prepare for the meeting and also, in the course of discussing an appointment, the salesperson may have the opportunity to gain some information about the prospect. Of course, this has the added advantage of having the prospect agree to hold the meeting, which may make them more receptive to the product than if the salesperson had followed the cold calling for presentation approach.

THE SALES MEETING

The core of the selling process is the meeting that takes place between the prospect and the sales team. At this stage of the selling process the sales team will spend a considerable amount of time presenting the product. While the word "presenting" may imply the seller is taking centre stage and does most of the talking by discussing the product's features and benefits, in actuality successful sellers find effective presentations to be more of a give-and-take conversation.

> The degree of success in the sales meeting reflects the degree of preparation made by the salesperson before the sales meeting.

Such meetings are highly beneficial to the salesperson as, besides discussing the product, it also enables the salesperson to establish a rapport with the prospect, know more about the prospect and understand his mind, and evaluate the current and future needs of the prospect. At times, it also helps to get some references that enable the salesperson to get more business in the future as well.

A salesperson should be very careful in his demeanour and responses during the sales meeting. He should be his natural self and should not look artificial, or over confident. A good salesperson should be a good listener, empathetic and try to customize his offer to suit the customer's needs.

HANDLING BUYERS' RESISTANCE

At times, a salesperson faces resistance from a prospect. Either the customer is not eager to take the product, or does not need it at all and is not willing to listen to the salesperson. The resistance is sometimes explicit where the customer states in clear terms what he feels about the product and even the salesman. On other occasions, the resistance presents itself

> It is said that sales start when the customer says 'no'.

in a non-verbal manner that may range from giving a cold shoulder to the salesperson to looking totally uninterested in the sales proposition.

'Your quality is not up to the mark'. 'Your price is too high.' 'Your company doesn't listen to its customers'. 'We're loyal to our current supplier.' 'I prefer your competitor's product.' These are some of the most common remarks that salespeople are accustomed to hear from their prospects.

Objections such as these are difficult to overcome and put a brake on a sales call after you have presented your company and your product, and think that the customer is convinced. Handling these objections is very important in finalizing a deal.

An objection is the customer's feeling or expression of opposition, disapproval, or dislike. In sales, such disapprovals or dislike may be the result of an experience he has had with the same product or services in the past or due to comparison *vis-à-vis* the alternatives available in the market. If you can ask all the right questions before making the formal product presentation, you can uncover every potential objection that could otherwise come back to bite you and you can modify your presentation accordingly.

> Resistance is a signal that the prospect is paying attention to the salesperson and may even have an interest in the product if the resistance can be effectively addressed.

Many people consider handling sales resistance as a difficult part of selling, most successful salespeople actually take it as 'part of the game' and regard as it as an inherent part of the selling process.

Some of the basic reflections of sales resistance are mentioned below:

Some Basic Statements of Sales Resistance

- We do not need your product. We are happy with the products that we are using/selling.
- Your price is too high.
- We have other problems to tackle now. So come later, we don't have the time to talk to you now.
- Our existing machines are doing well and we don't need anything new right now.
- We are not interested. Why? Why should I tell you that?
- What you are offering is not applicable here.
- I am very busy. I don't have time to discuss anything with you.
- Your product is very bad; your service is hopeless and your company doesn't keep its promises.
- Your competitor is offering it at a much cheaper price.
- Your payment terms are very rigid. Others are giving more lenient payment terms.
- Your supplies never come on time; that creates great problems and tarnishes my image.
- We are overstocked with your product. Your products don't sell.
- It's no point dealing with your company. Your company doesn't listen to its customers.
- Your company is very slow in settling customer complaints making my customers angry so I do not want to deal with you and your company.
- No customers ask for your product. Even if I buy it no one will ever buy it from me.
- Your company has no image. No one knows your products either, they will just not sell.

REASONS WHY CUSTOMERS RAISE OBJECTIONS

Success in selling means how best one can neutralize resistance. One of the basic methods followed by salespeople is to acknowledge resistance in the form of silence. Since objections are inevitable and are part and parcel of sales, a salesperson should learn the art of skilfully handling resistance.

A lot of resistance is the result of the prospect not knowing enough about their own needs and products that might fulfil their needs. There can also be resistance because of customers' bitter experience of the product, the company's slow response or indifferent attitude of the salesperson. Personal preferences and prejudices, and differences between what a prospect desires and what is offered often result in resistance. In any case careful handling of resistance holds the key to success in selling.

Some of the important reasons for objections raised by customers are as follows:

- Prospects might want to avoid a sales commitment because he is either too busy or too concerned about other matters.
- The salesperson has failed to deliver the promised offering in the past.
- Some customers enjoy objecting so that they can bargain in the process.
- The prospect resists change and is comfortable with the existing state of things. This might also happen because the customer does not find the new proposal very attractive.
- The customer fails to recognize how the product could make his life easier.
- The prospect has had a negative experience with the product or salesperson and does not want to have anything more to do with either of them.
- The prospect might lack information about or not understand the attributes of the new offering.

A salesperson who can understand the reasoning behind such resistances can handle it effectively.

Kinds of Objections

Objections of prospects can be of different kinds and can broadly be categorized as follows:

- Objections emerging because of inertia and apathy. This might occur because of unwillingness to change the status quo. The fear from moving from the existing state to a new one might prompt a customer to desist from buying.
- Product related objections which might pertain to its core quality, packaging, pricing or warranty.
- Service related objections that normally point to the poor quality of service, slow response or lack of empathetic attitude.
- Objections due to delayed response mainly in handling customer complaints.

- Objections related to the behaviour of the salesperson. Usually, street-smart or over talkative salespersons are not admired. Also customers will not entertain salespersons who do not deliver what is expected or keep their promises.
- Emotional considerations because of lack of sensitivity and courtesy of the seller towards the buyer. A prospect might also feel ignored and decide to abstain from buying.
- Lack of enthusiasm or energy on the part of salesperson might also lead the prospect to decide against buying from him. This often takes place when the salesperson is not trained adequately or is not 'cut-out' for this profession.
- Preconceived ideas can be barriers to sales. Prejudice is not only a recurrent and frustrating aspect of selling, but also one which is a true test of disposition for a professional salesperson. Such prejudices are the result of an unsatisfactory personal experience or that of others and are very damaging to sales.
- A reaction based on an illogical interpretation of clearly stated information or a reasonable assumption based on badly stated facts can be a potent cause of resistance to sales. Such cases are a failure on the part of the salesperson and should be rectified as fast as possible.
- At times, ego is a major reason for obstruction to sales. Thinking that he knows everything, the prospect is not prepared to listen to the salesperson nor is he ready to accept anything that is new to him.
- Some prospects are of the opinion that what they already have is the ultimate and all new things are inferior in quality and performance. Such people always take pride in having their age old possessions and develop an emotional attachment to them and are not prepared to replace them with new ones. Such people always raise objections to whatever new is offered to them.
- Often, the prospects are afraid to buy because they feel that the new product might not perform as the salesperson claims, or that the salesperson will benefit more from the transaction than they will. They fear that soon after the purchase, the salesperson will not be visible, the company will not extend support in case of any problem and they will face problems.
- Lastly another important factor is the lack of ability of the prospect to take a final decision. Though knowing his needs and the new products, prospects are at times confused or puzzled and are unable to come to a logical conclusion. In the process the sales are postponed.

OVERCOMING RESISTANCE

To overcome resistance, salespeople must be trained to make sure they clearly understand the prospect's concern. Sometimes prospects voice what appears to be an objection to the product but, in fact, they have other issues that are preventing them from agreeing to a purchase. Salespeople are rarely able to make the sale unless resistance is overcome.

Objections can be answered only if one is well versed in the information about the products (quality, quantity, and complaints) supplied to a particular customer; the services (offered versus those asked for). Performance of competitors' products with similar parameters could be valuable in this context. Some valuable points to overcoming resistance are given below:

> Effective handling of resistance requires a rational approach to the problem.

- Be empathetic.
- Do not disagree immediately with what customer says but put your viewpoint across in a logical way that makes the picture clear.
- Foresee objections and be ready with possible answers and with facts and figures to support your answers, so that the prospect is convinced by your logic.
- If a customer is unyielding, try to take a positive approach to the customer's perspective, empathize with him and try to find the truth behind it. If you find that what the customer is saying is correct, try to resolve it and give a feedback to the customer.
- Prepare a sales presentation that takes care of any objection, before it is raised.
- Eliminate objections by taking necessary steps in your company. This will enhance your competitiveness.
- Clarify the objections if necessary.
- Classify the objections.
- Maintain control at all times while handling objections.
- Never argue with the prospect.
- Be diplomatic in answering questions.
- Fit the answer to the prospect's concern.
- Minimize the objections.
- Capitalize on the objections, if possible.

Something More on Handling Objections ...

- **Always listen to the prospect** – The main objection of many people is that the salesperson or the company do not listen to them. A patient hearing solves most of the problems.
- **Ask questions** – This will convey the message that you are eager to solve a customer's problems. Probing or exploratory questions give the prospect assurance that a genuine effort is being made to solve his problem.
- **Give a guarantee** – Often a guarantee removes any doubts from the mind of the prospect and assures him that whatever is promised, will be delivered.
- **The "yes, but" technique** – This can often be useful in handling objections. Here are two examples of what salespersons might say when using this technique: (i) "Yes, I can understand that attitude, but there is another aspect that you might consider."

(ii) "Yes, you have a point here, but in your case, there are other issues that are also involved.

- **Admitting but reassuring** – When the reasons for the objections seem genuine, admit it. This will satisfy the prospect's ego and with the satisfaction of being the 'winner' he may like to give you another chance.
- **Demonstrate** – Many of the objections are clarified by seeing the product in use. It is a very good way of telling the prospect that the product is good and that he will gain if he buys it.
- **Evaluate the product versus the competition** – This will describe logically how your product is superior to other products and will satisfy the prospect.

CLOSING THE SALE

Closing the sale is the point when the seller finally asks the prospect to place the order. It is often believed that this is the most difficult part of the entire selling process. It is at this point that the salesperson should be very careful in reading the customer's mind and assessing his intentions. He should fit his offer to the requirements of the customer and ask him to sign the order book. Often, it is also the point when many customers, unwilling to make a commitment, say 'no'. For any salesperson, involved in sales, such rejection can be very difficult to overcome, especially if it occurs on a consistent basis. However, if handled carefully, closing the sale can actually be fairly easy.

It has been observed that many salespersons try to take a short cut to success. In their eagerness to sell and achieve their target, they are in a hurry to somehow transfer the material to the customer and take payment, without spending enough time to know the customer, understand his needs, know his likes and dislikes about similar products, his long-term expectations from the product, company and more so – the salesperson. The salesperson who has worked hard in developing a relationship with the customer, finds it easy to overcome such resistance. In the case of such buyers, salespeople must exercise restraint, patience, perseverance and persuasive communication skills as this will help and even persuade a buyer to place an order.

> It is always suggested that without rushing to sell, the salesperson must spend maximum time in the market, trying to know his customers, develop rapport with him and establish his own credibility as a reliable person.

The use of persuasive communication techniques is by far the most important aspect related to the selling process. Persuasion is the skill in helping the prospect to take a decision; it is not a technique for making someone make a decision. The difference is important. Where one is deceitful, the other is helpful and designed to benefit the buyer. Persuasion is not always necessary. Many times buyers take the lead in closing a sale since they are convinced that the product is right for them.

> The close of sale is not the end of the selling process but is the beginning of building a relationship.

MAINTAINING ACCOUNTS

In selling situations where repeat purchasing is always desired compared to a one-time sale, following up with a customer is critical to establishing a long-term relationship. Maintenance of past sales records is thus an important activity in the selling process, which really amounts to the beginning of the next sale and, thus, the beginning of a buyer-seller relationship.

> Once the sale is made, sales people should work hard to ensure that the customer is happy with the purchase and determine in what other ways he can help the customer to be even more satisfied with the purchase.

Generally, customers are forgotten after the sale deal is made and salespersons, in their anxiety to meet targets, start 'hunting' for other prospects. This is a highly improper approach as it tarnishes the image of the salesperson in a short time and damages the prospects of future sales.

On the contrary after the sale is made, salespeople should ensure that the customer is happy with the purchase and determine in what other ways he can help the customer to be even more satisfied. The level and nature of after-sales follow-up will often depend on the product sold. Expensive, complex purchases that require installation and training may result in the salesperson spending considerable time with the customer after the sale while smaller purchases may have the seller follow-up with email correspondence or periodic visits.

By maintaining contact after the sale, the seller tries to become more acceptable to the customer, which invariably leads the salesperson learning more about the customer and the customer's business. This knowledge will be useful to explore more selling opportunities.

THINGS TO REMEMBER

Walt Disney said: "*Do what you do so well that people want to bring their friends to see you do it again*. From my point of view, the greatest compliment for a seller is the customer's referral."

> Salespersons must always remember that selling does not mean manipulating the potential buyer to do what the seller wants, but it means trying to understand what the customer wants and providing it to him, so that he is happy and satisfied.

If you want to satisfy customers, and want them to be with you for a long time, you should:

1. **Treat customers right** – People want to feel like valued customers. They want to see that their time and opinions matter. If people cannot trust you to treat them right, then they certainly will not trust you with their money. Be ethical in your approach in dealing with customers.
2. **Make it easy and convenient for customers to buy your product** – Take care to see that each step in the order in this process provides the answers or serves your customers' needs. Be sure that they get what they came for.
3. **See that your presentation is fair and truthful** – No one wants to feel duped or to receive false information about prices, delivery dates, or terms of the sale. Even a hint of such intentions kills customers' willingness to listen to you. If a person feels

that he is cheated he will never buy anything from you again and will also spread a negative word of mouth publicity that could be very damaging to you and your business.

4. **Ensure that every step of the selling process is taken care perfectly** – If every part of the process works as an integrated whole, you may consider the customer well served. When the parts are mismatched it scares customers away.

FROM 'NO' TO 'YES'

Nothing can be more depressing than when your prospective customer says 'no', that they do not want your product/service, do not have time to listen to you and feel that your product and company is bad.

How to change 'no' to 'yes' is a question that every salesperson would like to know the answer to. It has been observed that while this is a vital aspect of sales, most salespersons fail to tackle it properly. This is due to one or more of the following reasons:

- Inability to understand customers and their needs;
- Taking customers for granted;
- A casual approach towards customers and sales;
- Over-confidence about the market and customers;
- Undermining customers' ability to buy;
- Pre-conceived notions about a customer;
- The 'know-all' attitude;
- Taking a shortcut approach for sales;
- Lack of optimism and enthusiasm;
- Inability to handle pressure of sales.

It is to be understood that not everybody will buy your product. A potential customer may not have the inclination or means to buy the product, nor any problem that you can solve. A potential client might not want his problem solved at present or does not want the problem solved at all. It must be remembered that you cannot possibly serve all the potential clients in your niche but you can serve all of those who are a perfect fit for you and your business.

In these situations a 'no' is the right response or outcome, and does not reflect on you and your products and services. In fact, there are also times when you will want to say 'no' to a potential client, e.g. if potential customers do not meet the criteria of your ideal client, you will know that you will not be able to offer them your best service. You may decide to say 'no' to them and refer them to some other person who can fulfil their needs. If you say 'no' to potential clients, they will find you more trustworthy. This may seem contrary, but then the sales game is full of contradictions. But that can be one of its most appealing aspects.

Assumptions: The Deadly Trap

Assumptions are deadly traps which can ensnare even the most prudent salesperson. Assumptions are a very natural aspect of human nature; they result from the experience that one has had with a person or in a similar situation. In either case past experience could furnish you with data for that help in making a decision in the present context. But under no circumstances should a salesperson assume anything that might not be true.

Listed below are few examples of common assumptions:

- A customer cannot afford to buy what you are selling.
- The person you are talking to is the only one making the buying decisions.
- Your customer always complains and does not want to do business with your company.
- You know the customer so well that you do not need to ask him/her what is wrong when they seem bothered.

Before assuming anything, a salesperson must ask himself the following questions:

- What are the underlying assumptions?
- How correct are these assumptions?
- What damage occurs when the assumptions go wrong?
- Should the decisions be based on objectivity or assumptions?

It is natural for everyone to assume things. Each one of us engages in a number of assumptions daily. Then one holds the assumptions to be 'accurate' and conducts oneself according to the 'assumed beliefs.' This is because we believe that assumptions are based on one's experiences or hearsay. In such cases, impressions gathered from experience might provide valuable data to the salesperson but a prudent salesperson should also consider the circumstance under which the prospect might have reacted. Hence past experience should be considered but it should not be the deciding factor in the present context.

You should think about the consequences that might arise if your assumptions are wrong. Normally, assumptions are the result of apathy, ignorance, lack of confidence or are due to fixed ideas about the market and customers, incorrect interpretation of the way some people might have reacted in the past or rigid predisposition due to a closed mind. A good salesperson should always get rid of the habit of assuming things and consider the facts while taking a decision.

- When you assume that you know what your customer wants – do you really know and how do you know it? Or, are you just assuming that you know?
- You assume the customer cannot afford what you are selling. How do you know? Did you ask or assume?
- How do you know that the customer will definitely complain about the product he has bought from you?
- You assume you know what motivates your current customers to buy but you have not made the sale. Why? Maybe your assumptions are wrong.

Hence assume nothing; when you assume nothing you ask lots of questions; when you ask questions you get responses; when you get responses you will draw accurate conclusions; when you draw accurate conclusions you are better prepared to understand your customer; when you truly understand your customer your chances of making and keeping the sale are much better; even if you do not make the sale, at least you will definitely know the reasons why. So, you should stop assuming and start asking! You will be amazed by the results.

Asking Leading Questions

Leading questions are queries that allow the salesperson to determine the prospect of sales from the buyer's perspective. They tell the salesperson which needs are most critical and should be addressed when presenting product features and benefits. Moreover, by clarifying the actual gains of the decision in the customer's mind, such questions serve the 'emotional instincts,' of the buyer, making the expected gains even more attractive.

As the salesperson asks open-ended questions to determine the customer's needs, he will realise that some needs seem very urgent to the customer. Whenever you perceive this to be the case, you can ask leading questions to confirm your gut feeling and clarify the situation. Good leading questions suggest what is at stake for the buyer's company, but the very best ones aim at discovering the customer's personal likes and dislikes. By clarifying what is really at stake with a business problem or opportunity, leading questions increase the customer's desire for a solution. And, they let the salesperson know how to present a product as the right solution to the right issues.

Leading questions offer the highest payoff when they are used in the context of a full-scale sales strategy – a strategy that spells how to build up to asking such questions and what to do with the information after you have uncovered it. By doing so salespeople now know where they stand at every stage during a call and can proceed strategically. They are better able to manage a sales call from start to finish.

To Confirm or Not to Confirm

Do you confirm every prospect's appointment before you go to meet him? Or you do not confirm, believing that it gives your prospect an "out?" Often a salesperson may feel that if he confirms a meeting it gives a prospect an opportunity to get out of it. Let us look at this statement and the beliefs that go with it.

The above statement means that the scheduled appointment is something that, given a choice, you feel a prospect would avoid. This must mean, therefore, that you somehow tricked or manipulated your prospect into agreeing to the meeting in the first place. Now on reflection, your prospect could only want to get out of it.

If, however, you truly believe that your product or service has value, if you have done your homework and are calling on qualified prospects then there is no reason that a prospect should want to avoid meeting with you. It is time to change some of our beliefs about the meeting. If a prospect schedules an appointment with you, that means they are interested in talking about what you have to offer!

Confirming a meeting avoids your having to race around your territory to meetings with prospects who do not want to meet you.

Some salespersons even feel that when a prospect stands them up, the prospect then feels guilty and "owes them." These sales professionals believe that their prospects will meet them in the future because of a sense of guilt. Perhaps some do, but barring a last minute emergency that takes a prospect away unexpectedly, someone who stands you up once, will more than likely have no qualms about standing you up again. This "guilt" approach goes hand-in-hand with the belief that prospects must be tricked or manipulated into meetings.

So, you should change the way you think about prospect meetings and confirm them! It is always desirable to call your prospect the day before or early in the morning on the day of the appointment. Try to reach the prospect directly.

If your prospect says the agreed upon meeting time no longer works, you must reschedule straight away! So that when you show up tomorrow or later the same day, your prospect will actually be there! (Leave your contact number so that the prospect can reach you if something unexpected happens.)

Confirming appointments makes far better use of your selling time. A prospect who will not meet you, is not a desirable prospect! Those prospects who do cancel and are unwilling, for whatever reason, to reschedule are doing you a favour. They are saving you the time and energy you would have spent going to see them, following up with them and then not selling anything!

REFERRALS

A referral is an introduction to a potential prospect that is made by someone the prospect knows and respects. One of the best (and most overlooked) sources of sales leads is through referrals.

Why are Referrals Important?

Think about it – what could be better than a respected business person talking about the quality of his products, services, and/or customer service to their equally well-respected friends and associates? Often this kind of input might jump-start some sales cycles. Moreover, it is more profitable – working with prospects who already think favourably about you and your company.

There are four categories of referrals, ranging from 'most effective' to 'least effective':

1. **In-person introduction** – This is when your contact personally takes you to the potential customer and introduces you in-person. Such introduction includes a very good testimony of you, your products or services, and your company.
2. **Telephonic introduction** – If time or circumstances do not permit a personal introduction, the next best option is a telephone introduction. Such an introduction also leaves a good impression about you and your business in the minds of the prospect.

3. **Electronic introduction** – If you cannot manage a personal or telephonic introduction, the next best option is for your contact to speak with, leave a voice mail for, or send an e-mail to the prospects before you contact them. When you make your introductory call, be sure to mention your referee's name and explain why he/she thinks it would be a good idea for the client to meet you.
4. **Authorized name dropping** – The least effective referral is when your contact gives you a prospect's name and telephone number and asks you to mention his name when you call the prospect. This is certainly 'warmer' than a cold call, but it is not as effective as the other types of referrals.

Dealing with Referrals

Like many of the activities involved in selling, asking for referrals requires care. The prospect should not feel that the name is being referred to pressurize or to indicate his power to influence the prospect. Also, referrals are to be used in rare cases only as many salespersons tend to drop the referee's name quite regularly thereby creating a disagreeable image of the referee in the customer's mind.

When should You Ask for Referrals?

You should ask for a referral if you have done a favour for a customer; when a customer places an order; when a customer is happy with you or your company or when you have helped a customer to solve a problem.

However, customers are not the only source of referrals. Anyone you talk to can be a potential source of referrals. If you feel you have built credibility with someone, or they seem interested in what you do, should not hesitate to ask them for referrals.

Referrals can be one of the most productive and profitable lead sources available to sales people. However, it takes some practice to be comfortable asking for referrals. Moreover, there are different kinds of referrals that produce different levels of results.

If you want to maximize the positive impact of referrals on your sales opportunity pipeline, follow these steps:

Practice what you are going to say when asking for referrals until you can say it easily and naturally.

Hold yourself accountable for asking for referrals at every opportunity. If you realize you had forgotten to ask for referrals during a specific meeting or telephone call, you should call your contact back as soon as possible and ask for referrals.

Keep in mind that not all referrals are equal. When you ask for referrals, always ask for a personal introduction first. If your contact cannot arrange a personal introduction, work your way down the list of referral types from the most effective to the least effective.

KEY CONCEPTS

- The selling process is a set of activities undertaken to successfully obtain an order and begin building long-term customer relations.
- Exploring sales opportunities prudently, validating sales leads properly, preparing for sales calls well, managing sales meetings, handling buyer resistance, closing a sale effectively and managing accounts properly are the key to success in sales
- Besides strengthening existing customers, efforts must also be made to bring potential customers into the fold.
- A potential customer is one who is either buying a similar product from the market to whom you can sell, or one who has not used it previously, but might require it now.
- Salespersons must prepare thoroughly for sales calls. Information about the market and prospects may help immensely in preparing the salesperson for the sales.
- A salesperson should be careful in his demeanour and responses during the sales meeting. A superior salesperson should be a good listener, empathetic and must try to customize his offer to suit the customer's needs.
- Sales start when the customer says 'no'. Most of the time, a salesperson faces resistance from a prospect. Resistances can be difficult to overcome and have to be handled very judiciously.
- Handling sales resistance is considered a difficult part of selling, but is actually an inherent part of the selling process.
- Success in selling consists of neutralizing resistance. Resistance is a signal that the prospect is paying attention to the salesperson and may even have an interest in the product if the resistance can be effectively addressed.
- Objections can be answered only if we are prepared well. Effective handling of resistance requires an empathetic approach and keenness to solve the problem.
- Use of persuasive communication techniques are very necessary to sell. Persuasion is the skill of helping the prospect to take a decision.
- Normally, customers are forgotten after the sale is made. It should be remembered that closing the sale is not the end of the selling process but is the beginning of building a relationship.
- By maintaining contact after the sale, the seller becomes more acceptable to the customer, which invariably leads to the salesperson learning more about the customer and the customer's business. With this knowledge the salesperson will almost always be presented with more selling opportunities.

CASE STUDY

CASE I: WARNER PUBLISHING HOUSE INDIA PVT. LTD.

Warner Publishing House India Pvt. Ltd. (WPH) is a leading publisher of reference books for the management profession. The company, headquartered in New Delhi, was established in 1953 and is held in high esteem by the profession it serves. It maintained its image as a leading publisher of management journals and reference books. They had maintained an advisory council to enhance the quality of its publications. Senior managers of this council would propose new titles in their selected areas, and then recognized management educators were commissioned to prepare these manuscripts.

WPH marketed its books via a network of aggressive, sales agents on a commission basis. WPH termed them as Associate Directors (AD) and they were reimbursed their expenses and were paid a good remuneration through a schedule of variable commissions, Mr. Shankar Waghel was one such AD serving the North Delhi municipal area. Shankar had been with the company for two decades and was considered to be in the top 10 percent of the firm's associate directors. Like other ADs of WPH he used to operate from his home, employed a secretary, and used an answering machine to handle his business calls.

Although he was happy with his present earnings, Shankar thought he could substantially augment his earnings if he could improve his selling productivity. He decided to seek advice from Dr. S. Valecha who was heading a sales organisation. He knew Dr. Valecha through a social group called "Kshitij", which was engaged in helping education among the slum dwellers in Delhi. Dr. Valecha listened to Mr. Shankar's problems. During that meeting it emerged that WPH provided sales leads for its ADs. Most of these enquiries were generated through good editorial reviews made in professional journals, direct mail, and through sponsoring international conferences. As Shankar told Dr. Valecha, "My concern really boils down to the fact that I only have time for four or five appointments per day. While my close ratio is very good in comparison to others in WPH I cannot predict the sales order from my existing clients vis à vis new young professionals. I wish there was some way of screening my sales leads as to the likelihood of their buying our books. This would allow me to concentrate on the better prospects and increase our earnings. So you see, my problem is not where to find prospects, since I have more than I could ever hope to cover. My problem is now how to translate calls into sales. I really don't know why of late I have seen that young professors do not give time to me to explain the new arrivals and other publications that would be of use to them. I have observed that they shy away from me and use some pretext or the other not to recommend books they get from us..."

Dr. Valecha said, "Have you tried to introspect why this has happened? You have been one of the best performers; your record has been excellent; and you have, in the past created many sales records. Is it that you have become complacent or egoistic; or perhaps you have started taking your customers for granted? Have you tried to think why your customers would buy from you? What is so unique in your offerings? And what will it require to get your customers' loyalty?"

Question

1. Do you feel Dr. Valecha's questions were valid, and if so why?

CASE II: NEW STYLE & CO.

The New Style manufactured a line of personal care products including hair dryers, razors, curling irons, manicure sets. Recently they introduced a new product called the "Shaper." Using the Shaper a person could trim, shape, or thin his or her hair. Two heads were provided – one called a "long cut" and the other a "short cut." The Shaper was available in different colours – brown, black, blue, green and yellow. The advertising theme emphasized the importance of a well-groomed appearance. For nearly two months the sales force had been calling on large retailers with little success, which was very disappointing, since a lot of money had been spent on advertising the new product. K.C. Chandra, the managing director of the company, was concerned about the poor market response to his new product. He firmly believed that the product was very good, and had no direct competition. The results of a focus group research backed up his opinion of the product.

Mr. Chandra learnt that his salespeople were finding it difficult to convince dealers that consumers would see a need for the Shaper and then buy it. The suggested retail price of Rs. 250 did not seem to be a problem.

Ms. Pramila Wirk, head of marketing research, told Mr. Chandra that the biggest question raised in focus group interviews was the consumers' inability to see themselves using the product. She added that consumers had no problem understanding the benefits of using the product.

Mr. Chandra was convinced that the Shaper had great potential and could become a top seller for the company. Chandra felt that the sales force was not performing its job. He believed that the salespersons needed greater preparation to get the major selling points across to buyers.

Question

1. Analyze the problems faced by this new brand and suggest a set of actions how sales team could convince the dealers to stock the brand.

REFERENCES

1. Berthon, Pierre, Pitt, Leyland, Halvorson, Wade, Ewing, Michael, Crittenden, Victoria L. (2010), Advocating Avatars: The Salesperson in Second Life, *Journal of Personal Selling & Sales Management*, Vol. 30 Issue 3, pp. 195-208.
2. Donoho, Casey, Heinze, Timothy (2011), The Personal Selling Ethics Scale: Revisions and Expansions for Teaching Sales Ethics, *Journal of Marketing Education*, Vol. 33 Issue 1, pp. 107-122.
3. Dubinsky, Alan J. Staples, William A. (1981/82), Sales Training: Salespeople's Preparedness and Managerial Implications, *Journal of Personal Selling & Sales Management*, Vol. 2 Issue 1, p. 24.

4. Graziano, John E., Flanagan, Patrick J. (2005), Explore the Art of Consultative Selling, *Journal of Accountancy*, Vol. 199 Issue 1, pp. 34-37.
5. Jolson, Marvin A. (1997), Broadening the Scope of Relationship Selling, *Journal of Personal Selling & Sales Management*, Vol. 17 Issue 4, pp. 75-88.
6. Miller, Skip (2011), Qualifying the Prospects: Seven Vital Questions to Ask, *American Salesman*, Vol. 56 Issue 1, pp. 24-30.
7. Miller, William "Skip" (2002), Applying the Proactive Selling Process, *ProActive Selling*, pp. 205-220.
8. Moncrief, William C., Marshall, Greg W. (2005), The Evolution of the Seven Steps of Selling, *Industrial Marketing Management*, Vol. 34 Issue 1, pp. 13-22.
9. O'Shaughnessy, John (1971/72), Selling as an Interpersonal Influence Process, *Journal of Retailing*, Vol. 47 Issue 4, p. 32.
10. Perry, Monica L., Pearce, Craig L., Sims Jr, Henry P. (1999), Empowered Selling Teams: How Shared Leadership Can Contribute to Selling Team Outcomes, *Journal of Personal Selling & Sales Management*, Vol. 19 Issue 3, pp. 35-51.
11. Reeves, Robert A., Barksdale, Hiram C. (1984), A Framework for Classifying Concepts of and Research on the Personal Selling Process... *Journal of Personal Selling & Sales Management*, Vol. 4 Issue 2, p. 7.
12. Selling Process, (1988), *Journal of Personal Selling & Sales Management*, Vol. 8 Issue 3, p. 68.
13. Szymanski, David M. (1988), Determinants of Selling Effectiveness: The Importance of Declarative Knowledge to the Personal Selling Concept, *Journal of Marketing*, Vol. 52 Issue 1, pp. 64-77.
14. Tyler, Philip R., Hair, Neil (2007), Teaching Professional Selling: A Relationship Building Process. *Journal for Advancement of Marketing Education*, Vol. 11, pp. 31-34.
15. Weise, Tracy (2010), Selling Franchises Online: Demystifying the Process, *Franchising World*, Vol. 42 Issue 10, pp. 11-13.

6 Sales Presentation Skills

"The precise presentation you develop will depend upon what you're selling, to whom you're trying to sell. For whom you're selling and you."

—*Russell, Beach, Buskirk*

CHAPTER OUTLINE

- Introduction
- Presentation skills defined
- Presentation – An art
- Key factors for an effective presentation
- 10 tips for preparing attractive slides
- Making an impact
- Signposting
- Refining delivery
- Body language
- Handling questions
- Things to remember while making a presentation

OBJECTIVES

After studying this chapter, you will be able to:

- Define the art of presentation skill and its important aspects
- Describe the key factors for an effective presentation
- Structure the presentation in a systematic manner
- Prepare attractive slides for presentations
- Make effective presentations

Opening Case: Steel India Ltd.

Mr. Raja Rao was a marketing executive for Steel India Limited, a medium sized company that specialized in ferro alloys.

Mr. Rao had been working with Steel India Limited for nearly three years. His job was basically that of contacting prospective firms and seeking orders for various types of steel products made by Steel India Ltd. Mr. Rao enjoyed his work. He had been selected for this position partly because of his extrovert personality, his knowledge about steel products and his vast contacts in the industry. Mr. Rao was also active in a number of extra-curricular activities while in college, including sports and drama. He had represented his college in several intra collegiate debates and theatrical productions. He was very popular amongst his peers because of his ability to take charge of a situation and he could fill in any silence with a witty comment.

Because of all these qualities, Mr. Rao was outstanding in getting presentation interviews with his clients. He was able to impress them with his presentations and often got rave reviews for his performance. However, Mr. Rao could not finally close as many sales as he should have. That is, though he had an excellent track record of meeting many new clients or prospects, his conversion into order records was not that impressive. Mr. John Mathews his territory manager one day said, "I'm not sure what is going wrong that Mr. Rao is not able to clinch the final deal, though he is able to get entry so easily. I want to help him for his own sake as well as the company's. But I'm not sure where to begin".

Questions

1. What do you think is the fundamental problem with Rao's approach here?
2. Suggest measures to solve Mr. Rao's (and the company's) problem.

SALES PRESENTATION SKILLS

Integral Design for Programmed Learning

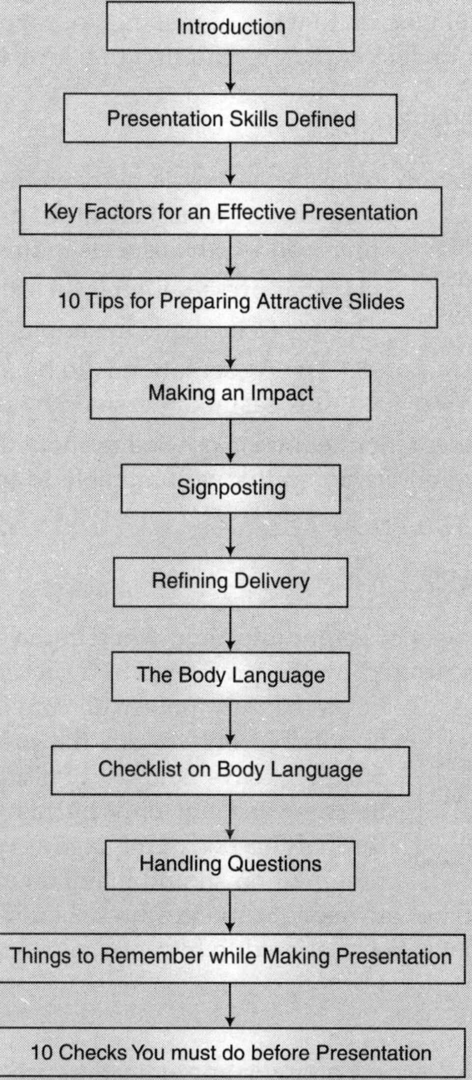

"Discretion in speech is more than eloquence; and to speak agreeably to him with whom we deal is more than to speak in good words or in good order."

–Bacon

INTRODUCTION

This chapter aims to discuss how to make excellent presentations, persuade your customers to buy and get orders. It will equip you with the tools and techniques necessary to make a winning performance, starting with some tips on preparing a plan – what to include and how to structure it – then moving on to ways of making your message clear and impressive, and finishing off with how to deliver the presentation to your valued customers.

PRESENTATION SKILLS DEFINED

The definition of a presentation given in the box is perhaps the simplest of all definitions available on what constitute presentation skills. There are three noteworthy aspects in this definition:

> A presentation is an art that explains about you and your knowledge in simple language and words, easily understood by the recipient.

1. That presentation is an art.
2. It is to be made in simple language.
3. The presentation is to be made in such a manner that it is easily understood by the recipients.

Making an effective presentation requires knowledge about the subject, conviction about what you are going to say and clarity so that you are able to translate your thoughts into words.

PRESENTATION – AN ART

A presentation is a formal way of communicating, wherein the objective is to persuade the recipient to act on what is desired by the presenter. In a presentation the communication has to be very powerful, convincing and persuasive. This is possible only when the presenter is convinced about what he says and is offering. This conviction should be conveyed not only by his words, tone and tenor but through his body language as well. The person making the presentation should maintain eye contact with the listener, and his expression, voice, hand movements and gestures should be such that they influence the listener to act upon what is being offered to him.

> In a presentation the communication has to be very powerful, convincing and persuasive.

Language

Language is visibly a critical aspect of any communication process. It is necessary that the language used should be simple and easy to understand. Many times, many people use slang words or difficult words or sentences in an attempt to impress the listeners about the vast knowledge that they possess. Such language is in fact a hindrance to communication. A salesperson should therefore make a conscious attempt to use simple and precise language in any presentation that he makes before customers.

Hence, use language that your audience understands. To drive your point home, use simple words and short sentences and see that your audience has understood what you have said. Remember the formula "KISS" – "Keep It Short & Simple" to make your presentation sharp. Some tips on "using a language that speaks" are:

> Use language that your audience understands. To drive your point home, use simple words and short sentences and see that your audience has understood what you have said.

- Use words of everyday speech, not jargon
- Avoid woolly, abstract nouns
- Try to avoid passive sentences
- Avoid long qualifying clauses

Easy Understanding by the Recipient

Communication is never complete unless what you are trying to say is understood by the recipient. It is therefore important to ensure that what you are presenting is easily understood by the customers. So the presenter must ask, during and after the presentation, whether what he has said is clearly understood by everyone.

Audience

The first thing that any good presenter must look into is the audience. When preparing your presentation, you must put the audience first, if you want to be persuasive and memorable.

The entire presentation must be prepared in view of who is going to listen to it. Your audience could be the top management of a multi-national corporation, a group of distributors in a distributors' meet, a big gathering of retailers or a select group of consumers invited to listen during a relationship marketing campaign. In each case the content, message, layout and time for the presentation will be different, even though the product/service being marketed is the same.

> The presentation must be prepared in such a manner that you are able to hold the attention of your audience during the entire period of your presentation.

It should be remembered that it is very difficult to hold people's attention for long. In fact few people can concentrate beyond twenty minutes. Hence, no matter how long or short a presentation is, the attention of an average audience wanders easily.

You are not going to get your message across if the audience is not attentive and active throughout. So, you need to make everything, i.e., the structure, the language, and the information, as clear and memorable as possible.

Hence the presentation must be prepared in such a manner that you are able to hold the attention of your audience during the entire period of your presentation. You could make the layout attractive by including visual aids like small video clippings about the company and its products, success stories and endorsement by some of your customers.

To find out about the audience and ask the following questions:

- Who are they?
- How well do you know them?
- How big is it?
- Why are they coming to listen to you?
- How much do they know? Should you start from scratch?

To ensure continued attention of the audience, the presenter must:

- Be clear about what "we" want to achieve
- Make "it" clear to audience
- Plan carefully before hand
- Always thank the participants
- Never ridicule or make fun of any participant

KEY FACTORS FOR AN EFFECTIVE PRESENTATION

There are three key factors that should be followed to make presentations effective:

- Preparation
- Planning
- Practice

Preparation

No presentation can be better than the preparation which precedes it. Prepare a checklist jotting down all the points that should be there in the presentation. For a thorough preparation this checklist should include the following:

1. Knowing the situation

- **When** – The time of the presentation will enable you to select the methodology, as the energy level of the audience fluctuates during the day – it is quite high during the morning, at its lowest ebb in the afternoon and medium in the evening.
- **Where** – It will help in selecting the audio-visual aids for the presentation. A formal presentation in a conference room can be made using modern electronic gadgets like an LCD projector, cordless mike etc. while a presentation in say a doctor's cabin or a small meeting room with some senior officials may not have such facilities.
- **Who** – As stated earlier in this chapter, knowing who the audience is, is very important. The content, layout, selection of colour, font and template etc. is to be decided accordingly.
- **How long** – The duration of the presentation. As has already been discussed, it is very difficult to hold the attention of the audience for long. Moreover, the presentation must have flexibility to suit the available time of your audience. You might have

prepared a 20 minutes presentation but your customer might tell you to finish it in 10 minutes as he has to go for another meeting.

It is therefore necessary to divide your presentation into three parts; namely **must know, should know and nice to know.** The concept is explained through Figure 6.1.

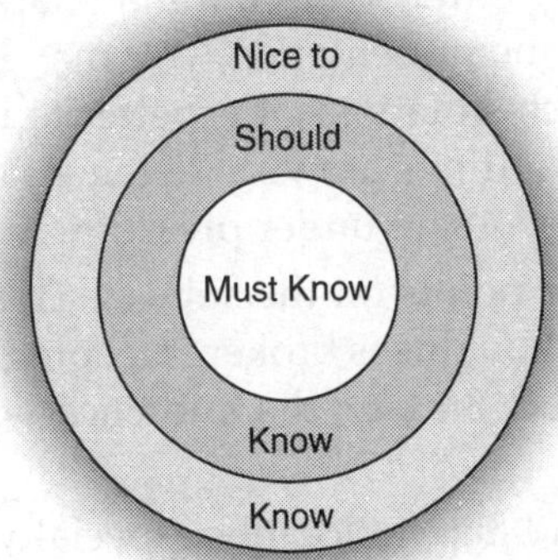

Fig. 6.1 *Categorizing the Presentation Material*

Must know – This is the aspect of your presentation that, in any case, must be conveyed to the audience. It should contain the critical aspects of your offer and the benefits that would accrue to the customers.

Should know – This should contain those aspects that are not critical but are important and conveying them would attract your customers to some degree.

Nice to know – This is the part of the presentation that supports your core message, e.g. videos, customer endorsements etc.

Why me

An equally important question to ask when making a presentation is "Why me?" You may discover that you have been asked to make the presentation because you are the best person who can present the subject to the audience; you have that skill of good delivery and are an incredible speaker. All this will give you confidence that will enable you to make the best possible presentation and ultimately clinch the deal!

2. Know your objective

The second important factor to be included in the checklist is to know the objective of the presentation. Your presentation could be to introduce a new product, or an aggressive promotional campaign, to persuade or to sell!

> The structure of presentation requires a different treatment for each objective. The presentation has to be tuned to address the objective specifically.

The presentation must be planned for a positive response in the early part of the speech. The presentation must reflect your purpose, that you want action. The presentation must have a balance between emotion and logic. Personal convictions should also reflect in your presentation.

3. Know your subject

It is obvious that you must know the subject of the presentation thoroughly. Though you may have made a thorough study of the subject, it may happen that when a member of the audience asks a question during the presentation, you may be unsure of the answer or your mind may go blank. To avoid such situations, it is better to make notes and keep them with you. However, if your notes and jottings are very detailed, finding your way through them may be difficult, especially when you are under pressure.

So it is best to have the major points on the subject. This will help you to come back to the subject in case your chain of thoughts is broken. Keeping notes does not convey that you are not confident about the subject. In fact, the audience will appreciate that you are well prepared for the presentation.

A4 sheets can be unwieldy and flap noticeably, especially if your hands are shaking with initial nerves. Index cards are a good option. Go through your text and highlight or underline key points and phrases. Make a note of where the visuals come in. Transfer these reminders onto the cards. Make them as clear as you can; it will help you during the presentation.

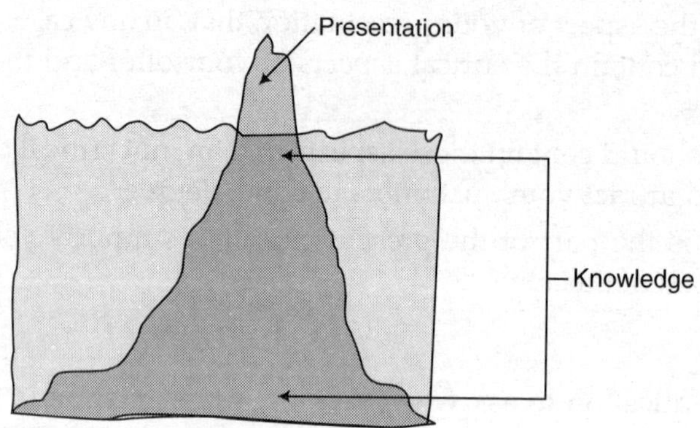

Fig. 6.2 *The Tip of the Iceberg*

4. Structuring the presentation

If your presentation has no structure, your audience will lose all interest in it. It does not really matter what sort of structure you choose, providing it is clear and logical to your audience and suits your needs.

A presentation should be structured in three parts:

- Opening
- Body
- Closing

Opening – This is the first part of any presentation and it introduces the subject to the audience. The opening is the most important part as it is during this time that the presenter "takes off". It is only during this time that you are able to connect to the audience, which helps to convey your thoughts to them during the entire presentation. In the opening, the audience's interest is aroused and they get a clear idea of where you are taking them.

The introduction needs to include the following:

- The starting line
- Central message – make it clear early on
- Overview – a hint of what is coming in each section
- How long you are going to take
- When they can ask questions

Body – This is the main part of the presentation in which the presenter explains the subject, often with the help of appropriate examples, and describes how it is beneficial to the audience.

Closing – This is the end of the presentation wherein the presenter summarizes and reinforces what he expects from the audience. The duration of the end part should not be more than 2 minutes irrespective of the length of the total presentation.

POINTS TO REMEMBER

In the opening - Tell the audience what you are going to tell them

In the body - Tell them

In the close - Tell them what you have told them

By now, you should have the audience's full attention. This is the last chance to drive home your central message.

Do not add any new information at this stage. Just briefly restate your main points in different words to avoid sounding repetitive.

5. Preparation of visuals

Visuals are the packaging in a presentation. A good visual is necessary to hold the attention of the audience during the presentation, though visuals should be used only as an aid and should not overwhelm the presentation. Visuals should be relevant, meaningful and must add value to the presentation.

Visuals include the template to be used in your presentation, colour combination, selection of font and its size; layout of the content and number of slides in your presentation.

There are four steps in preparation of visuals:

- Collection
- Visualization
- Format
- Practice

Collection of content – This is an important activity. It is the core of any presentation as it has to convey to the purpose of the presentation. The content thus has to be 'SMART' which means:

S = Simple
M = Meaningful
A = Action oriented
R = Relevant
T = Timely

Visualization – This is the second important aspect of presentation. It is not enough to write what you want to say on the slides; but it is equally necessary for you to ensure how beautifully the content is laid out in every slide. Some tips for preparing and presenting good slides are: Use visual aids to save time, to make abstract points concrete, to change pace or rhythm; above all, to make your point memorable and vivid. Do not assume that words are visuals. They do not always add to what you are saying. A well-produced chart or graph can help you get your message across more quickly and with greater impact than a verbal explanation on its own. Check that people sitting at the back will be able to see and understand the slides. It is especially important to check this if you are producing visuals from the printed page. Experiment with different colour combinations and look at the results with a fresh eye. Which point do you want to highlight? Does it stand out better in red or in black? What happens if you change the background colour? Stick to one idea per visual and keep it uncluttered. Use it to throw light on an otherwise complex point. You do not want all the visuals to look the same. Make them as varied as possible.

Stick to one idea per visual and keep it uncluttered. Use it to throw light on an otherwise complex point. You do not want all the visuals to look the same. Make them as varied as possible.

Format – The content should be formatted in a fashion to ensure that the presentation is 'seamless' and smooth. This is possible if the intent is clear, the flow of content is logical and the presentation appeals to the audience.

10 TIPS FOR PREPARING ATTRACTIVE SLIDES

1. The number of slides should be sufficient to justify the content.
2. Contents should be written in 'bullet form' and not in text form unless it is a quotation or a statement.
3. Slides should not be jammed with content; the number of words should be kept to a minimum in every slide.
4. Sentences should be written in "sentence case" and not in all capital letters.
5. 'Arial', 'Arial Narrow' or similar fonts should preferably be used for making slides. These fonts are soothing to the eyes and also look attractive.
6. The font size should preferably be 36 for the titles and 24 or 22 for the content.
7. Graphical description of data is always suggested in place of tables.
8. Template should be chosen very carefully; it should not be very flashy or gaudy, but should look attractive and should match the profile of the audience.
9. Relevant photographs add value to the presentation, though they have to be used judiciously.
10. Dark colours should be used while writing the content. This will add liveliness to the entire presentation.

Practice – This is the fourth important point in delivering the presentation. Rehearsing is necessary for this. It must be remembered that – 'Practice makes perfect'. The presentation should be crisp, focused, sharp, penetrating and clear in intent. All this is possible only through continuous practice.

> A good presenter should not fumble during the presentation. He should not overstretch his presentation and should not go blank for loss of words during the presentation.

How you sound is important, so practice your presentation out loud. Running it through in your head is not enough – and will not give you a clear idea of timing.

If you can, get a colleague to listen to you. If you cannot find a colleague, practice aloud before a mirror. Watch yourself and listen to your own voice. You may want to alter your presentation, taking into consideration what your colleague feels or how you feel you sound.

MAKING AN IMPACT

Variety is the key, it keeps your audience interested. Some techniques to do this are:

- **Keep your vocabulary simple** – Avoid jargon; use sentences in the first person; interject them with interesting facts that appeal to the audience.
- **Summarize and simplify details and figures** – Use pictorial forms like graphs, pie-charts or a photograph of a real life situation, as much as possible.
- **Give examples** – Relate success stories. Use a situation or story the audience can identify with.
- **Ask your audience questions** – This will keep the audience 'involved' in your presentation.
- **Put your points into lists of three** – This makes an impact. It is called "The Magic of Three."
- **Enhance the effect by using words with the same initial letter and sound** – For example, the three pillars of organizational success are people, product and profit.

SIGNPOSTING

Signposting is a method in which you make a conscious effort to keep the attention of your audience with you all through the presentation. This is done by breaking your presentation down into sections and conveying the specific messages of each part distinctly to them, when the audience's attention is best. At every stage, tell your audience where they are, where they have been, and where they are going. Remember, your aim is to help them grasp your ideas easily, not battle with your logic.

You may use signposts to establish an understanding between you and your audience. Show them that you:

- Understand their needs… "And this, of course, is why you want to …"

- Sympathize with their views... "You're absolutely right when you say..."
- Anticipate their questions... "You're probably wondering why we..."
- Appreciate their expertise... "I don't need to tell you that ..."

REFINING DELIVERY

Try to bring in as much finesse to your delivery part as possible. Here are some tips to help you inject interest and enthusiasm into your delivery.

- Punch it out
- Decide on key words and stress them for impact – "Our competitors are doing **well** but not as well as **we** are."
- Modulate your voice. A flat voice is a dull voice. Use the right intonation.
- Speak just as you do when you are having a conversation.
- Pause for breath.
- Aim to speak slowly, deliberately and clearly. Remember, as soon as you look down, your voice drops. As soon as you smile, your voice sounds brighter.

BODY LANGUAGE

Again, a colleague might be able to help you here. Any mannerisms that you have (scratching your head, pacing up and down, fiddling about in your pocket, waving your hands around) are fine unless the audience finds them more interesting than what you are saying. Throat clearing, *'ahs'* and *'hms'* between sentences, verbal tics (e.g. you know? ok? yeah? sort of, right?) can distract or irritate if they are too frequent.

Checklist on Body Language

- Eye contact – Make an effort not to look at the ceiling or floor. The audience will sense your lack of confidence.
- Remember to look at the audience and not your visual aids.
- Look around and establish eye contact, even with the people who are sitting at the sides of the room. If you focus on the person in front of you, you will make him feel uncomfortable and the others will switch off.
- Presenting with your arms folded can make you appear defensive, while if you stand with your hands in your pockets or lean back in your chair, you might seem too casual. Try the following techniques:
  - Stand still and lean forward slightly when making the main points, to express interest and enthusiasm.
  - Change position when you move on to another point.
  - Time your hand movements to coincide with a list of points you are making.
  - Do not turn your back on your audience to look at your visual aid or to point something out to them. Not only will they find it more difficult to hear you, but you will also lose contact with them.

HANDLING QUESTIONS

After you have researched, prepared and practised as much as you can, you are more or less ready to go, but what about questions from the audience? Some will be predictable, of course, but you cannot prepare for every eventuality. Whatever questions the audience has, the key is:

- Listen. Be honest. Keep control.
- Do not be afraid to think; your audience will be on your side by now, and they will appreciate that you need to switch from speaking mode to listening mode.
- People ask questions for various reasons – to attack, to test, to show off, to get information or to help you.
  - **Attacking** – The questioner may express a general objection. Try at first to reply, if he again asks questions, make him specify exactly what he disagrees with. For example the question may be – Is it the cost that's worrying you? Or repeat your argument briefly, concentrating on the benefits. You may also say – I take your point, but as against that there are the advantages of ... You could even rephrase the question in a non-attacking way.
  - **Testing** – Some people like to test your knowledge by asking for very detailed information. If it is relevant or interesting for everyone else, it is fine. If not, keep your answer short. In such cases, if you do not know the answer, be honest. Give a little more attention to those who like to show they know.
  - **Getting information, helping you** – It may not always be easy to answer. Some points can be remembered but not all. Whatever the reason for the question, direct your answer to the whole audience. Keep them involved too. Check that you have answered the question that was asked. Or else, rephrase the question if it is too long and unclear, or if the audience is large. Also, check your body language. Sitting down with them might create a warmer atmosphere.

THINGS TO REMEMBER WHILE MAKING A PRESENTATION

Some of the important tips that will help you in making your presentation highly effective are:

- Position yourself so that everyone can see you and your slides clearly. If you are right-handed, stand with the visual on your right.
- Signpost it briefly before you show it to them.
- Stay quiet while they absorb it before you start talking. A simple graph with two axes, one curve and a title takes at least seven seconds to absorb and understand; and that is assuming the audience are used to such visuals.
- Then make your point and explain the visual. Keep your eyes on the audience and talk to them, not the visual – even if their eyes are not on you.
- Switch the machine off or take the visual away when you have finished with it.
- Remember, you are there to persuade your audience through your presentation to achieve your objective. So do not rush through the slides; take your time to explain each and every point that you think "must be told".

- Give the audience time to absorb the visual, then explain it and draw conclusions from it. Ensure that you do not have too many slides. Strike a balance between visual aids and apt analogies or similes.
- Maintain eye contact with the audience. Make everyone feel that you are talking to 'each one of them.'
- Be audible. Ensure that everyone is able to hear what you are saying.
- Do not be stiff while making the presentation. Have positive body language. Be relaxed and smiling. Do not move your hands too much or move around too much on the dais. Be easy and natural. Do not keep your hands in your pockets or play with the pointer or the pen while you talk. It will distract your audience.
- Stick to the time that is scheduled to you for the presentation. Overshooting the time makes the audience restless.
- Do not bombard your audience with data. Convey the critical part of the content. A document containing the full details can be circulated to them beforehand for reference.
- Ask questions or tell them before starting the presentation that questions shall be invited at the end. Try to respond to the questions truthfully. No one knows the answers to all the questions. If you do not know the answer to any question, do not be afraid to acknowledge it to the audience. Tell them that you will try to find the answer and will come back to them.
- Never ridicule a person who asks a question. It may be an irrelevant question, but you should take it seriously and respond respectfully. Any disrespect to any member of the audience will be very damaging to your presentation.
- Thank the audience once your presentation is over. Request them once again to act on your request.
- Remember that the first 30 seconds are vital to the success of any presentation. You should ensure that your start should be so powerful that it 'captures' the audience and they listen to your presentation attentively. So start your presentation by arousing your audience's interest and giving them a clear idea of where you are taking them.

10 Checks you Must Carry Out Before a Presentation

1. Have you checked the profile of your audience?
2. Have you checked your timing? Are you sure you are not going to speak for too long?
3. Have you checked the venue? Where will you be standing or sitting? Will the audience be able to hear you and see you from the back? Is the lighting sufficient?
4. What about the equipment? Have you tried it out? Is it in the right position? Can you use it without fumbling?
5. Are you using visuals? If so, are they in order?
6. Do you have a back-up copy of your visuals for use in case the ones you are carrying fail?
7. Have you got your notes in order? Are they legible?

8. Is everything else you might need – paper, pens, pointers – to hand?
9. Have you got enough copies of any hand-outs you are planning to give out at the end of your presentation?
10. Have you planned to go to the venue beforehand to check the ambience of the place?

SUMMARY

A satisfying round of appreciation indicates that it was a successful presentation – persuasive and memorable. To summarize:

When you were producing the plan you created an appealing central message; chose relevant information that the audience could take away and remember; organized what you had to say in a clear, logical way.

At the presentation you made it easy for the audience to follow you by signposting; your language was clear and memorable; you had just the right number and variety of visual aids; you injected interest and enthusiasm into your voice and your body language was unobtrusive; your handling of questions was firm, friendly and informative.

In short, you put your audience first throughout – and that is the art of presentation.

KEY CONCEPTS

- A presentation is an art that explains about you and your knowledge in simple language and words, easily understood by the recipient.
- Making an effective presentation requires knowledge of the subject, conviction about what you are going to say and clarity to be able to translate your thoughts into words.
- Presentation is a formal way of communicating wherein the objective is to persuade the recipient to act on what is desired by the presenter.
- In a presentation the communication has to be very powerful, convincing and persuasive and is possible only when the presenter is convinced about what he says.
- Language is obviously a critical aspect of any communication process. A salesperson should therefore be conscious about the selection of language in any presentation that he makes before customers.
- Use language that your audience understands. Also, Keep It Short & Simple (KISS).
- It is very difficult to hold anyone's attention for long. In fact few people can concentrate beyond 20 minutes.
- Make your presentation in such a manner that you are able to hold the attention of your audience during the entire period of your presentation.
- No presentation can be better than the preparation which precedes it. The following checklist may be made for making a thorough preparation.

- While preparing the presentation you should know when the presentation is scheduled, its location, the profile of the audience and the duration of the presentation.
- You must also know the objective of your presentation – it could be to introduce a new product or an aggressive promotional campaign to persuade or to sell! The presentation requires a different treatment for each objective.
- Visuals in a presentation are the packaging of a product. A good visual is necessary to hold the attention of the audience during the presentation, though visuals should be used only as an aid and should not overwhelm the presentation.
- Practice is the most important part of a presentation. Rehearsal is necessary in this respect. It must be remembered that – 'Practice makes perfect'.
- The presentation should be crisp, focused, sharp, penetrating and clear in intent.

CASE I: AVON BUSINESS FORMS LTD

Vinod Kumar was a sales executive in Avon Business Forms Ltd. in Western Uttar Pradesh. The territory consisted of the districts of Agra, Meerut, Muzaffarnagar, Saharanpur and Aligarh. Avon was a newcomer in the business of business forms. Avon did not use much advertising to promote their products and depended a great deal upon its sales team to inform the potential customers about its product range. The company hoped that its sales people could sell complete systems rather than individual forms. The company had no proper training scheme for its sales force. Instead it expected its sales people to get acquainted themselves with the product attributes and company services themselves.

Vinod's first selling endeavour was to a big producer of automobile parts. This company Swift Automobiles was involved in revamping its accounting and book keeping system. Unfortunately, Vinod was not conscious of this fact. In fact, he had taken very little time to accustom himself with the operations of Swift Automobiles or the automotive part industry as a whole.

Vinod entered the office of Swift Automobiles and asked to see the chief accounts officer Mr. Akilesh Bhargava. Although he usually saw people only by appointment, Bhargava agreed to meet him. They met for a short time, and Mr. Bhargava called Dr. Tanmoy Sen, the systems analyst and asked him to join the meeting.

Mr. Vinod emphasized the low price of his products, their convenient size, their practicality in applications, the colour coding used to help the accountant, the ease of ordering, prompt delivery service and easy credit terms. The meeting was interrupted by several telephone calls for Mr. Bhargava and Dr. Sen. Vinod tried to point out the merits of each form but failed to present them as a totally integrated system. Both Mr. Bhargava and Dr. Sen raised several questions about the company's payment policy. Vinod found it difficult to convince them about their policy of 50% advance payment. When Vinod was about to leave, he offered them some sample forms to look at it and use. They declined his proposal and told him that they would contact him after they have ascertained their annual requirements.

Question

1. What is the essential principle of communication that Vinod did not follow which, had he observed, could have saved the situation for him?
2. Classify some of the barriers to effective communication in this case and propose ways in which they might have been eliminated or reduced.

CASE II: UNITED CYCLE COMPANY

Rahul Singh was a sales executive for the United Cycle Company. He covered the territory of central Maharashtra in India, which encompassed the erstwhile Vidarbha area that included Nagpur, with Gondia, and Bhandara in the east, Amravati and Akola districts in the west and Parbhani and Nanded in the south. All these district towns were the feeder markets for the adjoining smaller towns and villages of Maharashtra.

United Cycle Company was a reasonably big cycle manufacturer with three manufacturing units in Ludhiana. They were quite strong in north and south India. Though they had a presence in central Maharashtra, they were yet to consolidate in this area considering the fact that central Maharashtra had a huge potential and as per the estimates contributed to 18 percent of the total cycle sales in the country.

Newline Cycle Company was one of the biggest dealers of cycles in this area. Headquartered in Nagpur they had a chain of stores in each of the above district towns. Newline had been the single, largest, potential customer of United Cycle Company for a long time. They had been dealing with their competitor – National Cycles Pvt. Ltd. for many years and were quite happy with their products and services. Rahul was determined to break into this alliance and make them deal with his company.

Rahul started his game plan by obtaining as much information as possible about Newline Cycle Company. He called on all salespersons of other companies who were dealing with them in some way or the other. Rahul also obtained information about the strengths and weaknesses of United Cycle Company, its preferences, credibility in the market, financial position, warehousing capacity and plans for the future.

After analyzing the data, he found that, the relationship between Newline Cycle and National Cycles Pvt. Ltd., had seen some hiccups in the last couple of months.

While Newline Cycle was not happy with the rising complaints about their products, of late, the company was concerned about the deteriorating service of National Cycles. The latter was causing heavy inventory carrying costs and consequent losses. Moreover, Newline Cycle felt that National Cycles was not concerned about problems related to the poor quality of cycles and service. This led the Newline Cycle company to believe that National Cycles was no longer looking after its interests despite the fact that they had previously had very good relations.

Rahul decided that he would meet the owner of Newline Cycle, Mr. Raj Dua. Mr. Dua was an elderly man of 67 years. He was a highly principled person, kept his word and expected his suppliers to do so, considered his customers as the most valued assets of his firm and tried his level best to take care of them. This had earned him a very high reputation in the market which eventually helped when he expanded his business in other big towns of central Maharashtra.

Rahul took an appointment with Mr. Dua and met him as per schedule. After an exchange of pleasantries, he put his proposal on the table. Before the meeting, Rahul had planned to focus on only the things that Dua considered most important – quality and service. Rahul explained in detail about the products and service that his company could offer. Rahul drew Dua's attention to the new facility of his company about online registration of complaints, which he said were resolved within 72 hours! He also substantiated his statements with past data and some statements of appreciations given by some of his valued customers. When Rahul's presentation ended, he could understand from Dua's body language that Dua had a positive impression.

Two weeks later, Rahul got a call from Newline Cycles and he was given the message that Mr. Dua wanted to meet him to discuss the matter further.

Rahul again went at the appointed date and time and met Dua. Mr. Dua opened the conversation by saying, "Mr. Singh, I was impressed with the presentation that you made the other day. I am aware that your company is quite reputed and is known for offering good products and services. However, I am still not sure about your fulfilling the claims that you made that day. What happens if, whatever you claim is not met? Also, what about the payment terms? You know, we are a very big party. We have a chain of stores and though we shall place the order centrally, you have to give delivery wherever the cycles are needed. Mr. Singh, I would like to put a condition to you – "Quantity shall be yours while the rates shall be mine. You do not have to worry about the sales. But I can sell only if the rates are reasonable. Moreover, unlike your payment terms which specify that payments have to be made within a fortnight, I cannot make payment before 60 days."

Rahul was stunned by Mr. Dua's response. When he had received the message requesting a second meeting, he was sure that he had finally been able to get Newline as a customer and was sure that he was getting the order. Rahul gathered himself together and responded, "Sir, what you are saying is alright but as you know, our products and services are much better than what the market is offering. Moreover, I know that National Cycles is not giving you the necessary attention because of which you have been suffering a lot these days. Sir, I would request you to see my offer as a package and not stress upon the price front only." Dua retorted, "I agree that I am not happy with National Cycles these days. But you see son, this is part of business. We have been together for many years and I think we can overcome the problems. I am giving you time because I like your straight forward manner, your company's products and the fact that you are a young lad who should be encouraged and will go far. I do not need an answer just now. You can take your time, discuss my proposal with your seniors and come back to me whenever you arrive at a conclusion."

Question

1. What do you think will be Rahul's decision in this case?

REFERENCES

1. Collins, Robert H. (1989), Unleash the Power of Desktop Presentations, *Journal of Personal Selling & Sales Management*, Vol. 9 Issue 1, p. 70.
2. Delivering Great Presentations (2006), Bloomsbury Business Library - *Give Great Presentations*, pp. 15-25.
3. Farber, Barry (2007). Sales Success: Now Presenting, *Entrepreneur*, Vol. 35 Issue 6, pp. 76-77.
4. Fripp, Patricia (2011), 9 Timely Tips for Pre-Presentation Preparation. *American Salesman*, Vol. 56 Issue 6, pp. 13-16.
5. Hershey, Lewis (2005), The Role of Sales Presentations in Developing Customer Relationships, *Services Marketing Quarterly*, Vol. 26 Issue 3, pp. 41-54.
6. Johlke, Mark C. (2006), Sales Presentation Skills and Salesperson Job Performance, *Journal of Business & Industrial Marketing*, 2006, Vol. 21 Issue 4/5, pp. 311-319.
7. Kahle, Dave (2010), On Preparation and Presentations, *American Salesman*, Vol. 55 Issue 10, pp. 7-9.
8. Marshall, Trevor (2009), Presentation Hell, *Backbone*, pp. 10-15.
9. Miodonski, Bob (2003), Right Presentations Can Bring More Sales, *Contractor Magazine*, Vol. 50 Issue 4, p. 12.
10. Mueller, Van (2011), Believe in Your Message, *Senior Market Advisor*, Vol. 12 Issue 6, p. 96.
11. Namhata, Rima (2011), Smooth Talk, Smart Attire, Efficient Practice and a Tinge of Humor: Way to Presentation Skill for Beginners, *IUP Journal of Soft Skills*, Vol. 5 Issue 1, pp. 31-36.
12. Ryals, Lynette; Davies, Iain (2010), Do You Really Know Who Your Best Salespeople Are? *Harvard Business Review*, Vol. 88 Issue 12, pp. 34-35.
13. Super, Carol; Gold, Ronald D. (2003), Creating a Successful Presentation, *Selling Without Selling*, pp. 109-121.
14. The Sales Presentation - How it's Done, *Management Services*, (Winter 2007), Vol. 51 Issue 4, pp. 28-32.
15. Vishnevsky, Jennifer (2011), Presentation Transformation, *Wearables*, Vol. 15 Issue 5, p. 45.
16. Wagner, Judy A.; Klein, Noreen M. (2007), Who Wants To Go First? Order Effects Within A Series Of Competitive Sales Presentations, *Journal of Personal Selling & Sales Management*, Vol. 27 Issue 3, pp. 259-276.

7 Managing Customer Relationships

"A business absolutely devoted to Customer Service Excellence will have only one worry about profits. They will be embarrassingly large."

–*Sir Henry Ford*

CHAPTER OUTLINE

- ✦ Introduction
- ✦ Customer value management
- ✦ Customer relationship management
- ✦ Initiating customer relationship
- ✦ Assumption in sales
- ✦ CRM maturity
- ✦ Customer relationship and customer experience
- ✦ Reinforcing customer relationship
- ✦ Customer relationship through customer service
- ✦ Developing satisfied customers

OBJECTIVES

After studying this chapter, you will be able to:

- ✦ Understand the basics of customer relationship management
- ✦ Take steps to enhance customer relationships
- ✦ Develop initiatives to give outstanding customer service
- ✦ Build credibility to enhance sales through good relationships with customers

Opening Case: Modern Batteries Ltd.

Rohan was the new sales executive in Modern Batteries Ltd. in Delhi. An average student, Rohan graduated in arts and joined Modern Batteries as a sales representative. He was part of the six member sales team and was assigned the south Delhi territory. He was not very smart; rather he was a shy young man in his late twenties. Rohan was not a glib talker, but had incredible sensitivity and empathy. By virtue of his inherent qualities, Rohan outshined others and soon became the top salesman of his branch.

Like everyone else, every month of Rohan moved in a typical fashion: The first four days went in analyzing last month's performance, analyzing outstanding payments and planning for the current month; the next fortnight getting pushed consignments absorbed by the market and the last week in pushing the market for orders to achieve targets. But Rohan was never tense. His style of working was always carefree; he looked quite casual and his colleagues wondered how he was able to manage such a brilliant performance.

Rohan loved to work in the field till late hours; he always spent time listening to his dealers and their problems and tried to help them resolve them. He was always very conservative as far as his company rules were concerned; Rules were the Bible for him. He loved his products and also his dealers. Rohan always believed that selling did not mean taking dealers for a ride; he should build his credibility and be a trustworthy friend to his dealers. The rest will follow. He believed in his dealers and worked for them. For him dealers were not machines, but human beings with emotions. If he was able to touch their hearts, he would win them over.

Rohan's colleagues wondered how he could attain this feat again and again. They also visited the market regularly, met dealers, monitored competition and did everything that they could do as professional sales executives. Rohan was not as smart as them, not a very good talker, and an introvert, so how come he was able to beat them all in sales? What was the secret of his success?

Question

1. Was Rohan right in his approach?

MANAGING CUSTOMER RELATIONSHIPS

Integral Design for Programmed Learning

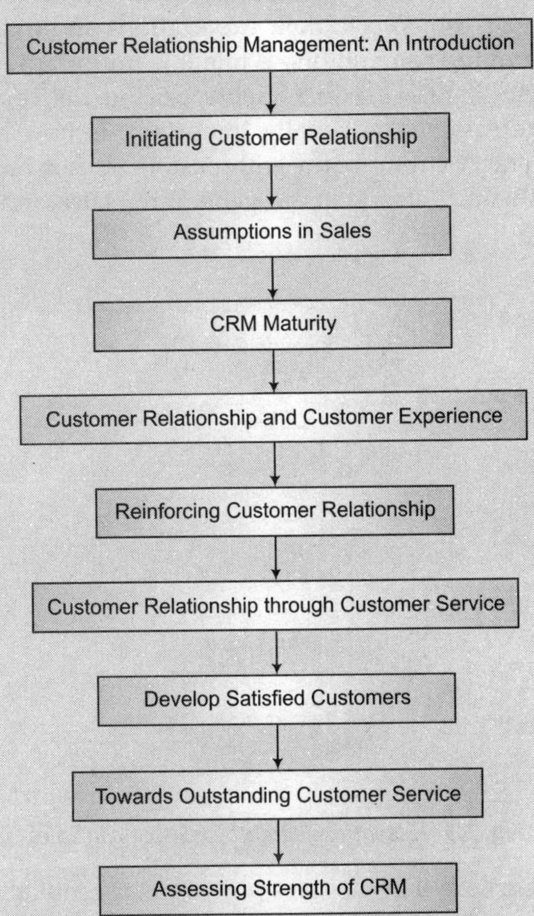

INTRODUCTION

Managing customer relationships is the essence of sales. The success of sales is directly proportional to customer satisfaction. Sales take place only if customers buy and they will buy only when the products come up to their expectations and they find the products and services better than those of the competitors. While it is important for a company to ensure that the total offering, including the product quality, pricing, delivery and post sales service, is excellent, a softer aspect, which is equally important, is how strong relationships are established with customers. A strong bond with customers not only helps in establishing a long-term bond with them, it also helps in generating sales and increases the "lifetime value" of customers.

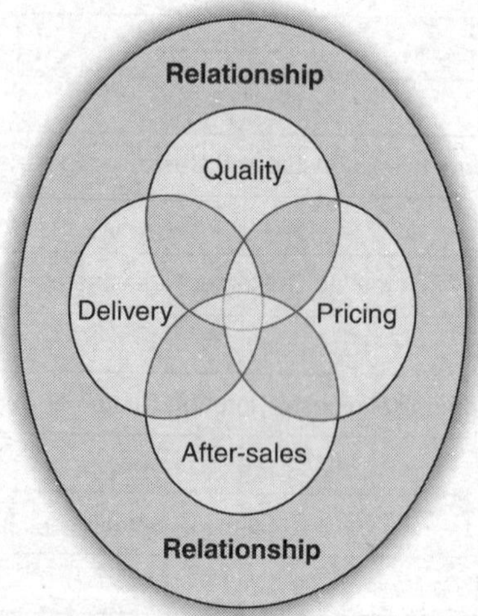

Fig. 7.1 *Essential Elements for Success in Sales*

Every company must ensure that the sales process transcends the usual steps of selling, and enter into a realm where customer and salespersons come to know each other well, have faith in each other and do what each other expects. Customer relationship management plays a significant role in this entire process of building and reinforcing bonds between the salespersons and the customers. It is therefore imperative that there is emphasis on managing positive relationships with customers – especially at the field level.

For customers or channel members, it is the salesperson who is the company; he is expected to solve their problems, guide them in doing better business and be their friend who will always be there whenever they need him. These hopes and expectations, rest on the faith and belief that the channel reposes in the salesperson. Salespersons must consider it their greatest duty to come up to these expectations of the channel if they are to succeed in the market. The rest follows automatically when this is taken care of. How this relationship can be nurtured is discussed in this chapter.

CUSTOMER VALUE MANAGEMENT

In today's competitive market, customer relationships are based on a company's ability to create, communicate and deliver competitive value to its customers. To meet the continually changing market needs, organizations have to constantly streamline processes, create systems, reinforce synergy, cut costs, and restructure for a quicker response to the customers' demands. In short, there is a need to 'customerize' the company; by configuring every function, not just marketing to work directly to fulfil customers' needs, by directing every process, just not selling, but also budgeting, planning and strategizing – towards this. It is these efforts that contribute towards enhancing customer relationships, and the strategy to do the same is termed as customer value management.

Customer value management is a strategy to attract and retain customers by building on the value they assign to goods and services. There are three critical steps that will enable this transition:

- Building a chain of internal customers
- Institutionalizing the process of innovative ideation
- Exposing every part of the organization directly to the external customers

The values of customer-service will thus cascade through the company. A constant stream of ideas will keep it ahead on the innovation curve. And an enterprise-wide culture of 'customerization' will blossom; empowering the company to leverage its resources to achieve customer focus; to be competitive.

The goal of Customer Value Management (CVM) is to deliver optimal value to customers, i.e. to align business metrics, improvement programs, capabilities, processes, organization and infrastructure with customer-defined values. In other words, to create the kind of business that can deliver to customers exactly what they want.

There are three critical "Rs" of the CVM Cycle

- Right customers
- Right relationship
- Right retention

Customer Value

While purchasing products/services, every customer looks for only two things – maximum value at the minimum delivery price. Value is a bundle of benefits that a customer expects to maximize and consists of all elements that a product consists of; i.e. its core, formal and augmented elements – all at the minimum possible delivery price. Every company attempts to focus on maximizing various aspects of this value and minimize its costs so as to offer the product/service at the lowest possible price. Any company that is able to do so has a chance of gaining and sustaining a competitive edge.

Customer Value Chain

Customer value chain is a chain of activities in the total marketing process to add value to the final product service that reaches the customer, and to do it in a way that sets it higher than competitors in the customer's perception. A company should focus on every stage in the value chain to fathom the customer's needs, wants and desires.

There are five steps by which a salesperson can build up a value for customers. These are termed as the 5 "P"s.:

- Probing
  - Understanding customers – What strategies and techniques marketers must employ to understand customer behaviour.
  - Mapping the markets – Gauging the real size of the target market and identifying what really drives the customers.
  - Segmenting markets – Are companies using deep-seated similarities in traits to carve out customer segments?
  - Understanding rural markets – How do companies comprehend the potential of the rural markets.
  - B-2-B marketing – Reinforcing relationships with customers in industrial marketing.
  - Targeting niches – As small customers prove to be highly loyal customers through rightly reading their needs.
- Prioritising
  - Translating needs into products – By employing the right strategies to meet the unique product needs of customers.
  - New product concepts – By innovating new products.
  - Developing customized products – By involving the customer in product design.
  - Launching new products – By ensuring that the value of the new product is conveyed effectively to the customers.
- Positioning
  - Creating the benefits package – Namely, what strategies marketers must apply to provide customers with differentiated value.
  - Positioning the brand – By ensuring that the brand is associated with a unique value proposition.
  - Extending the brand – By ensuring a means to add value while stretching the benefits of the corporate brand image to the new product.
  - Using differential pricing – By pricing the product in consonance with its value as perceived in different markets.
  - Using natural pricing – By identifying the key that pricing holds while occupying the same price slot as a rival.

- Provoking
  - Conveying the message – By understanding how customers process messages and what tools marketers must use to communicate the target markets effectively.
  - Advertising the brand – A company can use advertising to help customers to understand it is the value proposition of the product.
  - Selecting the media – The company should select the media in such a way that it cuts through the clutter of communication channels.
  - Integrating communication – When communicating with customers, the company has to make sure that its message has the desired impact.
- Penetrating
  - Delivering the product – By ascertaining the strategies that marketers must employ to add to the customers' buying experience.
  - Managing distribution – By creating distribution equity to maximize the benefits for customers.
  - Managing the retailing – By ensuring effective persuasion (in B-2-B) and merchandizing and outlet management (in case of B-2-C) distribution.
  - Using customer promotions – Using them as sales boosters and as instruments for renewing relationships with customers.
  - Servicing the customers – By providing effective servicing and by regularly monitoring its impact over that of rivals.
  - Building relationships – By recognizing and rewarding loyal customers.

CUSTOMER RELATIONSHIP MANAGEMENT

Customer Relationship Management (CRM) is a multifaceted process that aims at creating systems that ensure satisfied customers through a series of efforts that take care of the numerous problems that the channel members face on a day-to-day basis while doing business with the company. To create such systems, salespersons must have intimate knowledge of their customers, their needs, and buying patterns. Managing customer relationship requires a high degree of sensitivity on the part of salespersons, as they should empathize with their customers to resolve their problems and show them the right way so that they can do business more profitably.

> Managing customer relationship requires a high degree of sensitivity on the part of salespersons, as they should empathize with their customers to resolve their difficulties and show them the right way so that they can do business more profitably.

The fundamental grounding for CRM is an enthusiasm to nurture customers, be with them, resolve their problems and deliver more than what they expect. This process can be categorized into three parts:

- Pre-sales processes
- During the sales processes
- Post sales processes

Pre-sales processes include cordial interaction, conveying everything about the product/ service offered and recommend products that are suited to the customer. Services required during the process of sales are equally important for managing customer relationships successfully. This applies to processes during the time between ordering and delivery, and is also applicable to industrial as well as consumer products. Post sales processes include the responses that are expected by the customer in case he faces any problem after he has bought the product.

A positive response by salespersons during the entire process of sales sends a message to the customers that the salesperson understands them and genuinely cares for them. It means that throughout all his interactions with the customers, he knows who they are and what they want. It also means that the products and services developed are based on their requirements only. Thus the ability to control the customer's experience is what defines the capability of every salesperson. CRM supports customers by servicing the products and other services that help them through the various processes.

The ability to control customer experience is what defines the capability of every salesperson.

INITIATING CUSTOMER RELATIONSHIPS

The first step in creating customer relationship is to know that a salesperson must first dissolve that negativity in the minds of the customers before they can move on. How does one modify this 'no' to 'yes'? Every salesperson would like to know the answer to this question. It is seen that most salespersons are unable to do this, mainly because of one or more of the following factors:

- An inability to understand customers and their needs
- Taking customers for granted
- A casual approach towards customers and sales
- Over-confidence about market and customers
- Undermining customers' ability to buy
- Pre-conceived notions about the customer
- The 'know-all' attitude
- Taking a shortcut in their approach for sales
- Lack of optimism and enthusiasm
- Inability to handle pressure of sales

Assumptions in Sales

Assumptions are the result of apathy, ignorance, lack of confidence or otherwise–because of fixed ideas about the market and customers, incorrect interpretation of reactions about the way some people might have reacted (may be a couple of times) or rigid predisposition due to a closed mind.

Assumptions result from the experience. Though past experience can furnish us with data for decision making in the present context but under no case should a salesperson presuppose things which might not be there in the actual sense of the term.

Listed below are examples of common assumptions:

- Your customer cannot afford to buy what you're selling
- That the person you're talking to is the only one making the buying decisions
- Your customer always complains about your company and your products and does not want to do business with your company
- You know your significant other so well you don't need to ask him/her what's wrong when they seem bothered.

Before assuming anything, a salesperson must ask himself the following questions:

- How correct are my assumptions?
- What damages do occur when my assumptions go wrong?
- Should my decisions be based on objectivity or assumptions?

A good salesperson should always get rid of the habit of assuming things and go to the brass-tacks to take decisions.

- When you assume that you know what your customer wants – do you really know and how do you know it? Or, are you just assuming?
- You assume the customer can't afford what you're selling. How do you know? Did you ask or assume?
- How do you know that the customer will definitely complain about the product he has bought from you?
- You assume you know what motivates your current customers to buy but you haven't made the sale. Why? Maybe your assumptions are wrong.
- Hence assume nothing, as reactions based on assumptions destroy relationships.

CRM MATURITY

The success of customer relationship is judged by the level of its maturity. The different levels of maturity are illustrated below.

Level of CRM Maturity

Poor	*Average*	*Excellent*
No clear definition of customers	Definition exists, but no common understanding across the company	Uniform understanding of customer definition across the company
Incomplete & unreliable information on customers	Lack of analysis of available customer information	Meticulous analysis of available customer information
No appreciation of customers' expectations	Knowledge of customer expectations not shared	Knowledge of customer expectations fully shared
Inadequate customer value management	Customer value not considered while configuring offering	Offering planned after due consideration of customer value

A poor maturity of an organization with respect to its CRM maturity is exemplified by an unclear definition of customers, incomplete and unreliable information about them and lack of appreciation of customers' expectations. There is also a lack of customer value management in absence of which the value delivered to them could be inadequate which might lead to dissatisfaction.

In an organization with an excellent level of CRM maturity, there is a uniform understanding of customer across the company, available customer information is meticulously analyzed and customer expectations are fully shared within the whole organization. Also, the offering is planned only after due consideration of the customer value. This helps in reinforcing customer relationship immensely.

CUSTOMER RELATIONSHIP AND CUSTOMER EXPERIENCE

Most salespersons just sell. They get targets in the beginning of the month and keep chasing sales targets and outstanding collections. In the process, the important aspect of providing a 'memorable experience to the customer' often takes a back seat.

We buy different things from different shops every day but there are only a few of them which we want to visit again. Why is this so? May be the prices are better, but that is usually not the only reason. You would probably agree if I say that we like to go there because we like the warmth of the place, the gentle behaviour of the shopkeeper, and the way he talks to us. We feel happy and contended when we go there, and feel that we are wanted; a little bit of extra care makes the difference! This could all be summarized in the words – "It was a wonderful experience."

We create loyalty by consistently providing our clients with a positive experience. Some ways in which we can create loyalty through positive experiences are given below.

Take Care of Your Customer

Care about your customers and they will care about you.

Be Generous

If you have a customer who is currently passing through bad times, do something to let them know that you care and will stick by them during this time. Within the framework of official rules, whether you extend your invoice terms, offer them a discounted rate or otherwise "help" them during their time of need, they will remember it.

REINFORCING CUSTOMER RELATIONSHIPS

There are three primary actions that an alert salesperson will take to reinforce customer relationship.

1. Make customers happy by offering different products and services
2. Adapt to the relationship by trying to understand the customer. This is possible only through active listening and accordingly developing new products that the customer desires
3. Enhance the level of relationship by offering a unique product/service including reduced costs and superior customer service

The following are very useful to achieve this.

Appreciating Customers

Salespeople must be tuned in to the needs of customers. These needs are often hard to understand, as the customers do not usually verbalize them clearly. One has to be watchful in "reading" people, through their gestures and other non-verbal cues. As different customers have different ways of expressing themselves non-verbally, a good salesperson should not jump to conclusions, but try to determine the real concerns of customers before reacting to them. This is possible only if he is able to understand the customer and his difficulties. This demands a high degree of empathy on the part of salespersons. There should be sensitivity and the ability to distinguish between what is right and what is wrong. Customers will expect speedy response to their problems. This will enhance the credibility of the salespersons in the eyes of the customer and will build a long-term relationship with the organization.

Dealer Communication

The traditional asymmetrical relationship between the salesperson and the dealer/customer has been reversed today. Dealers/customers are now capable of acquiring knowledge that can give them an advantage in sales negotiations that normally take place at their end. Salespersons can respond to this change of circumstances in two ways. They can increase and refine their own knowledge base, thus upping the stakes; or they can adopt different methods and provide added value to the customer/dealer besides providing added information. The key to this is establishing a relationship based on trust, thereby improving sales and building customer loyalty.

It is essential that salespersons learn to understand the consumer's universe, their hopes and expectations, and the state of mind they are in when deciding to buy anything.

Understanding the New Dynamics

There are a number of aspects that can be instrumental in helping salespersons better understand and respond to the shifting dynamics of their relationship with customers.

Greater transparency is essential to improving the salesperson/channel relationship. The Internet, with its seemingly unending sea of information, has encouraged consumers to demand higher levels of transparency. And this trend shows no sign of abating. In this new era, where customers can get nearly all the information they need without even having to visit a dealership, dealer salespeople must view customers as partners on an equal footing. Their collaboration should be based on a transparent attitude and information sharing – in other words, a relationship based on trust. Their interaction should turn into a co-production, where both can obtain satisfaction.

While everybody acknowledges this shift in building relationships and recognizes the need to change, there remains significant work to be done. It is observed that there are numerous examples of negative interactions between customers and salespersons that reinforce traditional stereotypes.

The selling process is a set of activities undertaken to successfully obtain an order and begin building long-term customer relations. The more knowledgeable consumers are, the more the balance of power shifts in their favour. Although the interface does not exclude traditional dealership visits, the salesperson is justified in evaluating the growing use of this tool in the information-gathering process. Research has shown that the communication has an impact on the overall approach of the consumer. It is seen that customers can build up sound background knowledge, which can make them quicker and more strategic in their interaction with salespeople. This ultimately reduces the latter's influence.

Consumers increasingly demand a personalized and customized approach during the buying process. In today's world, customers want to be seen as individuals, as people in their own right. Success rests in the salesperson's ability to deploy formal sales methods in a personalized fashion. However, it is essential that the salesperson makes an effort to learn about the individual customer's wants and needs and factor that information into their approach. The move toward greater personalization and customization is an increasingly important element in the entire buying process.

Building an Equitable Relationship

The new relationship model between the salespersons and the customers can be conceptualized as the result of an interaction between two equal parties. In this case, there is transparency of information, with the same or similar information with both parties. This leads to trust and it enables both parties to feel comfortable while dealing with each other. Such trust reinforces a relationship and leads to a free and equal relationship.

The final purchase decision will only be made when both customer and salesperson consider that they have established a relationship based on trust and when both feel they are in a sufficiently balanced or symmetrical relationship. Approaching the relationship between customer and dealer in this way widens the possibility of a free and seamless relationship.

This does not imply that a situation of absolute transparency is always possible; rather, this is the ideal situation for which to aim. To achieve this balanced relationship, the salesperson must not sell; he must instead enable the consumer to buy; it is a subtle but critical difference. In response to changes in the market, including heightened competition, declining loyalty, more sophisticated consumers and the growing importance of the Internet in the buying process, salespersons must make corresponding changes in their relationship with customers in order to build this more symmetrical relationship.

Moving the Relationship to a Higher Plane

In some cases, the customer's higher degree of self-reliance is seen as being beneficial to both parties, moving their interaction to a higher plane. This requires that salespeople sharpen new interpersonal skills to improve their relationship with customers.

The customer/salesperson relationship varies considerably depending on a consumer's degree of advance knowledge as well as existing preconceptions on the part of both the customer and dealer.

The more dealers can demonstrate that they are trying to build a relationship based on trust, the better their chances of staying in the consideration set as customers narrow down their choices.

A Personalized Approach is Critical to Success

A variety of behaviour has been observed in establishing an effective customer relationship management process. Sales people tend to use certain tried-and-true sales techniques in their approach in dealing with customers. Although these methods are empirically developed and create a degree of achievement, they are more often than not insufficient to satisfy today's demanding customers and do not always lead to the desired result. Customers who feel that they are being given just the standardized treatment, and that they are perceived by the salesperson as "average," are often put off. Success thus rests on the salesperson's ability to organize a formal sales method in a personalized fashion. However, it is essential that the salesperson make an effort to learn about the individual customer's wants and needs and factor that information into their approach. The move toward greater personalization and customization is an increasingly important element in the entire buying process, from the features offered on manufacturer and channel, to advertising and promotional programs, to the approach taken by a salesperson to woo the customers.

It is observed that the customer/dealer relationship varies considerably depending on a consumer's degree of advance knowledge as well as existing preconceptions on the part of both the customer and dealer. These scenarios can exist on their own or as phases in a continuum, moving ultimately toward the third scenario. However, in each scenario, there are critical points where the potential for a breakdown in the relationship is particularly high.

It is essential that the salesperson make an effort to learn about the individual customer's wants and needs and factor that information into their approach.

15 Tips to Enhance Customer Relationship

1. Learn about your customers and explore how you can help them achieve their business goals. Suggest solutions that will alleviate their difficulties and help them to realize reduced costs, higher productivity or increased revenues.
2. Share what you know – not just sell. Customers expect more today than ever before. Share your expertise with them. Guide them and help them to take a correct decision. The value you add to your relationship with your customers will come back to you in the form of increased sales and customer loyalty.

3. Tell "what's in it" for your prospect and how a successful outcome will affect them personally. What do they hope to achieve by doing business with you? Find out how they will personally benefit from doing business with you.
4. Work with your prospects to prioritize their affirmed objectives. Whatever improvement your solution offers, it must support your prospect's priorities. Help them identify, rank and place a value on relieving their "pain points."
5. Remember that you are selling benefits, solutions and results – not features. Your customer just wants to know what your product will do for them. Describe how your product or service will rationalize operations, promote higher employee retention, augment sales, reduce costs or help them achieve their highest-level strategic goals.
6. Be a trusted advisor. Show that you will serve their best interests by staying informed about their business and their industry, by offering only those products or services that will truly benefit them and by providing pertinent, meaningful information to them before and after the sale.
7. Be disciplined. Plan your day carefully, keep appointments and deliver to customers what you promise. Make yourself do the things you know you should do and do them well and on time.
8. Systematize your process. Be clear in your mind as to how you would approach the sales, go with full preparation and convince the customer that your product and you are the best.
9. Follow up regularly. Execute and support your solution. Stay in touch with your customer. Continue to add value to your relationship. Be in it for long-term relationship.
10. Be customer-focused rather than outcome-focused only. This mindset will yield benefits to you during the entire sales process – from the early stages of prospecting to closing the sale – and beyond. It will help ease performance pressure and allow you to become a valued partner with your customers.
11. Narrate success stories to describe the benefits your prospect can expect by doing business with you. Customers do not want to be cheated. Many of them do not usually want to try something that is not tested. They just want to know that your product or service will give them the results they want and need.
12. Ensure that the quality of your products is good. Identify the prospects you wish to deal with to achieve your sales target. Determine what features are common among your best customers. Then contact these prospects and take them to logical sales. By doing so you will be selling to a highly focussed market.
13. Listen to complaints as they come to you. Resolve customer complaints with a cool head. Actively listen. Find a solution without delay. Delay in solving problems might disturb your customer.
14. Do not be impatient to jump from customer to customer based on which one appears to hold the most promise at any given moment. You must remember that only a sound relationship gets you sales. Be certain to take your customers along on your journey to sales success.
15. Welcome your customers to your business as if you were welcoming guests to your home. Customers are all you have. Treat each of them as if they were your only customer.

BUILDING CUSTOMER RELATIONSHIPS THROUGH CUSTOMER SERVICE

Business success is dependent on a variety of factors. These include a realistic business idea, a well thought-out business plan, an appropriate marketing strategy and an efficient customer service. While customer service is a part of marketing, it is considered as a prime mover for establishing an effective relationship. Customer service includes all aspects of interaction with a customer and speaks of the organization's image in the mind of a customer.

A customer provides an organization with that most organic of all advertising tools – word of mouth publicity. A happy and satisfied customer is much more likely to send more customers your way. Further, there is the potential for repeat business, which is the backbone of all businesses. Customer relationship management also enables the business to understand the deficiencies in the system and provide valuable customer feedback. When a business receives feedback, it is able to see the customer's image of the organization and the impression of its services. This tool is very useful in correcting systems as well as image management for the business. It is also a perspective, which provides the business owner or management a unique insight about how to take care of the ultimate objective of business – creating and keeping customers.

A pleased customer will be more likely to contribute in activities that help to generate customer preference data.

In fact, it would not be wrong to say that the old adage 'The customer is always right' has been the foundation of many organizations and what it really means is that keeping customers happy is the foremost principle of any business.

Regular and sustained interaction with a customer ensures that the customer feels connected with the business. For instance, a small restaurant owner who chats with his customers and knows them by name builds a relationship with them. Further, when he makes sure that the food is fresh and hot, he is providing customer service. The customers have a good experience and feel that the establishment treated them well. Once an organization grows or goes online, there is less potential for this face-to-face interaction and then the business must find creative ways to ensure customer satisfaction. The role of customer service to a business, online or offline is essential to its growth and survival.

Develop Satisfied Customers

In today's world we are flooded with new ideas, education and opportunities everywhere. Technology is changing at such an incredible pace that frequently it is demanding, and occasionally overpowering, to keep up with all the new growth possibilities that are being discovered and developed each day.

By having a goal of finding good customers, giving them great products and following up with excellent customer service, you will discover that many of them will be active advocates for your business. What that means for you is the best kind of publicity available – and it is absolutely without any cost!

The following seven stages will help you identify and carefully cultivate your customers as they grow into your most valuable assets.

1. **Suspects** – Initially, prospects might not believe what you say. They might have apprehensions about the quality of products and service that you are offering. So they look at you and your offering with suspicion. What is important here is to establish your credibility by helping them take a judicious purchase decision and introduce your product or service to them accordingly.
2. **Prospects** – Not everyone is going to want what you have. The next step is to qualify your suspects. Ask good questions to find out if they can benefit from what you are offering. Those that want or need what you have will become prospects for your business.

3. **Customers/Clients** – Your next step is to qualify your prospect. Not everyone that does want what you have will be in a position to do business with you. Again, the secret to success in this step is to ask good questions and listen to their answers.
4. **Repeat buyers** – The prospects that want what you have and qualify to purchase become your clients. Your next goal becomes retaining them and turning them into repeat buyers.
5. **Satisfied customers mean repeat business** – All long term businesses enjoy the benefits of repeat customer sales. In this increasingly impersonal world, superior customer service will make you stand out in any industry. Satisfied customers will generate referral business for you. They will gladly send their friends and family to you.
6. **Referral customers** – Take exceptional care of your repeat customers and your list of referral clients will grow and that will give you the best kind of customers there are! If you set your next goal to give them outstanding service, they quite possibly will develop into such great admirers that they will become active advocates for you.
7. **Active advocates** – When your customers reach this level, they will make it a point to tell all their friends, family and associates how good you are! As your best customers spread the word about your quality service, it will generate increased sales leading to high profits for your company. Four customer service ideas that can help you take your business to a superior level are:
   - Send a thank you note or card – A simple hand written note will cost you almost nothing, take only a few minutes of your time, but could generate enormous financial and personal satisfaction returns for you.
   - Find out what each of your clients like and keep a look out for articles of interest – either personal or professional – and either e-mail or snail-mail them to your customers.
   - Keep track of birthdays, anniversaries, and any special events in their lives, and acknowledge them.
   - Under promise and over deliver. Always give your customers more than they are expecting. Think about how you feel when someone goes this extra step for you.

All long term businesses enjoy the benefits of repeat customer sales. As we have seen there is a well-known principle in the business world called the 80/20 rule. In the majority of successful companies, 80% of your revenue will be generated from only 20% of your customers.

Things to Remember

Salespersons must always remember that selling does not mean manipulating the potential buyer to do what the seller wants, rather than providing the buyer what he wants. The greatest compliment for a seller is the customer's referral.

If you want to satisfy customers, and want them to be with you for a long time, you should:

1. **Treat them right** – They want to feel like valued customers and see that their time and opinions matter. If people cannot trust you to treat them right, then they certainly will not trust you with their money. Be ethical in your approach in dealing with customers.
2. **Make it easy and convenient for them to buy your product** – Take care that each step provides the answers or helps your customers in the order process. Be sure they get what they came for.
3. **See that your presentation is fair and reflects truthfulness** – No one wants to feel duped or to receive incorrect information about prices, delivery dates, or terms of the sale. Even a hint of such intentions kills customers' willingness to hear you. If a person feels that he has been cheated he will not buy anything from you again and also spread negative word of mouth publicity that could be very damaging to you and your business.
4. **Ensure that every step of selling process is taken care perfectly** – If every part of the process works as an integrated whole, you may consider the customer well served. When the parts are mismatched they scare customers away

Three ways to "check yourself" to enhance customer relationship by giving outstanding customer service are given below.

1. **Check your customer service attitude** – Make your attitude to say, "I will help you today." This means that you want to help, you want to take responsibility for the solution, and you are proactive in creating solutions for the customer. Make sure your attitude is positive.
2. **Check your customer service body language** – Ensure that your body language shows that you are keen to listen to the customers.
3. **Check your customer service voice** – Make sure your voice is energized and affirmative. This means that you do not sound monotonous and your voice has vocal variety. Check your voice to make sure you maintain a lively pace without cutting off the customers before they finish speaking.

KEY CONCEPTS

- Customer Relationship Management (CRM) is the essence of sales. It is a multifaceted process that aims at creating systems to satisfy customers through a series of efforts that address problems leading to their emotional fulfillment.
- CRM helps in creating ways and means that enable salespersons to have an intimate knowledge of their customers, their needs, wants, and buying patterns that helps them serve them to their fullest satisfaction.

- CRM requires a high degree of sensitivity on the part of salespersons, to empathize with their customers, to resolve difficulties faced by them and show them the right way so that they can do business more profitably.
- The fundamental grounding for CRM for any salesperson is to want to take care of customers, resolve their problems and deliver more than what they expect.
- More than just selling, CRM enables a salesperson to see beyond tomorrow and foster a strong relationship based on service, truthfulness, mutual trust and adherence to commitment.
- Salespersons must appreciate that if they care for their customers, they will care about you. An emotional bond that goes beyond the professional alliance and brings two lives together, leads to success in sales.
- Do not forget your customers once the sales are over. Remember, they can bring more customers for you in the future.
- Reinforce customer relationships by offering different products and services; listening to them and responding most effectively.
- The key to managing customer relationships is establishing a bond based on trust, transparency and confidence.
- Be customer-focused rather than outcome-focused only. This mindset yields benefits during the entire sales process and beyond. It helps ease performance pressure and allows you to become a valued partner with your customers.
- Listen to complaints as they come to you. Listen actively. Resolve customer complaints fast. Delay in solving problems might disturb your customer.
- Selling does not mean manipulating the buyer to do what the seller wants, rather than providing the buyer what he wants.
- If you want to satisfy customers, and want them to be with you for a long time, treat them nicely and make it easy and convenient for them to buy your product.
- Check your customer service attitude. Make your attitude to say, "I will help you today." Also, ensure that your body language shows that you genuinely want to help them. This will help you reinforce your relationship with customers.
- Share what you know – not just sell. Customers expect more today than ever before. Guide them and help them to take a correct decision.
- Tell your prospects "what's in it for them" and how a successful outcome would affect them. Find out what they hope to achieve by doing business with you and how they will personally benefit from doing business with you.
- Work with your prospects to prioritize their affirmed objectives. Whatever improvement your solution offers, it must support your prospect's priorities. Help them identify, rank and place a value on relieving their "pain points."
- Remember that you are selling benefits, solutions and results – not features. Your customers want to know how your product will benefit them. Describe how your product or service will rationalize operations, promote higher employee retention, augment sales, reduce costs or help them achieve their highest-level strategic goals.
- Be a trusted advisor. Show that you will serve their best interests by staying informed about their business and their industry, by offering only those products or services that will truly

benefit them and by providing pertinent, meaningful information to them before and after the sale.

- Be disciplined. Plan your day carefully, keep appointments and deliver to customers what you promise them. Make yourself do the things you know you should do and do them well and on time.
- Follow up regularly. Execute and support your solution. Stay in touch with your consumer. Continue to add value to your relationship. Be in it for long-term relationship.

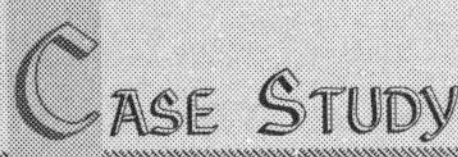

HI-TECH CONSTRUCTION

Rathin Verma, a builder, had a new house on the market for eight months. Usually he sold a house before it was finished, so it was understandable that he was very concerned about this one, which was located in a suburb of Kolkata and priced at about Rs.5,00,000 less than any house nearby. The style was traditional, not particularly different from neighbouring houses, except that it was slightly smaller.

In the past two months Verma had spent several thousand rupees on the house, adding a small garden with seasonal flowers, some trees, a brick walk, and tiling, and replacing many of the light fixtures. These additions and changes, plus the interest charges on his loan for the time this house has been on the market, had shrunk his profit margin considerably. Normally he cleared about 20 percent; but in this case, the extra costs and interest payments cut his margin to about 10 percent.

Mr. Neeraj Majumdar called Verma and asked for an appointment to look at the house. He did not ask the price, but he had some idea of the price. His appointment with Mr. Majumdar that same afternoon went off very smoothly. He said the house was not for him, but for his son and daughter-in-law, who were moving back to the area. His son was finishing his medical internship and was returning to set up practice as a physician. In fact, his new office would not be too far from the house.

In showing a house, Verma followed a regular procedure that had worked for him and his father for the past 30 years. He first showed the wife the kitchen and then talked about the closet space throughout the house. He focused all his attention on the wife. While he was doing this, he kept asking questions to find out her specific needs and what she was looking for in a house. In his opinion, there were only two types of customers. One type is interested in space, and the other in built-ins and extras. Verma classified Mr. Majumdar as the latter.

The second interview with Mr. Majumdar and his daughter-in-law, who had arrived to look at homes, was disastrous, even though it did end in a sale.

When Verma arrived at the house about 15 minutes before the meeting, he found Mr. Majumdar and his daughter-in-law already there. In fact, they had been looking at the house and the neighbourhood for quite some time.

Mr. Majumdar began the conversation by saying that the price of the house was too high. Verma responded by saying that they could talk about the money part after he had shown the younger woman the house. He started out in his regular pattern showing her first the kitchen and then the closets. She seemed impressed by the kitchen and the entire house as they went from room to room. However, starting in the kitchen, her father-in-law began to criticize everything about the house: "The finishing, particularly the woodwork is shoddy; there were very few cabinets in the kitchen; the carpeting also seemed cheap." These were just some of his remarks. Mr. Majumdar seemed to feel that, "Nothing was good about the house."

Verma noticed that the daughter-in-law, who seemed impressed initially, tended to change her mind and agree with her father-in-law. In criticizing the house, Mr. Majumdar did not talk about the part of the house they were looking at. This went on for a long time, at times almost becoming an argument between the two. The younger woman even told Verma, that though she agreed broadly with her father-in-law, she differed from him on some counts, and would take an independent decision. Verma became so confused and upset that he thought of ending the inspection tour.

He was perplexed; his whole selling procedure had gone wrong. He could not catergorize the daughter-in-law. The interruptions were very distracting to him.

Finally, Verma cut the price by Rs. 20,000, stressing that the price tag was already low in comparison with that of other houses in the neighbourhood.

Verma's last argument, was that the interest rates on mortgages were due to go up, which could further increase the price of any house.

The daughter-in-law asked him what he would suggest they do. He said that they could buy the house with the help of a loan which he could arrange. She finally agreed, and everything went smoothly from then on. Mr. Majumdar said nothing during the rest of the time.

Question

1. How would you analyze the sales approach of Mr. Verma?

REFERENCES

1. Bush, Robert P., Underwood, III, James H. (2007), Using CRM to Manage Marketing Productivity, *Journal of Relationship Marketing*, Vol. 6 Issue 2, p. 89.
2. Chakravorti, Samit (2009), Extending Customer Relationship Management to Value Chain Partners for Competitive Advantage, *Journal of Relationship Marketing*, Vol. 8 Issue 4, pp. 299-312.
3. Che Wel, Che Aniza Binti; Bojei, Jamil. (2009), Determining Relationship Marketing Instruments. *IUP Journal of Marketing Management*, Vol. 8 Issue 3/4, pp. 25-41.
4. Dorsch, Michael J.; Carison, Les; Raymond, Mary Anne; Ranson, Robert (2001), Customer Equity Management and Strategic Choices for Sales Managers, *Journal of Personal Selling & Sales Management*, Vol. 21 Issue 2, p. 157.

5. Eggert, Andreas; Ulaga, Wolfgang (2010), Managing Customer Share in Key Supplier Relationships, *Industrial Marketing Management*, Vol. 39 Issue 8, pp. 1346-1355.
6. Elmuti, Dean, Jia, Heather; Gray, Dane (2009), Customer Relationship Management Strategic Application and Organizational Effectiveness: An Empirical Investigation, *Journal of Strategic Marketing*, Vol. 17 Issue 1, pp. 75-96.
7. Injazz J Chen; Karen Popovich (2003), Understanding Customer Relationship Management (CRM): People, Process and Technology, *Business Process Management Journal*, Vol. 9 Issue 5, pp. 672-688.
8. Judge, Paul C (2001), Don't Just Listen Connect, *Fast Company*, Issue 49, pp. 140-143.
9. Kaj Storbacka; Tore Strandvik; Christian Grönroos (1994), Managing Customer Relationships for Profit: The Dynamics of Relationship Quality, *International Journal of Service Industry Management*, Vol. 5 Issue 5, p. 21.
10. Lee, Nancy (2007), It's All About the Customer: Commercial Perspectives on Customer-Centric Marketing and Managing the Customer Relationship, *Social Marketing Quarterly*, Vol. 13 Issue 3, pp. 12-16.
11. Ojasalo, Jukka (2001), Customer Expertise: A Challenge in Managing Customer Relationships in Professionals, *Services Marketing Quarterly*, Vol. 22 Issue 2, p. 1.
12. Pullman, Madeleine E.; Gross, Michael A (2003), Welcome to Your Experience: Where You Can Check Out Anytime You'd Like, But You Can Never Leave, *Journal of Business & Management*, Vol. 9 Issue 3, pp. 215-232.
13. Reinartz, Werner J.; Kumar, V (2003), The Impact of Customer Relationship Characteristics on Profitable Lifetime Duration, *Journal of Marketing*, Vol. 67 Issue 1, pp. 77-99.
14. Ryals, Lynette (2002), Are Your Customers Worth More Than Money? *Journal of Retailing & Consumer Services*, Vol. 9 Issue 5, p. 241.
15. Villanueva, Julian; Bhardwaj, Pradeep; Balasubramanian, Sridhar; Chen, Yuxin (2007), Customer Relationship Management in Competitive Environments: The Positive Implications of a Short-term Focus, *Quantitative Marketing & Economics*, Vol. 5 Issue 2, pp. 99-129.
16. Yousef, Robyn (2001), Managing Customer Relationships, *New Zealand Management*, Vol. 48 Issue 8, p. 39.

8 Retaining Customers and Building Loyalty

"The best portion of a good man's life, his little, nameless, unremembered acts, of kindness and love."

–William Wordsworth

CHAPTER OUTLINE

- ✦ Introduction: Why customers switch
- ✦ Dimensions of a customer's buying decision
- ✦ The Customer Value Added (CVA) approach
- ✦ The impact of customer retention
- ✦ Framework to improve customer retention
- ✦ The value creation process

OBJECTIVES

After studying this chapter, you will be able to:

- ✦ Understand the need to deal with customers with a human touch
- ✦ Describe the key factors for an effective presentation
- ✦ Apply the attributes necessary for delivering efficient customer service

Opening Case: Norton Eureka

Norton Eureka's vacuum cleaner and kitchen exhaust chimney were great success among the upper income households in India.

Rahul hailed from Ludhiana, an industrial town of Punjab. Rahul was a young man, decent, polite, soft spoken and very simple. After his graduation he was looking for a job. After struggling for almost a year, Rahul got a call letter from Norton Eureka. He appeared for the written test and interview and he was selected. Rahul was very happy and excited but wondered how he would cope with the ruggedness of the sales profession.

After Rahul joined Norton Eureka, his branch manager, Mr. Rathore, asked him to call on the customers and discuss his practical experience with him at the end of the day. He decided to visit the middle income families where both husband and wife are working. He found that they were not much aware of the utility of vacuum cleaners and exhaust chimneys at home.

In the evening Rahul went to brief his branch manager, Mr. Rathore about his first day's experience in sales. Mr. Rathore told him to sit down and relax for a while. Then he said, "Now narrate all your events during the first sales call." Rahul said, "I was extremely nervous and anxious, when I pressed the calling bell and knocked at the door. After a minute or so, an old lady, around 60 years old opened the door. After I introduced myself, she invited me inside her flat.

"As I entered, she said 'have a glass of water first.' I gulped the water all at once and somehow managed to talk about our vacuum cleaner and chimney. When I had finished, she asked the net price of the vacuum cleaner models. I told her that if she buys our best model it will cost (inclusive of tax) about Rs. 9000/-."

"After seeking some more information about warranty, after sales service and installation, the lady placed an order. She also said that she had already spoken with six other salesmen. All of them suggested that she should go in for the cheaper model. She said, "I was impressed by your bold suggestion that I should take your best model. You appear to be a novice salesman. But I liked your simplicity and straight forward talk, decent behaviour and politeness." She said she felt as if she was talking to her son! She did not bother about the extra expenditure. The other smart looking salesmen typically tried to somehow push a model, on the ground that it is cheap. The old lady followed her instincts and intuition, rather than getting trapped in the mechanics of bargaining and buying a low price model.

After hearing his experience, Mr. Rathore said, "You have the intrinsic quality to become a good sales person." The truth is, the first impression that Rahul gave was his simplicity, demeanour, courtesy, attitude, politeness and likability that helped him to get the order. No sales hype. No over-glorified talk about the product's superiority and benefits. His honest impression was all that was needed.

Mr. Rathore said, "Rahul, always be aware what impression you are giving to your customers. If you can impress them with your simplicity, then you have already won half the battle. If this means redesigning your presentation, or going out of your way to be polite, helpful and give the best possible shopping experience to your customers, then so be it."

Question

1. Is it really too much work to clinch sales? You need to ponder this.

RETAINING CUSTOMERS AND BUILDING LOYALTY

Integral Design for Programmed Learning

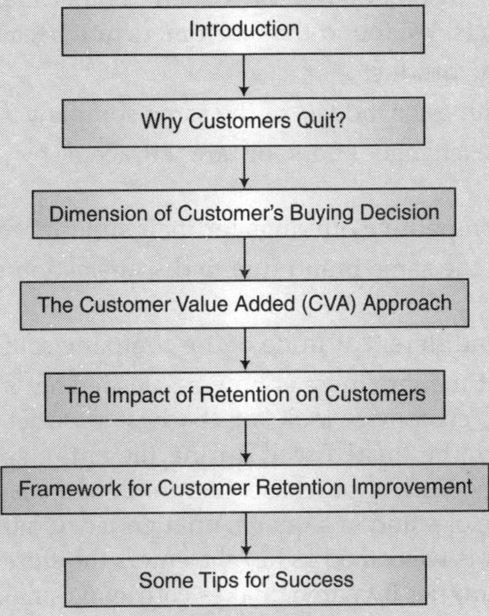

"Misunderstanding, politics, backbiting, blame and a number of factors stand in the way of satisfying relationships with even those who are very close to us."

–D M Silvera

INTRODUCTION: WHY CUSTOMERS SWITCH

The question 'Why do customers switch to other brands and leave?' has been the major cause of concern to any marketer. To know the underlying motives we conducted a research study on why household consumers in India switch to other makes of durable products. It revealed some startling facts. We found that customers quit because:

- 1% – Stop using the product
- 3% – Upgrade to superior models of the same company
- 15% – Avail of exchange offers or are attracted by festival deals from other companies
- 19% – Switch to competitive offerings for their superior features
- 24% – Do not buy the same brand due to dissatisfaction with the service offered by the company
- 38% – Due to the indifferent attitude of the company selling the products

It is evident that what matters most is how a salesperson is able to touch the heart of his customers. No doubt, customers look for the best product at the minimum possible price, but they also wish to be treated well during the entire span of time when they use the product and even at the time of purchase. Just think of a customer who has to wait in a store to make the purchase or stand in a queue, unattended. On the other hand, consider the situation when a customer is welcomed as he/she enters the store and is given full attention. The salesperson knows him/her by name, makes courteous small talk and is also willing to deliver his purchases to his home – at no extra cost. He knows his likes and dislikes and goes out of the way to make the customer happy!

Customers do not wish to be treated as faceless entities who just buy a product and pay a price but want to be treated as "human beings". Another research study has revealed that 70% of a customer's decision to buy is based on interactions and only 30% is based on product attributes. It is the "personalized approach" that stands out in the mind of the customer. Although in the 21st century all companies claim to maintain good "customer relationships," in reality very few actually do. Most of the customer initiatives are aimed at how to "sell more" rather than how to serve them better.

Kirpatrick Charles & Russ FA found that the following qualities were important to sales people to excel in the market.

Making Interactions Humane

A series of interactions occur over the course of product ownership and repeat buying. Interactions might cascade in a sequence, such as placing the initial order – delivery-installation – after sales service (repair, annual maintenance contract), (note: it may not always follow only this sequence). Regardless of this, companies must strive for a consistently human interaction every time, because how the customer feels about the business is made up of all of these interactions. Research reveals that a customer perceives a business as a chain of interactions between the company and himself where, besides the explicit needs

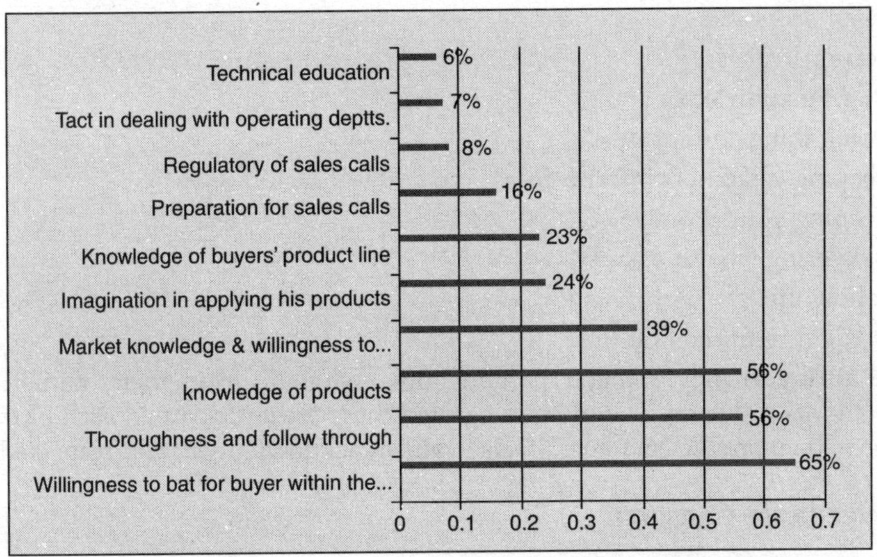

Source: Kirpatrick Charles & Russ FA (1981) Effective Selling, South Western Publishing, Cincinnati, p-298.

Fig. 8.1 *Important Qualities for Sales People to Excel*

of having a quality product, low price and good services, he also expects honesty, sincerity, respect, attention and warmth from the supplier. He expects the company representative to treat him as a human being with specific emotional needs. Despite knowing this, many companies fail to understand the humanness of customer interactions.

DIMENSIONS OF A CUSTOMER'S BUYING DECISION

There are three aspects of a customer's buying decision:

1. What they get, i.e. product and service features.
2. How they get it and how they are treated after they get it, i.e. interaction humanness.
3. How much they pay, i.e. price.

In most cases, the customer's perception of "how they get it" is determined predominately by how "humanly" the business interacts with the customer using different channels of interaction. All these human perception factors must always be thought of as relative to a competitor's ability to provide them.

Human Touch: Attributes of a Highly Human Interaction

Consumer research has shown that the majority of a customer's perception of a business is linked to a distinct set of human interaction attributes. There are nine specific core human interaction attributes that are most important to customers. These nine distinct human interaction attributes are:

1. Being accessible
2. Responsiveness
3. Sharing knowledge
4. Doing things promptly
5. Keeping customers informed
6. Keeping your promise
7. Delivering what is assured
8. Follow up
9. Doing it right the first time

These attributes play a major part in how customers form their opinion about the company and its products. The more integrated these attributes are in each of the business interactions, the more the customer "feels" valued, acknowledged, and respected.

Human Needs are Constant

These nine attributes, essentially say "we care for you". For instance, each of these attributes can be translated as follows:

1. Accessibility – Customers need help when they ask for it.
2. Responsiveness – Responsiveness does not necessarily translate into helping the customer quickly but rather into showing a genuine caring for the customer's personal needs. The fact that a retail store decides to be "more responsive" to its customers by opening earlier every day has little value if, when customers walk through the door, no one shows any genuine attention in responding to them.
3. Knowledgeable – Knowledgeable does not mean only having knowledge about products or services, but also knowing what a human being really needs. A business cannot acquire this type of knowledge until it understands the customer as a person.
4. Prompt – Being prompt means delivering a product or service when the customer expects it.
5. Keeping the customer informed – Means providing information to counter any potential human anxiety from uncertainty surrounding the purchase or consumption of a product or service.
6. Keep your promise – Delivering on any promise the business makes to a customer.
7. No surprises – No surprises unless it is a well-thought-out good surprise, because no human being likes bad surprises.
8. Follow-up – This is showing the customer simple courtesies such as thanking them, making sure certain activities happened, checking for closure.
9. Do it right the first time – Making sure that the product or service was done right the first time to avoid rework and failure costs.

Another aspect to these human factors is how adept a business must be at any one of these interaction attributes relative to their competitors. In order for the business to truly comprehend how well it can satisfy these nine attributes, it must first understand what the customer perceives as "excellence in service" in any one of these attributes compared to the business's competitors. It is these attributes that are the primary building blocks of a relationship. This "human touch" is different from what many companies are today striving for – customer "relationships" that focus on maximizing profit by reinforcing relationships. Customers expect something more, such as recognition of customers, meeting their desires, emotions and sentiments etc. which are based on three expectations:

- Acknowledgement
- Respect
- Trust

The areas on which salespersons should focus are:

1. Acknowledging customers
2. Treating customers with respect
3. Building trust with customers
4. Communicating humanly
5. Continuously touching the customers' heart

1. Acknowledging customers

Understanding how best to fulfil the human need for recognition and acknowledging the customer's existence, importance, individuality, and way of thinking is the first step in sales. It is also important to focus on eliminating behaviour (intentional or unintentional) which creates feelings of being ignored and unattended.

While acknowledging customers can be an intuitive act, which should be encouraged on an individual basis, creating consistency and unanimity requires that these acts of acknowledgement be standardized to the greatest extent possible.

One of the critical factors behind customer defection is that they feel ignored and neglected. It is important to acknowledge customers' presence, give credence to their views, respond to their grievances and interact with them with sensitivity.

Customers need to feel they are being heard and that their feelings are valid. Asking questions, such as "What do you feel about..........," is the key to obtaining useful information to assess whether the series of multiple interaction channels most companies utilize are effective or not.

Follow-up activities are critical in this respect. Whether customers "feel" they have been taken care of, or the company has been insensitive can quickly damage customer company relationships. One of the ways to acknowledge a customer's importance is to respond to customer problems quickly. This is also the key to minimizing negative emotions with customers and a unique opportunity to create higher customer fulfilment than if there had been no problem in the first place.

2. Treating customers with respect

It is often seen that customers are given importance by the salespersons only till the sale order is received. Once the customer has purchased the product, he is forgotten and sales persons 'hunt' for new customers. This is most unfortunate.

Customers have a strong need to feel respected. It is these softer areas that need special consideration. The following are some essential points that should be followed by the sales people.

Show empathy – One of the important ways for a business to check itself is to put itself in "their shoes." Salespersons should be sensitive to customers' problems, understand their difficulties and try to solve them. They should think of it as their problem and so sort it out. This will win the hearts of your customers and pass on an important message to them that "you care".

Be polite and courteous – Always be polite to your customers. Pay attention to them and listen to them. They may not always be right but never ridicule them or brush them off. Even when you cannot agree to their requests, tell them politely and give reasons for the same. Treating every customer with respect not only helps in increasing the probability of a favourable buying decision but such customers are more likely to buy more of the same and/or different products, and also recommend the company's products to others. Some things that salespeople should remember are stated below:

- Always try to feel the emotions and sensibilities of your customers.
- Every activity should demonstrate some sign of admiration for them.
- Never demean your customers.
- Never embarrass or humiliate them when they approach you to solve their difficulties.
- Always be grateful that they have chosen your products over those of your competitors.
- Good behaviour helps in touching the hearts of your customers.
- Genuine warmth towards a customer will help to align you with most of your customers.
- Always treat your customers as the basis of your existence.

Respect your customers' time – Time is one of the most precious things that customers have today. When a salesperson is punctual, he is admired and earns respect for the company too. Customers deeply appreciate such gestures and like to deal with such companies and sales people.

Respect the privacy of customers – Respecting the customers' personal space while being proactive in acknowledging them and offering them help, is critical in almost any business situation. However, while being close to your customers is important, it does not give the company the right to infringe upon their personal space. Many salespersons without having any consideration for the time of customers just intrude at odd times and try to sell them something. This antagonizes the customers a lot. The call centres are an apt example of such intrusion. Whether one likes it or not they call up at any time of the day, and try to sell whatever they have. This is to be avoided at any costs. Salespersons must take an appointment with the customers before meeting them. While this will ensure that your customers are mentally ready for the sales talk, they will also feel happy that you have respect for them and their valuable time.

Show respect by trusting customers' integrity – The feelings of your customers must be considered seriously. Treating customers with suspicion must be avoided. Even if the customer is wrong, the message must be conveyed to him very carefully, so as he is not offended. Directly pinpointing his mistakes might embarrass, frustrate, and even humiliate the customer. Believe in your customers and do not give them a "hard time" during such activities as returning items.

Enable control through choice – Customers have an emotional need for respect. Salespersons must allow customers to have control over interactions by communicating with them respectfully. Enabling customer control is done through choice. Choices show respect for the customer's freedom and ability to choose. Recognizing this personal freedom and ability is acknowledging their dignity as human beings. Sales people must therefore proactively create choices for customers prior to interactions. The choice could be a product feature, a service option, or to address the specific customer service problem.

Address customer issues as anxieties – Many times, it is far more effective for a business to approach business issues for what they really are – manifestations of human anxieties. A customer's concerns (anxieties) are fundamentally a reflection of their management's concerns (anxieties) driven from their respective business objectives. The three primary anxieties facing the customers are Price, Time, and Quality (PTQs). In particular, new customers have a high level of anxiety because there is uncertainty and lack of trust. In contrast, regular customers have less anxiety because they have some prior knowledge in all three areas. This requires constant communication between the customers and the supplier in order to enable the client to change priorities or focus on any one of the three attributes. This flexible approach is effective because many clients start off with only a rough idea about any project. The more projects accomplished by the supplier and client, the lower the PTQ anxieties and the more efficiency, both for supplier and client, is realized.

3. Building trust with customers

Building trust is at the very foundation of every purchase made by every customer. A customer will not purchase without trust. The customer must believe that the company will conveniently deliver the best product for them at a fair price, and treat them humanly. When the term "customer loyalty" is used, one is actually referring to extended "trust" from a behavioural and social science perspective. When a customer says, "I am loyal to that company's products and services," they are really saying, "I trust that the company will consistently deliver the best value to me over time." Trust helps forgive occasional performance issues. The trust built between business and customer fosters tolerance for intermittent operational issues.

Customers do not buy until they trust – Provide complete knowledge of the products and services so that the customer begins to develop sufficient trust to make a buying decision. This is very important because every customer is continually assessing a company and its salespersons as to whether or not they are knowledgeable enough to be trusted with the customer's business. Focus on activities that build trust and avoid creating distrust. Customers are continually judging firms as to whether to conditionally trust them. From the human perspective, any time a customer decides to give a firm their money in exchange for a product or service they are essentially "trusting" them to deliver something of value. In the period after they have paid for the product or service and before they have actually used the product or service, they have made themselves vulnerable to the firm they chose to patronize. Therefore, it is their vulnerability that the customer is actually deciding to entrust to the firm, not specifically their money. This alliance is in the form of conditional trust until such time as the relationship experiences some form of trauma. When a traumatic situation occurs, the firm's reaction to this trauma causes the customer to decide the degree of their trust.

It is not until trust has been tested that the customer is able to validate their initial trust of the firm. If the firm's reactions support an added sense of a customer's self-survival, the customer feels:

1. I was right to depend on this company.
2. I did the right thing by placing initial trust in them.
3. My trust in them will be less conditional moving forward.

Trust (and therefore loyalty) is created during trust "proof points" which can range from a typical interaction to handling a major customer crisis. The more significant the trust proof point is, the greater the trust that is built, and therefore, the greater the loyalty. A customer's relationship to a business will generally "coast along" with minimal degrees of trust and loyalty until some event happens to threaten a human being's sense of emotional security. When a business begins to consistently respond to problems in an exemplary way, the relationship will typically evolve into a higher degree of trust and loyalty.

Do what's right, do it right the first time – Doing the "rights" is a useful strategy for building trust. Doing what is right lays the foundation for customer fulfilment. Doing it right is a more rewarding and satisfying way to work. Doing it right the first time saves time, as the task does not have to be redone later.

4. Communicating humanly with customers

It is important for every salesperson to understand the importance of respectful communication with customers. While a cordial communication may keep your customers with you forever, an arrogant interaction will probably make them leave. Salespersons must learn how to be both good listeners and good communicators. This reinforces the emotional bond of customers with you. While customers need to be treated nicely, often this is not the case. These emotional needs must be fulfilled through your communication.

The behaviour of salespersons is a combination of face-to-face behaviour with customers and behaviour that builds supporting infrastructure, processes, interfaces, and systems which either enhance acknowledgement, respect, and trust or decrease the fulfilment of these central needs in customers. In order to achieve a positive result, a salesperson must first become a good listener. Communicating the message of acknowledgement, respect, and trust is probably the weakest point of most businesses. Given below are some key insights into the art of communication.

- **Be an attentive listener** – It is always important to be a good listener first. Only when a salesperson listens well can he be a good communicator. The very act of listening without judgment leaves an impression of genuine caring and compassion. Listening carefully and with concern can solve the significant emotional issues involved with many customer problems.
- **Be compassionate** – Achieving the goal of being compassionate and empathetic with every customer each day depends on the salesperson's own value systems and ethical mores.
- **Be non-judgmental** – Salespersons must listen to the customer's perception of a situation objectively. The goal should be to take an empathetic view of each customer's problem. The validity of the customer's perspective should not be questioned at all. It is the customer's perception of the problem that should define the nature of the interaction, not the salesperson's perception.
- **Communicate** – Many times, the worst possible situations are resolved by continuous communication with your customers. This will also help salespersons manage problems well by informing the customers of the real situation and then managing the problem with honesty and efficiency.
- **Let them tell you how to tell them** – A business should be constantly sensitive to subtle signals from customers revealing the degree and manner of communication desired. Do not try to force information by unwanted communication; instead recognize signals from the customer that reveal how much they want to talk and the level of familiarity with which they are comfortable.
- **Respond fast** – One critical component of listening well is the ability to respond after listening. Speed should also be complemented with the quality of response. Your response will determine your concern for the customers and their problems.

One of the most effective ways to create trust is to freely admit your own mistakes, if committed. Admitting your own mistakes openly and in good humour shows character, strength, and honesty, and almost everyone can relate to mistakes because everyone makes them – no exceptions.

Tracking regular customer issues and their resolution does little good unless the issues are widely and quickly communicated. This is the start of creating a systemic solution to reoccurring issues. In the case of negative customer feedback, information should include both the customer issue and also the actions the employee took to overcome the issue. Both positive and negative comments should be taken with equal importance. Customer feedback should be used to educate everyone as to how customers are reacting to a business experience. If these issues are not communicated quickly, the employee who experienced the problem resolution may have ended their workday without sharing the problem, thus creating an opportunity for the same problem to reoccur during the next shift.

5. Continuously touching the customers' heart

There are three aspects of a customer's buying decision:

- What they get, i.e. product and service features.
- How they get it and how they are treated after they get it, i.e. interaction humanness.
- How much they pay, i.e. price.

In most cases, the customer's perception of "how they get it" will be determined predominately by how "humane" the business is with the customer using different channels of interaction, e.g. face-to-face, web, call-centre, kiosk. All these human perception factors must always be thought of as relative to a competitor's ability to provide them. Otherwise, the factors are meaningless, unless the business is a monopoly. Once all three of these factors are understood, the business can begin to understand and manage how the customer perceives the value of the business's products and services.

THE CUSTOMER VALUE ADDED (CVA) APPROACH

Customer Value Added (CVA) can be applied to understand, measure, and manage this perception of value. The CVA approach is based on providing products and services to customers that have a greater value than they could expect from purchases from competitive companies in similar markets.

Was it "Worth what I paid for it?"

The central concept used to help define the measurement of a customer's perception of relative value is called Worth What Paid For (WWPF), i.e. "Is it worth what I paid for the product or service relative to my other choices?" The answer to this question is a strong loyalty indicator. If the business receives an excellent score on the overall customer value measurement, i.e. the degree to which the customer perceives that the product or service was "worth what they paid for it" relative to the competitors' product or service, there will be a very high probability for strong customer loyalty. This customer loyalty is indicated by measurements that track the responses to questions such as:

- Will you buy again?
- Will you tell your friends?
- Will you buy more from us?

From a strategic perspective, the CVA approach helps a business understand and manage the three necessary components of business success:

- Choosing the right value proposition for products and services to be delivered.
- Managing the delivery of that value better than the competitors.
- Successfully communicating that value because customers need to know.

The most surprising downfall of most firms is that they fail to communicate the value they created to their customers. They dedicate so much of their resources to choosing and delivering value that they end up under-resourcing the step that communicates value. As a result, they fall short of actually communicating that value to their customer. In this scenario, the value to the customer does not exist.

The CVA Journey

In order to implement the CVA approach effectively, businesses must first clarify their vision and mission. Then they must endeavour to understand themselves and their market not only by collecting good data but also by teaching themselves how to use the data. These data must drive the changes in business priorities. As priorities change, efforts must focus as much on "what not to do" as on "what to do". From these priorities, new process changes and their respective measures must be put in place in a process-oriented culture for systemic change.

This entails first analyzing what the customers want. This is accomplished through applying market research and statistics. The next step is to understand how well the business is doing relative to its competitors. Once this is done, economic models can be created to prioritize the business's focus. Then, quality improvement teams can be created and taught quality process improvement skills by quality experts. The business will then need to be taught how to understand and accept the data as meaningful to the business objectives. Once this is accomplished, the measurements can be turned into actions through quality improvement programs.

- Analyze what customers want.
- Apply market research and statistics.
- Compare the business's success with that of its competitors.
- Create economic models to prioritize focus.
- Create quality improvement teams and teach quality process improvement skills.
- Teach the business how to understand and accept data.
- Turn measurements into actions through quality improvement programs.

THE IMPACT OF CUSTOMER RETENTION

Why should retention have such a great effect on profitability? There are a number of reasons:

- Acquiring new customers involves costs that can be significant and it may take some years to turn a new customer into a profitable customer.
- As customers become more satisfied and confident in their relationship with a supplier, they are more likely to give the supplier a larger proportion of their business, or 'share of wallet'.
- As the relationship with a customer develops, there is greater mutual understanding and collaboration, which produces efficiencies that lower operating costs. Sometimes customers are willing to integrate their IT systems, including planning, ordering and scheduling, with those of their suppliers, and this further reduces costs.
- Satisfied customers are more likely to refer others, which promotes profit generation as the cost of acquisition of these new customers is dramatically reduced. In some industries, customer advocacy can play a very important role in acquiring new customers, particularly when there is a high risk involved in choosing a supplier.
- Loyal customers can be less price-sensitive and may be less likely to defect due to price increases. This is especially true in business-to-business markets where the relationship with the supplier becomes more valued and switching costs increase.

FRAMEWORK TO IMPROVE CUSTOMER RETENTION

Given the dramatic impact that improved customer retention can have on business profitability and the fact that many organizations continue to place too much emphasis on customer acquisition at the expense of customer retention, there is a strong need for a structured approach which organizations can follow to enhance their retention and profitability levels. Three major steps are involved in such an approach: the measurement of customer retention; the identification of root causes of defection and key service issues; and the development of corrective action to improve retention.

Step 1: Measurement of Customer Retention

The measurement of retention rates for existing customers is the first step in improving customer loyalty and profitability. It involves two major tasks – measurement of customer retention rates and profitability analysis by segment. To measure customer retention, a number of dimensions need to be analyzed in detail. These include the measurement of customer retention rates over time, by market segment, and in terms of the product/service offered. If customers buy from a number of suppliers, the share that your company is getting should also be identified. The outcome of this first step should be a clear definition of customer retention, a measurement of present customer retention rates, and an understanding of the existing and future profit potential for each market segment.

Step 2: Identification of Causes of Defection and Key Service Issues

This step involves the identification of the underlying causes of customer defection. Traditional marketing research into customer satisfaction does not always provide accurate answers as to why customers abandon one supplier for another. All too often customer satisfaction questionnaires are poorly designed, superficial and fail to address the key issues – forcing respondents to tick pre-determined response choices. The root causes of customer defections should be clearly identified.

Step 3: Corrective Action to Improve Retention

The final step in the process of enhancing customer retention involves taking remedial action. At this point, plans to improve retention become highly specific to the organization concerned and any actions taken will be particular to the given context. Some key elements include: marshalling top management commitment; ensuring employee satisfaction and dedication to building long-term customer relationships; utilizing best practice techniques to improve performance; and developing a plan to implement customer retention strategy. Increasingly, organizations are recognizing that enhanced customer satisfaction leads to better customer retention and profitability. Many organizations are now reviewing their customer service strategies to find ways to boost retention rates as a means of improving their business performance. This often entails a fundamental shift in business emphasis from customer acquisition to customer retention. Achieving the benefits of long-term customer relationships requires a firm commitment from senior management and all staff – to understanding and serving the needs of customers.

Step 4: Building Trust with Customers

Understanding the role of trust is key because customers don't buy without trust. Actions to build trust in customers should be focused on honesty, ethics, integrity, openness, educating customers, and most importantly operational excellence. It is also important to focus on eliminating behaviour which creates distrust.

Step 5: Communicating Humanly

Understanding and developing the skills to create the most human communication with customers is vital. This involves becoming a better listener as well as a better communicator to customers both verbally and non-verbally.

Step 6: Implementing the Human Touch Consistently Across Interactions

Salespersons should view their interactions with customers as a series of opportunities that must be consistently given a "human touch". Each human touch can be viewed as one step linked to many other interdependent steps to make up an entire process. Businesses should focus on human touch as a process that not only enables a high degree of consistency in delivering their humanness but also helps to isolate activities that dehumanize.

THE VALUE CREATION PROCESS

A Checklist to Review Your Value Proposition

1. Is the target customer clearly identified?
2. Are the customer benefits explicit, specific, measurable and distinctive?
3. Is the price, relative to competition, explicitly stated?
4. Is the value proposition clearly superior for the target customer (superior benefits, lower price or both)?
5. Do we have, or can we build, the skills to deliver it?
6. Can we deliver it at a cost that permits an adequate profit?
7. Is it viable and sustainable in the light of competitors and their capabilities?
8. Is it the best of several value propositions we considered?
9. Are there any impending discontinuities (in technology, customer habits, regulation, market growth, etc.) that could change our position?
10. Is the value proposition clear and simple?

Understanding and undertaking the value creation process is crucial in transforming the outputs of the strategy development process in Customer Relationship Management (CRM) into programs that both *extract and deliver* value. An insufficient focus on the value provided to key customers, as opposed to the income derived from them, can seriously diminish the impact of the offer in terms of its perceived value. Only a balanced value exchange will ensure that both parties enjoy a good return on investment, leading to a good (long-term and profitable) relationship.

Achieving the ideal equilibrium between giving value to customers and getting value from customers is a critical component of CRM and requires competence in managing the perception and projection of value within the reality of acquisition and retention economics. To anticipate and satisfy the needs of current and potential customers, the supplier organisation must be able to target specific customers, and demonstrate added value through differentiated propositions and service delivery. This means adopting an analytical approach to value creation supported by a dynamic, detailed knowledge of customers, competitors, opportunities, and the company's own performance capabilities. Increasingly sophisticated technologies provide essential aids in developing and deploying 'intelligence' for competitive advantage. Many companies have achieved greater organisational efficiency and market place effectiveness through automating the business processes that deliver value to their customers (as well as suppliers and employees). However, such innovations do not negate the vital role fulfilled by employees. Indeed, excellent customer care remains the key determinant of winning and keeping customers.

Some Tips for Success

- Acknowledge the client's needs. Begin with the client's needs, not your product or service.
- Convey your recommendation in the form of a structure.

- State specific benefits, not just good attributes.
- Use the language that your customer understands.
- Be concise and clear.
- Ask for feedback by checking.

Creating a Real Experience for Your Customers

While obviously, what exactly your customers will want will depend very much on the industry in which you operate and the goods and services you offer, there are some key rules that can apply to any business:

- Give high-quality service and value for money.
- Tailor the services to your customers' specific needs.
- Make sure your first point of contact is efficient and friendly.
- If you say you will contact customers within, say, two working days, stick to that promise, without fail.
- Be consistent and reliable in everything you do: deliver on time and on budget and if you do run into any problems, talk to the customer.
- Cater for, and be accessible to everyone, especially if they have mobility problems or other challenges.
- Make sure the design, comfort and safety of your establishment are appropriate for your market.
- Deal with queries or complaints promptly and effectively, and keep relevant customers informed of their progress.
- If you sell anything that requires after-sales service, follow up regularly to make sure your customers are happy.
- Continually strive to improve your services and look at your customers' needs.

Sales is a Challenge: Accept it

Customers are increasingly demanding, and there may be days when it feels like the world is against you. However, no effort should be spared in pleasing the customer, regardless of how you are feeling or how the customer is behaving towards you.

Next time they give you their order they will expect to receive the same service and so it becomes the norm. Make sure, therefore, that when you do give a customer 'that little bit more', the business can afford it. A few tips to help you provide what customers want are given below.

- Treat your customers as you would want to be treated yourself.
- Talk to them! Passing the time of day with customers and visitors, asking them questions and picking up on their perceptions of your business is an excellent way to understand what they like and what you need to work on.

- Use your friends and family as sounding boards. What is most likely to encourage them to purchase a specific product or service? What techniques or offers do they respond to positively?
- Be visible. There is no better way to get to know your customers than being 'on the shop floor' and interacting with them. I would like to give a personal example here – *I regularly shop at a local small boutique. The owner knows my taste in clothes and always calls me when she has something new in stock that she thinks might appeal to me. She is careful not to harass me and only calls when she is almost certain I will like the new stock. I am always delighted with this personal attention because it saves me so much time and energy. The boutique gets more business, as I've become a loyal customer and have also recommended it to friends. The owner is also astute enough to recognise that I am a walking advertisement for her. She realises that she is in the business of selling and that selling is everything.* In a small business you are not only selling a product or service, but you are selling your 'personal brand' too.
- Whenever possible, keep a record of your customers. You do not only want their name, address and telephone number but any other relevant information you can make a note of that may help you discover what they like and (hopefully) initiate another sale in the future. This information helps you to stay close to the customer. Gather feedback in different ways. Some customers will happily share their experiences of your products, but many others may find it very difficult to express their views face-to-face. Try to break down the formality so that customers feel relaxed and are able to tell you what they want. Train your staff how to communicate with, understand and delight your customers. Make sure they realize very clearly that if customers are not happy with the service they receive, they will go elsewhere.

KEY CONCEPTS

- Over and above an excellent range of products, aggressive advertising campaign, a top notch sales promotion campaign and highly differentiating sales strategies, what matters most is how a salesperson is able to touch the heart of his customers.
- Customers do not wish to be treated as faceless entities who just buy a product and pay a price but want to be treated as "human beings." It is the "personalized approach" that stands out in the mind and memory of the customer.
- A customer perceives a business as a chain of interactions between the company and him where, besides the explicit needs of having a quality product, low price and good services, he also expects honesty, sincerity, respect, attention and warmth from the supplier.
- Responsiveness does not necessarily translate into helping the customer quickly but rather into showing genuine care for the customer's personal needs.
- Acknowledgement, Respect, and Trust (ART) are the cornerstones of sales and define the success of salespersons in the marketplace.

- Understand how best to fulfil the human need for recognition and acknowledging the customer's existence, importance, characteristics, and feelings.
- Customers defect when they feel ignored and neglected. They want to feel that they are being heard and that their feelings are valid.
- Customers have a strong need to feel respected. Like all of us, they also wish for love, affection and warmth from every interaction with the company and its sales people. Today, when every good company is delivering standard product quality, it is these sotter areas that need special consideration.
- Pass on an important message to your customers that "You care and you care because you respect them and their words".
- Be polite to your customers. Treating every customer with respect not only helps in increasing the sales but such customers are more likely to buy more of the same and/or different products and also recommend the company's products to others.
- Respecting the customer's personal space while being proactive in acknowledging them and offering them help, is a critical for almost any business situation.
- Treating customers with suspicion is one thing that should be avoided at all costs. A customer might be wrong at times, but this message must be conveyed in a very careful manner so that he is not offended.
- Building trust is at the very foundation of every purchase made by every customer. The customer must believe that the company will conveniently deliver the best product for them at a fair price, and treat them humanly. Customers do not buy until they trust.
- Keep your promises and you can do so by making only those promises that you can keep. Unfulfilled promises will cause tremendous damage to trust.
- It is critical for every salesperson to understand the importance of respectful communication with customers. While a cordial communication may keep your customers with you forever, an arrogant interaction will probably result in your customers leaving.

RETAINING CUSTOMERS & BUILDING LOYALTY

Mathew, a short man in his early forties, had a rather unassuming personality. He hailed from a small town in Kerala. He was a graduate and had joined Vibgyor Paints Ltd. at their Nagpur branch. Mathew was part of the sales team that looked after the sales in Maharashtra. Mathew was assigned the Marathwada area. The important towns in his area included Aurangabad, Nanded, Latur, Jalna, Beed, Parbhani, Osmanabad, and Hingoli. He was handling the dealers in his area well and this was well reflected in a steady growth in sales in his area. Mathew was highly concerned about the issues of his dealers and tried his best to resolve them once he was back in his office. At the same time he was conscious of the interests of his company, and tried to maximize his sales within the framework of rules.

One morning Mathew heard the terrible news of a fire gutting one of the major godowns of one of his main distributors in his territory. He talked to his branch manager immediately and asked permission to rush to Parbhani where his distributor R.K. Agarwal was in deep distress. Agarwal was one of the biggest distributors of that area and had a good hold on the market. He had been dealing with Vibgyor Paints since the last 28 years and had contributed immensely to the growth of the company in that area. Mathew had known him since he joined this company. He had been with Agarwal through thick and thin all these years and had worked hard to build up the market. With his sheer hard work, honest approach and sincerity, he earned high credibility for himself in the eyes of Agarwal and also his retailers.

What Mathew saw after reaching Agarwal's godown was unimaginable. The biggest of the five godowns was completely gutted. According to Agarwal, it contained paint worth over Rs. 80 lakhs. Unfortunately, the insurance of the godown had expired three days back and before Agarwal could revive it, the fire erupted and reduced everything to ashes. Mathew consoled his distributor and friend, and assured him that he would do whatever possible, to help him.

Mathew returned to his office with a heavy heart. Once he was back, he went straight to his branch manager and narrated the agony Mr. Agarwal was going through. He also pointed out that standing by his distributor in his hour of need was not only a moral responsibility of the company but would also reinforce the bonds that he and his company had created over the years. Mathew argued that if the company could share 50% of the loss, it would be an investment towards building customer relationship. The branch manager could see the reason in Mathew's arguments and discussed it with his seniors. His branch manager decided to consult the vice president of marketing of Vibgyor to approve Mathew's proposal of sanctioning Rs. 40 lakh as a special case.

Question

1. What decision should the vice president of marketing take in this case?

REFERENCES

1. Anderson, James C., Narus, James A., van Rossum, Wouter (2006), Customer Value Propositions in Business Markets, *Harvard Business Review*, Vol. 84 Issue 3, pp. 90-99.
2. Bates, Brooke (2010), Customer Care, *Smart Business Houston*, Vol. 5 Issue 4, pp. 10-15.
3. Bielski, Lauren (2002), The Rise and Fall and Rise Again of Customer Care, *ABA Banking Journal*, Vol. 94 Issue 8, p. 46.
4. Brooks, Ian (2011), Getting Serious About Customer Care, *NZ Business*, Vol. 25 Issue 2, p. 63.
5. Cowling, Mike (2010), Know Your Audience, *Smart Business South Florida*, Vol. 2 Issue 9, p. 26.
6. Flint, Daniel J., Blocker, Christopher P., Boutin, Philip J. (2011), Customer Value Anticipation, Customer Satisfaction and Loyalty: An Empirical Examination, *Industrial Marketing Management*, Vol. 40 Issue 2, pp. 219-230.

7. Graham, John (2011), Words That Betray Our True Motives, *American Salesman*, Vol. 56 Issue 1, pp. 12-17.
8. Graham, John (2011), Twenty Customer Care Actions that Build Sales, *American Salesman*, Vol. 56 Issue 7, pp. 10-14.
9. Hedley, George (2009), Customer Care = Cash, *American Salesman*, Vol. 54 Issue 3, p10-13
10. Junjun Mao (2010), Customer Brand Loyalty, *International Journal of Business & Management*, Vol. 5 Issue 7, pp. 213-217.
11. Kakabadse, Andrew P., Savery, Lawson, Kakabadse, Nada K., Lee-Davies, Linda (2006), 1% for 10%: Executive Strategies for Customer Care, *Strategic Change*, Vol. 15 Issue 2, pp. 103-111.
12. Magee, Jeffrey (2011), Service Ratings, *Sales & Service Excellence*, Vol. 11 Issue 2, p. 14.
13. Santo, Brian (2011), Satisfaction as a Weapon: Innovation in Customer Care is as Important as it is in Network Equipment, *CED*, Vol. 37 Issue 6, pp. 16-19.
14. Shehab, Thomas M., Adler, Larry A. (2009), The Quest for Service Excellence - One Group's Journey, *Physician Executive*, Vol. 35 Issue 4, pp. 40-45.
15. The Economics of Customer Care (2001), *Customer Relationship Management*, pp. 23-38.
16. Waring, Joseph (2010), The Winning Ingredient: Customer Care, *Telecom Asia*, Vol. 21 Issue 3, pp. 30-34.

9 Customer Service

"A sale is not something you pursue; it is something that happens to you while you are immersed in serving your customer."

–*Anonymous*

CHAPTER OUTLINE

- Customer service in today's business environment
- Customer service: Crucial facets
- The ABC of customer service
- 10 simple steps to customer service excellence
- The most important customer service question
- Action plan to improve customer service

OBJECTIVES

After studying this chapter, you will be able to:

- Understand the importance of customer service in today's business environment
- Be able to describe the important facets of customer service
- Be able to make an action plan to improve customer service

Opening Case: Speedstar Courier

Speedstar was a leading courier company in India. It had three basic activities -

- The Pace Courier that provided counter services to the high street customers.
- India Mail that managed the delivery of letters and packets.
- Parcel Force that provided express parcel delivery services for businesses and consumers.

With over 30,000 business customers in India, Speedstar handled over 200,000 parcels a day and had a turnover of Rs. 382 crores. In 2010-11, its revenues grew by 8.3% over the previous year. With its 23 partners across the country, it operated in all towns with a population of over 50,000.

Mr. S.R. Sharma was the owner of a very big publishing house called Quality Printing Pvt. Ltd. Quality Printing was the biggest printer in eastern India and was primarily involved in undertaking printing jobs for institutes in the corporate sector and various departments of the government of India, like the state examination boards. The company had a turnover of over Rs. 150 crore. Mr. Sharma had placed orders for some new state of the art machines and was planning to expand his business and desired to cover more institutions within the next year. But the recent change of response of Speedstar was causing him a lot of concern.

Mr. S.R. Sharma was not happy with the service of Speedstar. Mr. Sharma had been dealing with Speedstar since 1985. All these years he found Speedstar courier company to be reliable, efficient and trustworthy. However, of late, Mr. Sharma had been observing that the quality of service of the company was deteriorating. Speedstar was not only causing inordinate delays in delivering his packets and printed material but also exhibited an indifferent attitude towards him and his company. He felt that they did not even try to solve the problems caused by their delay in service. Mr. Sharma was even more worried because he was an old customer of Speedstar and had always referred them to his friends and other business colleagues as an excellent courier company. So his concerns, about the deteriorating quality of service provided, were two-fold. Speedstar did not appear to have any intention of looking into his problems. In fact he felt that Speedstar could no longer be considered a partner in his progress.

As part of its sales strategy to attract and retain key customers, Speedstar recruited a team of professionally qualified salespersons who were supposed to create and retain customers by offering them solutions to their courier needs and ensuring timely delivery of articles booked through them. The key parts of this customer service were:

- Time – making sure that deliveries are on time.
- Visibility – letting the customer follow a parcel through online tracking.
- After-sales service – ensuring that any problems are dealt with courteously and promptly.

Mr. Vijay Kumar was one such sales executive who was assigned the task of handling the account of Quality Printing. Kumar was a young man of 25 years, he had two years experience in a logistics company before joining Speedstar. He was jovial and had good communication skills. He had high aspirations to make a mark in sales, with a dream to grow to become a senior executive in the future. Mr. Kumar had the task of ensuring timely delivery, prompt response to queries and clear documentation. He was told to keep in regular touch with Mr. Sharma and other people of his company and resolve any difficulties that they might face at any point in time.

Mr. Kumar was flamboyant, and always tried to have the last word. He would often ridicule his colleagues and felt that by handling the account of Quality Printing, he was doing a favour to the company.

When the accounts department told him about the long due outstanding payments of Quality Printing, he cut his colleagues short, saying that since Quality Printing was a big customer they should be given extra facilities and Speedstar should not be too concerned about timely payments. He also said that the company's strict policy with regard to payments had led to the downturn in relations with Quality Printing.

Mr. Sharma was a forward looking and highly disciplined person. He was aware that they had some outstanding dues with Speedstar. But he used to justify his delay because of his delay in receiving payments from the government organisations. After all he never kept bills unpaid beyond 3 months. On the contrary, he expected Speedstar to live up to its old quality of service. Mr. Sharma was not able to accept any delays and lapses on the part of the courier company and finally decided to write to Mr. Menon, the managing director of Speedstar, and sort out the matter.

Questions

1. How would you assess the approach of Mr. Kumar towards his customers and his colleagues?
2. Is his approach conducive to sales growth or is it detrimental to the growth of his company in the long run?

CUSTOMER SERVICE

Integral Design for Programmed Learning

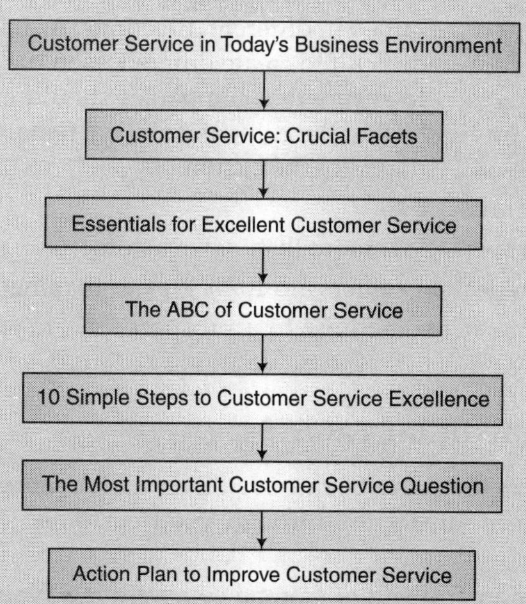

Don't tell people how good you make your products. Tell people how good your goods will make them.

–Kenneth M Goode

CUSTOMER SERVICE IN TODAY'S BUSINESS ENVIRONMENT

"What makes a great company?" A great company from the consumer's point of view is one that offers excellent products and efficient customer service.

However, due to the tremendous pressure to meet sales targets, customer service is generally perceived as that part of the contract that has to be fulfilled out of compulsion rather than as a wonderful opportunity to come closer to the customers and reinforce a business relationship with them.

As is rightly said, *"In a world where instant satisfaction and big results rule the playing field, we have all witnessed and experienced customer service pushed aside for a higher profit margin. Even companies who stood above the rest and prided themselves on the belief that 'The customer comes first' have fallen victim to the philosophy of corporate giants, profit maximus, but when it comes to customer service nothing beats one on one service delivered sincerely, swiftly and with a smile."*

Customer service is a critical factor to success in business. In today's environment of demanding consumers, those who deliver memorable customer service consistently create superior value and have competitive advantage. Indeed the creation of these services is increasingly becoming both the leading edge and a standard practice for business.

> Holding on to existing customers is crucial, but acquiring new customers is equally important as a satisfied customer is always likely to help in acquiring new ones by word-of-mouth publicity about the outstanding customer services of a particular company.

An increasing number of organizations are realizing that with growing competition, new technological innovations and constantly improving services, consumers are being pulled in different directions. As it is becoming increasingly difficult to create differences in the products, it is necessary to ensure that companies should excel in customer service so that the company always remains a preferred one in the minds of the customers.

Research shows that:

- Repeat customers spend 33% more than new customers
- Referrals among repeat customers are 107% greater than new customers
- It costs 6% more to sell something to a prospect than to sell the same thing to an existing customer

CUSTOMER SERVICE: CRUCIAL FACETS

Good customer service is defined as, "Giving customers a little more than what they expect." The mechanics of customer satisfaction through good customer service can be explained through Figure 9.1.

To create service as an instrument of gaining competitive advantage, then the following elements are essential:

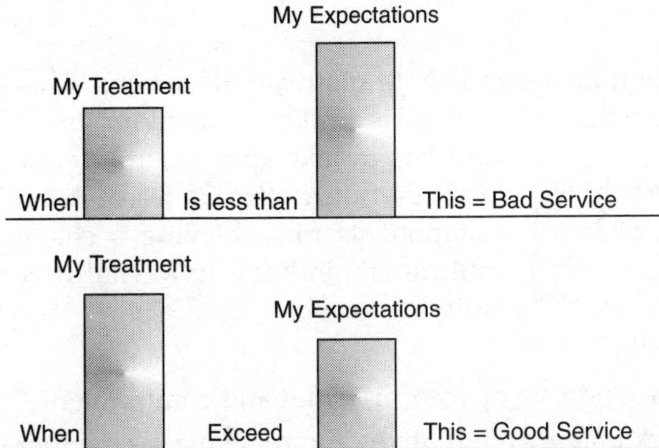

Fig. 9.1 *The Mechanics of Customer Satisfaction Through Good Customer Service*

Decide on Your Core Business

As Peter Drucker says, "*One of the most important things an organization can do is to determine what business it is in.*" Most of us are often unable to pin point what business we are really in. Normally there are different perceptions about the nature of selling which may lead to very different attitude and approaches. The way one recognizes business will decide the sales priorities and strategies.

> Wilkinson Sword does not think that it is manufacturing blades but is making any metal edge sharp. Walt Disney does not think that it is in the business of cartoons, it says that it is in the business of entertainment and offers service accordingly.

Companies need to revisit this question from time to time. The managing director of a company may be certain about what his core business is, but does everyone in the company think the same way?

Know Your Customers and Your Competitors

It is said, "*The only real measure of business success is a satisfied customer, all else is a distraction.*" Here the important question is, "How much do you know about your customers?" Do you know their likes and dislikes, their whims and fancies, and their pains when you deal with them? A good salesperson has to be a prudent psychologist who is capable of understanding his customers so well that he always tries to satisfy the customer's demands. This will also help him to:

- Deal with customers with sensitivity
- Take care of customers' implicit or unspoken needs fully
- Gain the customer's confidence by addressing his behavioural needs
- Know what the customer wants and convert it into sales orders
- Strike an emotional chord that will help build a strong relationship with the customer eventually helping him in sales.

Create a Vision

Everyone needs a vision or a purpose, to motivate his actions. This is especially so in the sales profession where the salesperson is under tremendous pressure to achieve targets and has to take split second decisions that may make or mar his future. Recent research into what the important components for achieving a change to a quality service culture are, indicate how vital it is to have a motivating, unifying vision.

> A clear vision helps in driving the energy of a salesperson to a fruitful conclusion.

A strong vision will:

- Provide visible evidence of your priorities and commitment
- Ignite the spark to launch initiatives and remain a visible reminder as it unfolds
- Be the clarion call which gathers the troops and focuses on the task ahead
- Help you to move forward in a pre-decided manner to achieve your goals
- Excite and inspire you to serve your customers better

Statements like:

- I exist only to serve my customers and I wish to be the best in our business
- I hope that my customers are happy in their dealing with us and that they feel the dealings are beneficial
- I want my company to be remembered for its excellent service.

Portray Your "*moments of truth*"

These words defined by Jan Carlzon explain the meaning of the various facets of customer-company relations very aptly. Moments of truth are moments when the customer comes in contact with the company in his effort to buy the product. Whether he will buy the product or not depends upon the direct result of his experiences with the company and its products. Purchase decisions are not usually made in a long thought-through analysis but through brief encounters with all the components of service that are labelled as the packaging around the core business.

> Purchase decisions are not usually made in a long thought-through analysis but through brief encounters with all the components of service that are labelled as the packaging around the core business.

Whether you are in the business of selling perishables or consumer durables, there will often be times when you and your customer come in touch with each other. How you respond in these moments of truth will determine whether that customer

- Buys from you or not
- Remains your customer
- Recommends you to other customers or not

Any experience of your customers will eventually be decided by the four **P**s: **P**eople skills, **P**rocess, **P**resentation and **P**roduct, as shown in Figure 9.2.

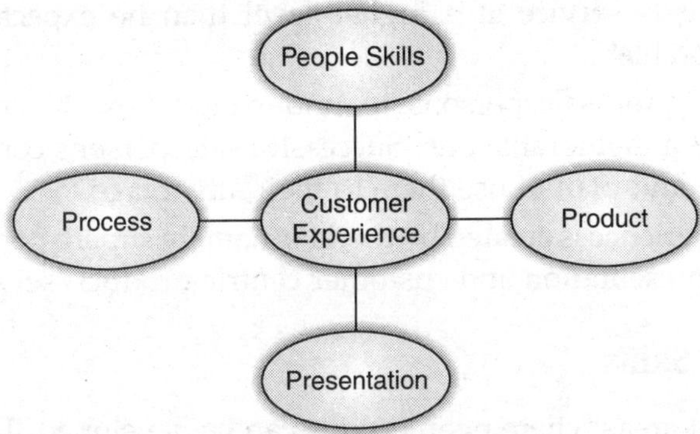

Fig. 9.2 *The Four Ps: People Skills, Process, Presentation and Product.*

To achieve success through service one needs to manage the customer's experience with the salesperson, his product and his company by ensuring that:

- The salesperson has superb people skills
- One is selling outstanding products
- His presentation is exceptional
- The process of delivering the product or services is customer centric

"Good service is giving people a little more than they expect; Excellent service is enjoying giving people a little more than what they expect." To make it happen, one must have a passion for service excellence. Anyone who pursues excellence in service should do it with energy and enthusiasm. Marketing can create a customer but it is only service that can keep the customers with the company.

Create a Customer's Delight

Good service is not just smiling at your customers, but getting your customers to smile at you. Wherever we go, whether it is a bank, a shopping mall or a showroom, our experience is being managed. This means that companies or banks make a conscious effort to create an ambience that will make you comfortable, relaxed and happy. However, there are many instances when companies lose sight of the basics. The same is true for individuals who work in the market and sell what the company produces. People working like this understand that at every "moment of truth" there are the following three possible results:

> Excellent salespersons see their job as not simply selling a product or service, but rather pleasing the customers.

- The customer will get less than what he expects and be disappointed (the service is awful).
- The customer will get exactly what he expects and therefore it is no big deal (it is forgettable).

- The customer gets service at a higher level than he expects and is delighted (it becomes memorable).

It is thus necessary for salespersons to understand how to create your customer's experience and make it a memorable one. Successful salespersons continuously examine all their moments of truth and plan to use them to their advantage.

The customer's experience is created by the 4 Ps; namely superb people skills, outstanding products, exceptional presentation and customer centric product/service delivery.

The First P – People Skills

There are six important areas where people skills can be developed. These are:

- Making people feel special
- Managing the first 30 and the last 30 seconds
- Outstanding attitude
- Clarity in communication
- Displaying a high energy level
- Performing well under pressure

To remember them the following has been aptly coined.

The customer comes 1st where "the first letter in the phrase 'comes 1st'" stands for:-

C	Clarity in communication
O	Outstanding attitude
M	Making people feel special
E	(show positive) Energy
S	Service
1st	First and Last 30 seconds

These five elements can be put into practice through actions as shown in Fig. 9.3.

The Second P – Product

As Tom Peters says in his book *In Search of Excellence, "A good service is not a substitute for junk."* Often, many companies are convinced that they can sell mediocre products with the sheer strength of their aggressive advertisement and sales promotion.

A company must commit itself to improving its product quality continuously. As stated by Barrie Hopson and Mike Scally in *12 Steps to Success through Service,* Edward Heath, after visiting China, quoted Dong-Xiao Ping to sum up what customer oriented production is really about. *"The Americans and Europeans come to us offering splendid goods and enquiring how much we want to buy ... the Japanese approach is to ask us what we want, how much we can afford to pay and then produce the goods."*

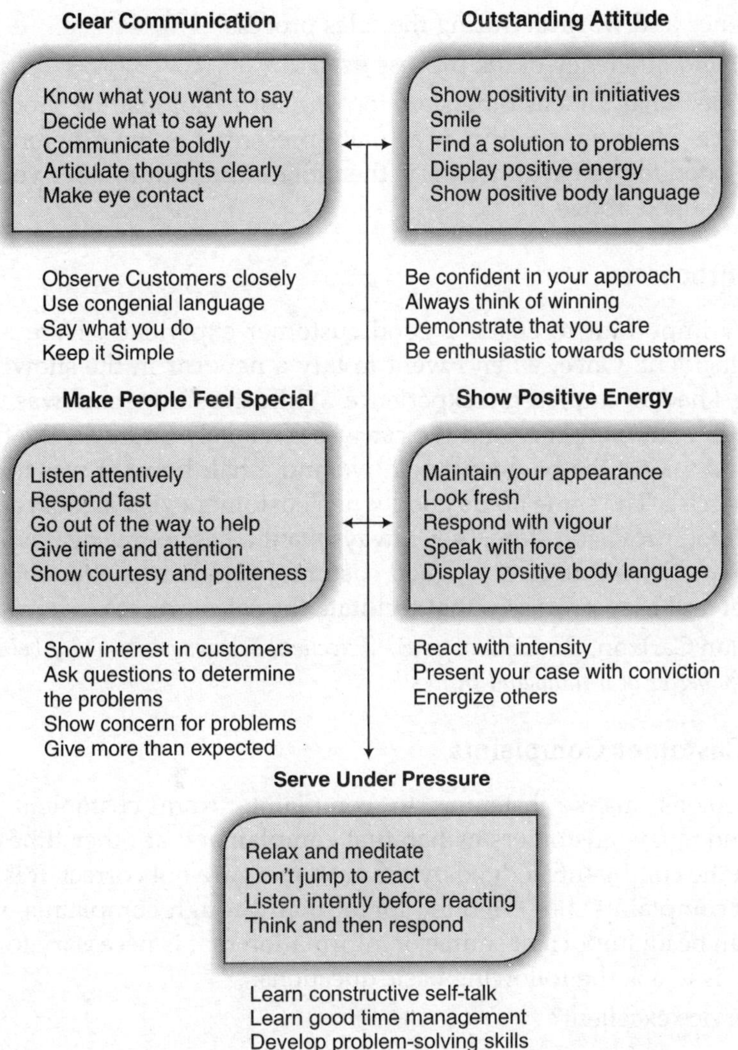

Fig. 9.3 *Elements for developing people skills*

The Third P – Presentation

Presentation is extremely important to create an excellent customer experience. Customers are generally influenced, for better or worse by the 'packaging that wraps the product'. This 'wrapping' includes:

- The physical ambience in which the customer actually buys the product
- The appearance of the sales personnel interacting with the customer
- The quality and richness of the sales catalogues and point-of-purchase material

- The ambience and warmth during the sales process
- The speed and efficiency of the process itself

Most of the time, what the customers are looking for is not just the product, but a total customer experience. How the product is actually presented is the difference between the various offerings extended to customers. It is therefore important to offer your product in a nice 'packaging' as stated above.

The Fourth P – Processes

Processes are very important to create a good customer experience. Here I would like to share a personal incident. Once, when I went to buy a new car in the showroom of a very famous car dealer, I had an unpleasant experience. While the show room was very plush, the behaviour of people extremely nice and the car was obviously fantastic; the final process of preparing a bill and taking the payment took two and a half hours! I was totally disgusted with the whole exercise. The same holds good when customers visit a bank, a shopping mall or our neighbourhood provision store, they always want a hassle-free deal while buying any product. If a company wishes to create a good customer experience, efforts must be made to ensure simple, fast and easy processes that facilitate the sales process.

According to Jan Carlzon, Ex-CEO of SAS, *"Excellent service is not about being 1000% better at one thing, but 1% better at a thousand things!"*

Learning from Customer Complaints

Normally salespersons dislike listening to complaints from customers. Often, many salespersons 'brand' some customers as habitual complainers; at other times, many others think that most of the complaints lodged by the customers are not correct. It is true that none of us like to hear complaints. But we often forget that through complaints, we can learn a lot. Complaints can be an important source of information that is necessary for any business. What is necessary is to ask the following basic questions:

- Is your service excellent?
- Do you care to resolve customers' problem fast?
- Do your customers have faith and trust in the quality of your service?
- Do your customers feel that it is useless to complain, or
- Are they fed up of complaining as they feel that your company is insensitive to solve their problems?

As we mentioned earlier complaints can be a source of learning. The biggest difficulty is to unearth them. It has been found that:

- On an average, 96% of the customers are dissatisfied, but do not complain.
- For every complaint received, there will be another 26 customers with problems out of which at least six will be serious.

- People do not complain because they think it is not worth the time and effort, they do not know how or where to complain, or they believe the company will be indifferent to them.
- Non-complainers are the least likely group to buy from the company again. A complainer, who gets a response, is more likely to come back. Between 65% to 90% of the non complainers will never buy from you again and you will never know why.
- A company needs to welcome complaints as a second chance to retain customers.
- Even if a complaint that has been made is not satisfactorily dealt with, it makes the customer 10% more likely to come back – just being able to complain helps.
- When a customer complains, and the matter is dealt with satisfactorily, 54% will buy again.
- If the complaint is dealt with quickly and efficiently, the retention rate rises to 90 – 95%. (The above figures refer to major purchases such as domestic appliances, motor cars or an insurance policy).
- For smaller purchases such as food items, clothes or household goods, 37% of unhappy non-complainers will not purchase again, 82% of complainers will, if their complaint is handled well.
- Damage may not be restricted to the person with the complaint. A customer who has had an unpleasant experience will tell an average of 9-10 other people; 13% of those with a complaint will tell more than 20 others.
- When a complainant has received a satisfactory response they will tell only half the number of people and will talk about it positively.

(*Source:* Barrie Hopson & Mike Scally; *12 Steps to Success through Service*, p-100)

So, take care of customers' complaints. They will help you to improve.

Stay Close to Your Customers

The importance of staying close to the customers cannot be underestimated. As Tom Peters and Waterman Jr. have clearly emphasized in their famous book *In Search of Excellence, "Marketing strategies should not be made in the antiseptic environment of the ivory tower but in the mud of the marketplace."* The basic question here is "How do we stay close to our customers?"

> The most significant part of any business is to understand the customer and his needs, and be in touch with him all the time – by walking around, talking to them and not just sitting in the office and basing decisions on the basis of presumptions.

The following simple steps will help in this respect.

- Have a continuous dialogue with customers
- Senior management should interact with customers periodically
- Have a dialogue through company newsletters and magazines
- Have a collaborative relationship with customers

- Reinforce the relationship with customers through excellent service
- Educate the customers
- Treat customers as your appreciating assets
- Offer them a little bit more, as good service is giving a little more than they expect

Set Service Standards

It is necessary to set benchmarks in service if you want to excel in it. A typical organization with exemplary service level has the following three attributes:

- A commitment to quality by everyone in the company.
- An understanding by everyone of what represents quality service in the eyes of customers (internal as well as external).
- A translation of those expectations into specific performance standards which are the basis of assessment and rewards.

Service standards are important as they help us to take concrete steps to ensure quality. To make them more effective, service standards should be set in accordance with the following principles:

- Service standards should be decided after talking to the customer and after studying the competition.
- They should be finalized after interacting with the persons who will implement them.
- They should identify critical success areas of business that affect the customers most and start with these areas.
- Standards should address both 'soft' and 'hard' aspects of service.

Some of the key standards of service include:

- Written correspondence
- Speed of response through telephone
- Response time after complaint
- Queuing time
- Ease of access to information
- Periodicity of customer contact etc.

Establish a Customer Service Culture

In-depth interaction with customers reveals that most customers are not displeased by poor products, but rather by a disappointing customer experience. The eight critical steps to establish a customer service culture are briefly given below.

1. Customers are the reason for work, not an interruption of work

Though this is an obvious fact, most companies ignore it. How many times have you waited to get attention from the customer care executive who was perhaps busy on the telephone or busy doing something urgent? How many times have you failed to talk to the senior managers of the company trying to tell them your grievances but they were busy in meetings configuring sales strategies? Employees often lose sight of the significance of the customer and spend their energies in lesser day to day tasks. Good customer service must be a priority for you and your team.

> Without your customers, you have no company!

2. Skill development through training

Salespeople need to enhance their competencies continuously to meet the challenges of the market. Competence primarily has three aspects – knowledge, skills and attitude. While it is absolutely necessary for salespersons to upgrade their knowledge base and learn new facets of sales management, it is equally important for them to sharpen their selling skills continuously and learn new tools and techniques that can be applied in the field to maximize the results. It is also necessary for them to keep their spirits high to face the odds that come daily in the market.

> Training should not be looked upon as leisure time but as time to think, time to look into your own weaknesses, analyze your failures and find answers to overcome these weaknesses.

Enhancement of competencies can be done by training. However, training should not be looked upon as leisure time but as time to think, time to look into your own weaknesses, analyze your failures and find answers to overcome these weaknesses. Behavioural training is significant in this respect as ultimately it is these soft skills like inter-personal relationships, keeping commitments, sticking to time schedules and truthfulness that create a liking for a particular salesperson amongst customers.

3. Empowerment

You should delegate powers to your sales people so that they can take decisions on the spot for serving the customer better. This needs the backing of a strong system that ensures speed, exceptional service and resolution of issues should a customer become disgruntled. There should be a structured system that helps to serve customers. These decisions might relate to local advertisements, settlement of some minor claims or giving some extra discounts for gaining a big order. Such positive gestures will create a "memorable" customer experience and can go a long way in business relationship with your customers.

4. Make service personal

Try to greet customers by name, if possible. Welcome them with warmth and give personalized attention to them. Listen attentively to what they say and respond to their queries speedily. Your body language should be highly positive and your eye contact with your customers should be perfect. Creating service that is personal will not only retain customers, but help diffuse difficult situations should they arise.

> Your body language should be highly positive and your eye contact with your customers should be perfect.

5. Offer a solution

The customer may flood you with problems when you meet him. Do not get upset; keep your cool and try to note them down in your notebook. Try to find immediate solutions for your customer's problems. If this is not possible, assure them that they will be solved once you go back to your office. But, do not forget to solve them once you are in your office. Consider it a priority, solve them with the help of your superiors if necessary, and inform the customer immediately. However, if the problem cannot be solved due to company rules, clearly explain any limitations that exist and make the customer understand why they cannot be solved.

6. Ask your customers what they think of your service

The best way to find how satisfied your customers are is to ask them. Go out and talk to your customers and staff informally. Ask them how they feel about the service you are providing. Ideally, use a combination of visiting the market and talking to your customers. Do not always look for positive comments only. Negative comments from your customers may be crucial in helping you to improve customer service. Other methods include customer surveys, questionnaires, interviews or suggestion.

7. It is alright to say "yes", even when you should say "no"

Be with your staff when they take customer service decisions. Often, they may be wrong. An employee can act without concern for repercussions, when fulfilling a customer's need. This normally comes with a strong urge to serve the customer. Saying 'no' to a customer can have huge implications on your business. Salespersons should be guided and counselled about this. Sometimes, however, a salesperson might be afraid of losing a customer and say 'yes' when it would have been better to refuse the customer, because his needs cannot be fulfilled by your product.

Most customers do not voice their disappointment with your level of service. They will simply leave and never return. If you do not ask about the quality of your service, you are liable to make wrong assumptions and become complacent. You may also feel that you need not improve your service levels further because you get few complaints and so are doing very well.

Every interaction is a customer service opportunity. Asking your customers about their satisfaction sends a message to them that you are concerned about them and their problems. While you are sure to hear some criticism, you might also learn what you are doing right and what you should improve upon. Moreover, such interactions also help in creating and reinforcing bonds with your customers which are invaluable for long-term business.

> One has to be continually alert about the customer's difficulties and find ways and means to resolve them.

Most of us wish to do business with people who give good service. We might not say anything, but we reward good service providers by continuing to do business with them. If the service is exceptional, we will probably tell our friends and colleagues about it. However, if we receive poor service, we are liable to just leave.

It is therefore necessary for a steady and dedicated customer support service that will reinforce relationships with customers through excellent customer service. Understanding their problems, sensing their irritations and delivering what they want, is an important factor in an organization's success. Since the market is in constant flux, one needs a consistent and committed approach in order to gauge and be in touch with the changing whims of consumers. The fact that there needs to be an intense focus on customer care is indisputable. Acquiring new customers as well as keeping existing customers satisfied by anticipating their needs can only be done through excellent customer support.

Customers' needs can be met through physical service needs such as timely delivery, responding to complaints, ensuring easy availability of spare parts and products; or fulfilling their emotional needs, i.e., how a customer feels about the service. While the former is part of the offering and is essential for customer satisfaction, emotions are part of their overall experience. We often forget that fulfilling emotional needs of customers is also a key part of our offering and something we have to deliberately design into the experience. We want to connect with our customers and make sure that through fulfilment of emotional needs, we build a relationship that over a period of time creates loyal customers.

> Connecting on an emotional level is an important part of the brand experience and helps in our journey from a share in the market to a share in the mind and finally to a share in the heart.

THE ABC OF CUSTOMER SERVICE

If you want your customers to be happy and loyal to you, there is no better way to reach them than through the ABC of customer service.

A – Attention to detail
B – Benefits for the customers
C – Commitment
D – Dedication
E – Empathy
F – Fairness
G – Giving
H – Helpfulness
I – Impact
J – Justice
K – Kindness
L – Loyalty
M – Meticulousness
N – Newness
O – Openness
P – Pride
Q – Quality
R – Responsiveness
S – Sincerity
T – Truthfulness
U – Understanding
V – Value
W – Weight
X – eXtraordinary
Y – Yes
Z – a good night's Zzzzz

A sharp salesperson must practise these attitudes and skills, he will then love his job and his customers will love him.

Keeping Promises

Today, very few companies enjoy customer loyalty, as consumers are suspicious about company promises. This is because companies often do not deliver what they promised resulting in unpleasant experiences for the customer. Many times, the products do not have the attributes projected in the commercials, assurances given by their dealers are generally not met and there is always a lot to be desired in the services given by the companies.

> Making a promise is not enough to get customers flocking to your door. One has to demonstrate by living the promises and giving customers a reason to believe that your promise is not another empty one.

Today, consumers are more realistic. Their desires are now based on experience rather than expectations. Consumers now expect results from companies. They have become distrustful and assume that certain things will likely not go their way. When the inevitable letdown occurs they look for a similar product or service provider elsewhere. Consumers who have been disappointed with the company's service for some time, often not only do not buy but also spread the word that the products and the company, manufacturing the products, are unreliable.

Companies need to change these negative expectations. A good salesperson has to communicate the "what" and the "how" to your customers. The promise is "what" you say you are doing. The reason to believe is "how" you do it. Marketers call these the pillars of the promise. However, customers will believe in you if you keep your promises and deliver to your customers.

SIMPLE STEPS TO CUSTOMER SERVICE EXCELLENCE

Often, customers are not happy because of the unsatisfactory product or service or slow response of the company to his calls or emails. Maybe they did not do what they promised. Or they made the customer run around when he called to report a problem or ask a question.

All these negative experiences reflect lack of customer service, which usually stems from lack of passion to serve the customer. It has been seen that many customers are lost because the salesperson simply lost sight of whom he has to serve and how. Of course, there could be numerous occasions when you come across totally unreasonable customers who are unhappy with you and your services most of the time. Instead of shying away from them, you have to deal with them. You have to understand that basically all customers are good and assess whether they come within the scope of your sales operations; if they do, all efforts have to be made to resolve their complaints. There is however a catch here, because at times, customers complain either because they do not want to take the material or they do not have the money to pay for it. A good salesperson will have to evaluate the situation and take a decision in this regard.

So make it a point to listen to your customers genuinely. Take a pledge to take care of your entire customers well. After all, giving impressive customer services is one of the finest marketing tools available to increase sales. When you care for your customers well, and deliver beyond their expectations, customers will respond happily. These contented clients will refer you to their acquaintances who will also buy from you.

The opposite is also true. If you dissatisfy a client, or do not deliver what you assure, or you just treat them shoddily, they will likely tell all their acquaintances about their bad experience. In fact, those displeased customers are more likely to talk about you than your contented clients.

Below, are ten tips to help you deliver excellent customer service.

1. Be Available

Your customers should have easy access to you, or someone in your company, as and when they need service. Your availability to your customers should be "24 x 7". To ensure that, you have to provide multiple ways for your customers to get in contact with you, such as email, phone, mail or fax.

2. Respond with Speed

Make it a point to respond to all customer queries within the shortest possible time. If you cannot commit to that, then determine what timeframe you can manage and let your customers know upfront that they can hope to hear back from you within that specified amount of time.

3. Listen to Your Customers

Often when a customer calls or writes to complain, they just want to be heard patiently. In fact, sometimes, just listening is all you need to do. Take time to listen to what your consumers have to state before you start reacting or defending your product or service. They may just have a point.

4. Respect Your Customers

Even when the customer is behaving irrationally, or is discourteous, do not lower yourself to their level by reciprocating. You must treat every customer with respect. It will help resolve the customer's problem amicably. Sometimes, the customer might have had a bad day, and his undesirable behaviour with you could be the result of that.

5. Never Argue with Your Customers

Long back, Dale Carnegie made a million dollar point in his famous book *How to Win Friends and Influence People*, *"The best way to win an argument is to avoid it"*. In fact you can never win an argument with a customer, because if you do win, you will have alienated the customer and you will lose the business. We all know the customer is not always right, but instead of focusing on what went wrong and defending yourself, think of how you can solve the problem or fix the situation.

6. Honour Your Commitments

It is vital to honour the commitments made to your customers. Be sure you do not make false commitments to meet your sales targets. If you say you will settle a customer's claim, settle it come what may. If you have given a discount to the customer on a certain invoice to get more sales, send a credit note as fast as possible after you go back to the office. If you offer a guarantee, then honour it. Nothing damages customer relationship more than not honouring a promise.

7. Do What You Say You are Going to Do

If you say you are going to call someone on Tuesday, call them on Tuesday. If you have an appointment at 5 pm, meet your customer at 5 pm sharp. It builds your credibility as a person who values his words. If you want your customers to trust and believe you, you have to do what you say.

8. Build Relationships

The long-term success of your business rests on your ability to have a long-term relationship with the customer. If you sacrifice relationships to make short-term sales or do not base your sales on facts, your business will be short-lived.

9. Be Honest

Be honest in your dealings. Here honesty means transparency and fairness in whatever you do in your business with your customers. This can be achieved by implementing company policies justly and equitably, tackling customer problems with fairness and creating examples through fairness and honesty so that the customer has faith and trust in you. Do not promise things you cannot deliver just to make a sale. Be honest and direct about what your products and services can deliver.

10. Admit it when You make a Mistake

Often, salespeople commit mistakes in the market. Mistakes are a part of our learning and help us to perform better in the future. So when you make a mistake, do not cover it up or deny it. Just confess to it and if necessary, do something to amend it. Your customers will understand and they will be more likely to remain loyal customers.

Make it a point to follow these ten guidelines religiously. Make them the purpose of your business. It is one of the important keys to marketing success and best of all, does not cost much!

THE MOST IMPORTANT CUSTOMER SERVICE QUESTION

It is said that "If marketing is the fuel for your business then customer service is the octane." The higher the octane, the better your business will run. Customer service is actually the most critical part of the marketing process. When it becomes increasingly difficult to differentiate your products from those of your competitors, differentiation by offering excellent and unique services, holds the key to selling success. It affects word of mouth marketing and your credibility and reputation; excellent customer service helps to establish you as a brand.

It is thus important to answer the most important question – Will your customers recommend your products or services to someone else? The question is critical as recommendations of your product or services to friends and family demonstrate your customers' confidence in the quality of your products or services. It is also a tribute to your business that your customers become your spokespersons, through word of mouth publicity.

Word of mouth publicity is one of the best, most trustworthy and cost effective forms of converting prospects to actual buyers. There really is nothing better than the testimonial of a customer regarding your products and services to others. Not only does it help to establish a pattern of loyalty and influence the purchasing behaviour of potential buyers, it also helps customers to take buying decision speedily. Consider the products or services you support. A product or service suggested to you means much more to the prospect than any advertising or sales promotion activity initiated by the company.

Word of mouth publicity is one of the best, most trustworthy and cost effective forms of converting prospects to actual buyers.

Customer recommendations make great marketing tools. An endorsement, testimonial or case study is an excellent tool to help establish validity of the quality of your service. Your sales promotion campaign can explain how your product or service solves your customer's problems but when a customer says it, it is more effective.

An endorsement, testimonial or case study is an excellent tool to help establish validity of the quality of your service.

So find out what kind of service your customers want and what services are not offered by others. The following steps will be helpful in making a comprehensive service plan for your sales territory.

- Determine the service needs of customers and prepare an action plan to give these services.
- Design systems to find out whether customers advocate your products or services. This can be done through surveys, incentive programs where customers receive a benefit by recommending you to others or by simply tracking how customers heard about you.
- Ask your customers to involve themselves in a referral programme. Every time someone recommends your product or service and a sale is made, reward them for this nice gesture. Build strong relationships with your customers and strike an emotional bond with them. Let them feel that they are part of you. This is the key to getting customers who are more than happy to recommend you to others.

ACTION PLAN TO IMPROVE CUSTOMER SERVICE

Customer service is all about the customer's perception. You have to do more than just get the job done. You must deliver on all the things (big and small) that affect the relationship with your client. You may think of finding opportunities for improvement in the following areas.

Understanding expectations – Try to understand the expectations of your customers. These expectations may not be very difficult to fulfil, but are important – a smile when you meet them, warmth when you talk to them, paying more attention to what they say, etc. May be a customer wants to talk to you and share his happiness and sorrows. Most of these expectations are "implicit". They are latent and you will have to identify them as does a trained psychologist. These seemingly trivial things can mean a big difference to your business.

> Try to understand the expectations of your customers. These expectations may not be very big to fulfil.

Communication – Most of the time, we do not communicate with our customers. We meet them with some preconceived notions and prejudices. This creates cracks in the relationship and we lose a good customer and his precious sales. Create mechanisms to ensure direct, open and free communication with your customers at every stage of the engagement, from initiating the sales to the post sales service as and when required. Be absolutely certain about your objectives, what has been initiated, what is coming up next, who is responsible, what results you can expect, etc. Above all find out if your customer is happy with all you are doing for him?

> When you meet your clients, see that you have done your homework and are prepared to make them feel comfortable and taken care of.

Spadework – Are you prepared? Even though you have done it hundreds, maybe thousands of times before, do you take the time to organize and prepare to make it the best customer experience possible?

Committing to the little things – Do not ever underestimate the power of little things. Together they can make all the difference and really distinguish you from the competition. Returning calls and emails in a timely manner; providing valuable information to customers on a regular basis; showing your appreciation for your clients through things like thank you notes, exclusive client-only briefings, and open house, etc. are very important.

Clearly these are not the only significant areas for creating great customer service. I am sure you can think of more. But, start following just one of these areas and create an action plan to improve your business. Make a commitment to continuously improve the level of service you are providing and see how it pays off. When you have worked on one area, pick another area and work on that area.

Customer service is more than just smile training – it is about treating people the way they want to be treated. It is also about giving the clients what they want, when they want it and how they want it. It really comes down to the fact that good communication and human relations skills equal good customer relations.

KEY CONCEPTS

- Customer service is a critical factor to success in business; creation and delivery of services is increasingly becoming the leading edge and a standard practice for business.
- When price wars fail to increase sales, excellent service helps in giving competitive advantage to companies.
- Good customer service is defined as: "Giving customers a little more than what they expect."
- A good salesperson has to be a prudent psychologist capable of understanding his customers so well that he always tries to satisfy the customer's demands skilfully.
- Having a vision helps in directing your energies to a fruitful conclusion and ignites the spark to launch initiatives.
- To achieve success through service you need to manage the customer's experience with you, your product and your company.
- Good service is giving people a little more than they expect; Excellent service is enjoying giving people a little more than what they expect.
- Create a customer's experience; good service is not just smiling at your customers, but getting your customers to smile at you.
- Remember that good service is not a substitute for junk. Service, supported by aggressive advertisement and sales promotion, can never substitute mediocre products.
- Presentation is extremely important to creating an excellent customer experience. Customers are generally influenced, for better or worse by the 'packaging that wraps the product'.
- Processes are imperative to create a good customer experience. Remember that excellent service is not about being 1000% better at one thing, but 1% better at a thousand things!
- Complaints can be good lessons in a business. The biggest difficulty is to unearth them.
- Customers are the reason for work, not an interruption of work. Though an obvious fact, most companies ignore it. Remember, without your customers, you have no company!
- The best way to find how satisfied your customers are is to ask them.
- Most customers do not voice their disappointment with your service levels. They will simply leave and never return. If you do not ask about the quality of your service, you might make wrong assumptions and become complacent.
- Every interaction is a customer service opportunity. Asking your customers if they are satisfied sends a message to them that you are concerned about them and their problems.
- If you want your customers to be happy and be loyal to you, you must have a positive attitude.
- Keep your promises; making a promise is not enough. One has to demonstrate by living the promises and giving customers a reason to believe that you mean what you say.
- Listen to your customers genuinely. Take a pledge to take care of your customers well. Giving impressive customer services, is one of the finest marketing tools available to increase sales.

- Respond to all customer queries with speed. If you cannot commit to that, then determine what timeframe you can manage and let your customers know upfront that they can hope to hear back from you within that specified amount of time.
- Take time to listen to what your consumers have to state before you start reacting or defending your product or service. They may just have a point.
- Do not promise things you cannot deliver just to make a sale. Be honest and direct about what your products and services can deliver.
- Remember "If marketing is the fuel for your business then customer service is the octane." The higher the octane, the better your business will run.

METRO MANUFACTURING CO. LTD.

Metro Manufacturing Co. Ltd. was a big manufacturer and distributor of commercial chemicals. It was situated in an industrial city in Noida, near Delhi. Last year, about 73% of its sales volume came from New Delhi and adjoining areas.

S. Pillai, Metro's head of purchasing, had been with the firm for nine years. Before that he was in the purchasing department of a major steel company in Durgapur.

One day last January, Pillai had granted an appointment to Mr. R.K. Roy, a sales representative for a well-known office equipment manufacturer in Chandigarh. Pillai and Roy had never met each other before the meeting and Metro had never bought any equipment from Roy's company. About 20 minutes before the planned 10:30 appointment, Pillai received a long-distance call from Roy in which the conversation went as follows:

Roy: Mr. Pillai, I'm sorry, but I will not be able to keep the appointment I had fixed with you last week. I have some other important assignments here in Chandigarh and I will not be able to reach Noida to meet you before 2 pm. The urgent assignments just came up yesterday morning.

Pillai: Oh, that is too bad!

Roy: I am sorry that we won't have a chance to meet, since I have to be in Mumbai tomorrow morning. But could we set up an engagement next month, when I'll be in your area?

Pillai: Yes, that would be alright with me. Let me transfer you back to my secretary, who will make an appointment for you.

Roy: That's great.

Pillai: However, if you run into similar 'important assignments' again, please give me a little bit more notice. This has upset my entire schedule today.

Roy: Don't worry about this happening again. I shall take care in future and will see that I keep my promise.

Subsequently, another meeting was scheduled between the two men in late February. At the prearranged time, Roy entered Pillai's office.

Roy: Good morning, Mr. Pillai, I am happy that we finally have an opportunity to meet. I do apologise again for missing the appointment last month.

Pillai: That's OK. Now, let me see, as I recall you wanted to tell me about that new range of filing systems your company has brought out.

Roy: Yes, I do! We've had astounding success with these filing systems. It seems that just about everyone is ordering them... We think that they will end up with 45 to 52 percent of the market.

The company did some very careful research on matching filing systems to the physical distinctiveness of the individuals who use them. As a consequence, we came up with three general kinds of users. We termed them as Stile, Esteem, and Pride user profiles. Our studies demonstrated that people using the right size filing systems were more productive. Let me show you how these filing systems work.

Roy showed Pillai booklets and graphic displays of the new product. After an extensive sales presentation, during which Pillai sat and listened patiently, Roy said:

Roy: Aren't they wonderful? Like I said, we think they will transform the industry.

Pillai: Possibly yes.

Roy: Mr. Pillai, we would be happy if you could come down to Chandigarh at our expense to look at the new filing systems. I'm sure that once you see them, you will concur that they are just the thing for those brand new offices you are going to be opening.

Pillai: Well, I don't think I'll have a chance to get down to Chandigarh for another month or so. Besides, I kind of like the cushioned stuff offered by Newtech Designs. In fact, their representative was in here to see me last month, the same day you had your 'important assignments'.

Questions

1. How do you feel Mr. Roy handled Mr. Pillai?
2. If you were Roy, how would you proceed?

REFERENCES

1. Armstrong, Robert W., Pecotich, Anthony (1993), Does the Sales Manager Make a Difference? The Impact of Sales Management Succession Upon Departmental Performance, *Journal of Personal Selling & Sales Management*, Vol. 13 Issue 4, pp. 15-24.
2. Asugman, Gulden, Johnson, Jean L., McCullough, James, (1997), The Role of After-Sales Service in International Marketing, *Journal of International Marketing*, Vol. 5 Issue 4, pp. 11-28.
3. Bundschuh, Russell G., Dezvane, Theodore M. (2003), How to Make After-sales Services Pay Off, *McKinsey Quarterly*, Issue 4, pp. 116-127.
4. Cohen, Morris A., Agrawal, Narendra, Agrawal, Vipul (2006), Winning in the Aftermarket, *Harvard Business Review*, Vol. 84 Issue 5, pp. 129-138.

5. Das, Gopal, Kumar, Rohit Vishal (2009), Impact of Sales Promotion on Buyers Behaviour: An Empirical Study of Indian Retail Customers. *Globsyn Management Journal*, Vol. 3 Issue 1, pp. 11-24.
6. Davidson, Craig (2011), If You Want to Sell, Paint a Picture, *Employee Benefit Advisor*, Vol. 9 Issue 4, pp. 70-71.
7. Davidson, Craig J. (2010), Pre- and post-sales Tactics. *Employee Benefit Advisor*, Vol. 8 Issue 8, pp. 64-65.
8. Heselbarth, Rob (2009), Managing Post-sale Relations, *Residential Design & Build*, Vol. 74 Issue 2, pp. 24-28.
9. Hull, Sam (2010), Transferring Client Trust. *Journal of Financial Planning, Practice Management*, pp. 24-26.
10. Ives, Blake, Vitale, Michael R (1988), After the Sale: Leveraging Maintenance with Information Technology, *MIS Quarterly*, Vol. 12 Issue 1, pp. 7-21.
11. Kabiraj, Sajal, Shanmugan, Joghee (2009), Indigenous Customer Relationship Management Practices in Indian Automobile Companies: Strategic Implications, *International Journal of Management Perspectives*, Vol. 1 Issue 4, pp. 1-25.
12. Kurata, Hisashi, Nam, Seong-Hyun (2010), After-sales Service Competition in a Supply Chain: Optimization of Customer Satisfaction Level or Profit or Both? *International Journal of Production Economics*, Vol. 127 Issue 1, pp. 136-146.
13. Posselt, Thorsten; Gerstner, Eitan (2005), Pre-sale vs. Post-sale e-satisfaction: Impact on Repurchase Intention and Overall Satisfaction, *Journal of Interactive Marketing* (John Wiley & Sons), Vol. 19 Issue 4, pp. 35-47.
14. Shih, Stephen C. (2007), A Three-stage Field Service Management Model for Effective Post-sales Service Supply Chain Management. *International Journal of Manufacturing Technology & Management*, Vol. 12 Issue 4, pp. 384-404.

10 Managing Yourself for Success

"The greatest discovery of my generation is that human beings can alter their lives by altering their attitudes of mind."

—*William James*

CHAPTER OUTLINE

- ✦ Introduction
- ✦ Managing yourself
- ✦ Analyzing productive and unproductive activities
- ✦ The aims of a salesperson
- ✦ Managing yourself for success
- ✦ Self discipline
- ✦ Managing time
- ✦ Sales reporting

OBJECTIVES

After studying this chapter, you will be able to:

- ✦ Understand the importance of managing yourself to achieve success in the sales profession
- ✦ Distinguish between productive and non-productive work and concentrate more on the former to obtain positive results
- ✦ Rise to a high level of ethical rectitude that is essential for success in the field of selling

Opening Case: Bass Electronics

Mr. Dilip K. Poddar passed B.Sc physics honours from Loyola College, Chennai. After that Mr. Poddar did a one-year course in sales and marketing from IGNOU, an autonomous educational institution set up by the Government of India. Poddar joined Bass Electronics as a territory manager and was assigned to western Maharashtra. His company manufactured a wide range of consumer electronics products like televisions, DVDs, CD players and CDs and marketed them through a network of dealers. He was asked to develop a strong distribution channel in western Maharashtra. So Poddar's job involved appointing authorized dealers in major towns and establishing a service network. Poddar had previous experience in selling electronics goods in a small company in Delhi where he was the sales executive for five years before joining Bass Electronics. He knew that setting up an entire sales network was really difficult. But at the end he found the challenges really enjoyable and a great experience. As he stepped into his new task he realised the difficulties in setting up a sales network in a fiercely competitive market like western Maharashtra. He had to work hard to do the ground work at the start.

Within a year Mr. Poddar was able to establish a network of 37 dealers spread over 9 towns. The sales grew by 26% in that period of time, 88% of the sales target could be achieved and there was a 23 days outstanding level in the market.

However, Poddar faced some typical problems. As the familiarity of his company's name and products was not very high, dealers were not very enthusiastic to stock larger quantities. In fact, he had to push his products to the dealers by devising different trade promotion schemes. As a result the dealers' outstanding payments were increasing and within a year the outstanding levels touched 50 days. The profile of his dealers showed that out of 37 dealers, there were only 3 big dealers and 7 medium category dealers, the rest were small dealers. As a result his sales growth was not consistent. In the current year, Bass Electronics set ambitious targets, such as, a 35% growth in sales turnover, expansion of the dealer network to 60 and outstanding levels to reduce to 30 days.

Poddar knew that if he was to succeed and meet his targets, he would have to manage himself well, plan his time and tasks well, and approach the market in a systematic manner.

Question

1. Suggest how Poddar should manage himself.

MANAGING YOURSELF FOR SUCCESS

Integral Design for Programmed Learning

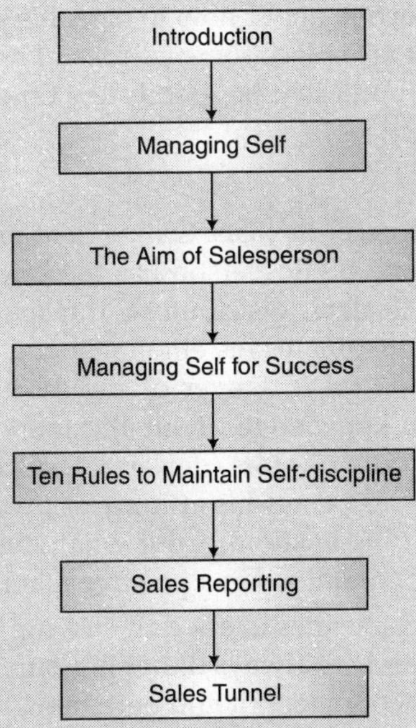

"To be what we are, and to become what we are capable of becoming, is the only end of life."

Robert Louis Stevenson

INTRODUCTION

The daily routine of a typical salesperson is something like this: He goes to meet his distributors/stockists, enquires about the present stock level, talks about the next order and meets some of the dealers/retailers, and collects the payments, which is essential. Towards the end of the month he gets worried about how to meet his sales target. At times he cajoles or persuades his channel members to place some additional orders or else 'dumps' the goods without orders. It is invariably found that he spends less time for his personal growth.

MANAGING YOURSELF

Self-management is essential to excel in sales. Selling as a profession requires tremendous self-discipline and self-regulation. A salesperson has to network or manage diverse group of people, such as customers, dealers, distributors, transporters etc. However, unless he regulates his emotional and physical self carefully, there is a great danger of success eluding him in spite of all his knowledge about the market and his skills of handling distributors/dealers or customers. What is crucial in this respect is his attitude or predisposition towards his duties, his wisdom about what is right and his ability to face all situations in a positive manner.

> Self-management is the unique ability to handle emotions, feelings, sentiments, thoughts and attitude with the single objective of winning in the marketplace.

Salespersons face different challenges every day, striving to meet newer expectations of customers. They face new odds and are always under pressure of time. Efficient management of all these requires tremendous courage, grit and determination on the part of salespersons. Those who overcome these odds, emerge as the winners. They are successful and are admired for their ability.

Self-management is the unique quality to handle emotions, feelings, sentiments, thoughts and one's attitude. Managing oneself means managing time, controlling emotions, avoiding distractions and focusing on the targets.

THE AIMS OF A SALESPERSON

The aim of any salesperson is to achieve his targets with respect to sales, collections; appoint new dealers; gauge competitors' activities etc. However, there are both productive and unproductive activities, but all activities are important as they have a bearing on sales. Some of these specific activities are as follows:

Productive Activities

- Sales calls
- Maximizing collections
- Handling customer complaints
- Meeting customers' expectations

- Managing stocks at distributors'/stockists' level
- Setting up sales promotion and point-of-purchase materials at the outlets
- Ensuring a steady flow of supplies from the factories
- Monitoring competitors' activities including prices
- Exploring new customers and markets
- Solving old, pending issues/problems of customers
- Contacting customers, transporters, etc.

Non-productive Activities

- Travelling
- Waiting to meet customers/dealers/distributors;
- Administrative work like writing reports, preparing statistics and getting ready for sales conferences.

Productive Activities

Sales calls

Making sales calls is the first most important activity for any salesperson. It is the first step to sales and the foundation to success in business. Every company has a set rule as far as making sales calls is concerned and every salesperson tries his best to convert his sales calls into productive ones. Though most of the time, they may achieve their aim, at times they fail. The main reasons for failure are:

- Lack of thorough homework before meeting prospects.
- Actions not taken on problems raised by them in the previous meeting.
- Inadequate time and attention given to them.
- Inability to meet their expectations.
- Not keeping promises.

Things to remember:

- Visit the prospect when he gives you an appointment and not at your convenience.
- Offer proper solutions to their problems.
- Do not waste prospects' time.
- Do not thrust your products on your customers.
- Deliver what you have promised previously.

Maximizing collections

No sale is complete until payments for the same are collected and deposited with the company. Once orders are procured, and goods are sent to the customer, payments have to be collected as per the established norms of the company. It is seen that collecting payments is the most difficult task of the entire sales function. In a cut-throat competitive market, supply far exceeds demand and in such a situation, the notion of indispensability pervades the channel – distributors, dealers, retailers and salespersons find it a hard task to collect payments in time.

The basic difficulty could be due to many reasons:

- The market does not know about the product or its attributes.
- The distribution channel is not keen to promote the product either because they are too busy dealing in other products/companies with greater "pull" or your product is not giving sufficient margins.
- The channel of distribution is such that the outlets are far away and are not easily accessible.
- The product is not available all the time.
- The product quality is not up to the mark.
- Service quality is unsatisfactory.
- The offering does not give "value for money."

The net result is a high outstanding in the market, which has a cascading effect on the liquidity of the company and also demoralizes the salespersons or the channel to promote the product for higher sales.

Handling customer complaints

A salesperson should be totally customer-focused and respond to customer complaints effectively. Research has shown that for every formal complaint there are over 25 unregistered complaints. Many dissatisfied customers simply withdraw and take their business elsewhere. Therefore, organizations that are truly committed to delivering superior customer performance work hard at providing their customers opportunities to complain. No organization is so perfect in the delivery of superior customer performance that dissatisfaction or complaints do not exist.

> Organizations that are truly committed to delivering superior customer performance work hard at providing their customers opportunities to complain.

Types of Complainers and How to Respond Effectively

Types of complainants	*Nature*	*Response*
Submissive customer	Generally, will not complain.	Must solicit comments even if no complaints are made and act appropriately.
Aggressive customer	Readily complains, often loudly and at length.	If a problem exists, indicate what will be done to resolve it and how soon. The aggressive customer does not like excuses.
Perfectionist customer	Expects the best and is willing to pay for it. Likely to complain in a reasonable manner, unless a hybrid of the aggressive customer.	Always listen and carefully ascertain the situation. Like the aggressive customer, these types of customers are not interested in excuses.

The rip-off customer	Try to to get the complaint resolved and also get something which the customer is not entitled to receive.	Remain unfailingly objective. Use accurate information to back up your response.
The chronic complainer customer	Is never satisfied; there is always something wrong.	To tackle such customers extraordinary patience is required. Unlike the rip-off customer, most chronic complainer customers will appreciate your efforts to make things right. Such customers appreciate your effort at the end.

There is a general saying that that for every customer complaint received, there are more complaints that are never expressed. Furthermore, a customer with a complaint is likely to tell others about his complaint. Therefore, every organization needs a mechanism or procedure to quickly resolve customer complaints.

Eight-step customer complaint process

Follow the eight-step customer complaint process, given below for dealing with customer complaints in your company:

1. Provide customers with the occasion to criticize.
2. Give customers your full and undivided attention.
3. Listen fully.
4. Ask the key question: "what else?"
5. Agree that a problem exists; never disagree or argue.
6. Apologize.
7. Redress the complaint. (Ask again: "what else?")
8. Thank the customer for bringing the complaint to your attention.

Use answers to these questions to improve your customer complaint.

Meeting customers' expectations

When we talk of meeting customer expectations, the basic question with which we can start is: What do customers want? One may cite a number of things that customers want – good quality products, efficient service, low price, discounts, delayed payments, credit, free maintenance guarantee (if required), speed in delivery etc. The question here is that most companies know these things but how many of them really fulfill these needs? Surveys have shown that most products and companies fail because of the companies' inability to deliver what they promise their customers. What is required is to first understand that customers want only two things – maximum value at the minimum delivery cost. Value is a bundle of benefits and includes everything that customers want. The degree to which a company delivers what is expected defines its success in the market. As sellers, you should therefore identify three things:

> Most products and companies fail because of the companies' inability to deliver what they promise their customers.

1. What value you propose to deliver.
2. How you are going to deliver the defined value.
3. How you are going to communicate the value that you have delivered.

Managing stocks at the distributors'/stockists' level

One of the expectations of customers is ready availability of stocks. More often than not, many salespersons face the problem of no stocks when they have orders for the same. At times, they blame the manufacturing set up or the transporters who have held up the material at some transit point.

Non availability of stocks mars the sales, annoys the dealers and gives a chance to the customers to shift to other manufacturers.

The only solution is to keep stock ready at hand to meet any sudden demand. The stock can be kept ready at three levels.

1. Branch warehouses
2. Stockists' godown
3. Retailers

While it is most desirable to keep stocks at the company warehouses and feed the market as and when needed, it adds to the inventory and the inventory carrying costs. Moreover, if a customer is in a hurry, getting stock from the warehouse to the dealer point may take more time than the customer's willing to wait for.

Retailers are generally reluctant to keep stocks because of two reasons: Retailers operate with very little liquidity and they have limited space to keep stock. Salespersons may try to stretch the retailers' capacity by having their products occupy the maximum "shelf space," but not beyond that. This can be achieved by organizing display contests or similar promotional campaigns.

The only option thus left is to ensure that your distributor/stockist keeps adequate stocks that are readily available to retailers. To ensure this, sales function should continuously have attractive discounts for the retailers so that there is a steady flow of goods from the distributor's end to the retailer on to the customer.

Setting up sales promotion and point-of-purchase materials at all outlets

Sales promotion refers to communication with individuals, groups or organizations to directly or indirectly facilitate exchanges by informing and persuading one or more audiences to accept an organization's products. Companies must communicate with their customers, and this communication should not be left to chance. Communication must be designed to address your specific target audience:

> Companies must communicate with their customers, and this communication should not be left to chance. Communication must be designed to address your specific target audience.

Some sales promotion methods

There are several methods to encourage and kindle the customers' desire to patronize a specific retail store or to try a specific product. Some of them are as follows:

- **Coupons** – These usually reduce the purchase price or are offered as cash. They need to state the offer clearly and make it easy to recognize.
- **Demonstrations** – These are excellent attention getters, though they involve high labour costs.
- **Frequent user incentives** – This is being followed in airlines and credit card companies and it helps to promote customer loyalty.
- **Point Of Purchase (POP) display** – This includes outside glow signs, window displays, counters, display racks. The POP display helps in keeping customers at the counter, ensures recall and persuades them to make a purchase decision. It is believed by retailers that point of purchase materials sell products.
- **Free samples** – This is done to stimulate trial of a product, increase sales volume at the early stage of the product life cycle and obtain desirable distribution. This is perhaps the most expensive sales promotion technique and it should be remembered that this method is not suitable for mature products and slow moving products.
- **Money refunds/rebates** – In this method, customers have to submit proof of purchase and they get a specific refund on multiple purchases. It helps to promote trial use, though due to the complexity of the refund, it has little impact. It is seen that customers have a poor perception of rebate offered products.
- **Consumer contests and sweepstakes** – In this method, consumers compete on the basis of their analytical or creative skills. This must be devised very carefully or be prepared to invite the wrath of customers/retailers. This is a method that evokes maximum response and has quick results.

Ensuring a steady flow of supplies from the factories

It is very important for a salesperson to ensure a steady flow of supplies from the factories. The salesperson must see that the product is always available to the customers/consumers. To make it happen he must make sure that there is no obstruction in the flow of goods from the factories to the company warehouse to the distributors and finally to the retail outlets. If there is any bottleneck, it is his responsibility to remove it and ensure a free flow of goods through the channel.

> The salesperson must see that the product is always available to the customers/consumers. To make it happen he must make sure that there is no obstruction in the flow of goods from the factories to the company warehouse on to the distributors and finally to the retail outlets.

If the delays are unavoidable, then a sharp salesperson will book orders in line with the goods available with the company at that particular point of time. In marketing terminology, it is called de-marketing where the demand of a particular product is underplayed and those goods, which are in supply, are promoted. Another way to tackle such a situation is to distinguish between good and not so good customers and supply goods to the former and request the latter to wait for some time (may be when any outstanding payments are cleared).

Monitoring competitors' activities including prices

Monitoring the activities of competitors is an arduous task. More often than not information about their activities is gathered by talking to the channel members. Though this provides important information, it can be quite confusing at times. This is so because such information is often modified by the prejudices of the channel member towards you and the competitors and can also be guided by his own business interests. What is important for salespersons is to explore the genuineness of the information received and cross-check it with information from other sources, which often is not the case.

Exploring new customers and markets

One of the tasks found difficult by salespersons is exploring new markets and sourcing new customers. The reasons why salespeople explore new markets and source new customers continuously are:

- Growth in sales depends a lot on the depth of your channel members and how widespread your distribution channel is.
- An extensive channel helps you to avoid over dependence on certain dealers who may not support you when you need them most.
- It helps in building confidence of customers in the product and company.
- It helps you to reach more and more customers and increase your market share.
- A widespread channel is an asset to any company and salespersons.

Solving old pending problems

One of the major sources of irritation for dealers/distributors etc. is non-settlement of old, pending problems. The magnitude of the problem might vary from big issues, involving huge financial implications, to trivial issues like replacement of a small quantity of some product/spares or settlement of a financial claim. As the channel members are very busy in various businesses, they often assume that once the problem is brought to the notice of the salespersons, it will be solved. However more often than not, this is not the case. While the salespersons, in their eagerness to get orders write down everything that the channel members tell them and promise to solve the problem, as soon as they go back to their offices, they often forget about it. Promises are not kept or even if efforts are made by them to solve the problem in their offices, it is not followed up seriously, with the result that the issue remains

As the channel members are very busy in various businesses, they often assume that once the problem is brought to the notice of the salespersons, it will be solved. However more often than not, this is not the case.

unresolved and next time when they go to the field and face the same channel member, they cut a sorry figure.

It must therefore be remembered that orders are procured only when channel members are happy and satisfied with your products and services. And solving old pending problems are an essential part of the services that you offer to them. So remember that:

- Do not promise what you cannot fulfil.
- Once you promise something, you must fulfil it even if it means stretching yourself to the maximum.
- Solve problems first before asking for orders.
- Give feedback to your dealers/distributors about the progress made in solving their problems and when they will be solved.
- Ensure speedy settling of claims.

Contacting customers and transporters

One of the important functions of salespersons is to contact customers on a regular basis. This includes keeping track of the supplies from the company to them, monitoring their inventory levels and liquidating dead stock, if any, redressing their problems and concerns and managing defectives. The salespersons also must monitor the outstanding payments and keep the receivables as per the company norms.

An important function that a salesperson should efficiently perform is coordination with the transporter. Transporters are a key link in the entire sales process, and any anomaly in the transportation might lead to a stock-out situation for non-availability of goods resulting in dissatisfied customers and loss to the company.

Non-productive Activities

Travelling

Travelling is perhaps the most tedious part of a sales job. What is required is careful planning of an itinerary so that the salesperson gets the maximum productive time for sales, is not tired while travelling and also can relax after long hours of working in the market. This can happen only if the following aspects are followed meticulously.

- A salesperson should be in the market by 11 am and remain there till 6 or 6.30 pm. Travel plans should be made accordingly. Thus the salesperson should either travel during the night and reach the destination in the early hours of the next morning, or else, his travel time should not exceed three to three and a half hours. This will ensure that when he reaches his destination, he is fresh enough to take on the challenges of the market.
- The travel must be comfortable and once he reaches the destination, he must have enough time to get ready for another gruelling day.
- The travel plan should be made in such a way that the salesperson can come back to headquarters at least after about 3-4 days. This will help him in getting physical and

mental rest. He will also get time to settle customer complaints and discuss important developments of the market and competitors with seniors.

Waiting time

Another difficult but necessary unproductive job in sales is the waiting time. Waiting bores the salespersons, disrupts their call plan and upsets the quality of their interaction with the prospects. Though you cannot help but wait, you can make productive use of this time for organizing the day's work, thinking about how to approach other customers and make necessary plans to meet the targets. This time can also be utilized for contacting your office to settle customer complaints.

Administrative work

Normally salespersons like to be in the field and consider paper work most boring. Though paper work is very important, a lot of unnecessary paper work is thrust upon them, which takes up a lot of their precious time, which they could have used productively in the market. Such work includes writing long reports on market trends, internal meetings, preparing statistics and attending sales conferences. Such activities divert attention of salespersons from their core activity i.e. selling and dilute the efforts that they put in to maximize sales. This is not to say that reports are not important or salespersons must not attend conferences, but what is a waste of time is the frequency at which these events happen in some companies.

MANAGING YOURSELF FOR SUCCESS

The first challenge of managing yourself is to understand oneself. Various words prefixed with 'self' such as self-made, self-esteem, self-worth, selfless, self-evaluation, self-improvement, self-discipline, self-control etc. are important and must be understood.

From selfishness to selflessness is one continuum, with the self as the centre; the same self moves from one end of the spectrum to the other. But the locus of control is within us, influencing the decision of moving either towards selflessness or towards selfishness. So knowing where you stand in relation to each of these 'self' words is the starting point of self-awareness.

Understand Yourself

Often we do not realize how we perform or how we learn. We live in our own world and think that it is the best. Perhaps, at times we are in a state of "I am ok you are not ok." Or at best "I am ok and you are ok." This creates a disillusionment from which we are unable to get out and this eventually destroys us but by the time we realize it, it is too late. So what is important for us is to ask ourselves 'how do I learn better?' Do I learn better when I read something, or when I isten to something or is there any other way that I learn better?

> An excellent salesperson must be a great leader and at the same time an equally excellent team member.

The other important thing for you to do is find out whether you enjoy sales and if yes, are good at it? If a wrong person is put in sales you will not get any output from him. On the other hand, if a person has the basic attributes of a salesperson he can achieve the unimaginable. What then are the attributes of an excellent salesperson? He must be honest, sincere, hardworking, have good communication and interpersonal skills and great adaptability.

An excellent salesperson must be an outstanding leader and at the same time a good team member. Play to your strengths, rather than trying to be somebody completely different and lead your team to success in the market.

Radiate Positive Energy

Do you know how many 'encounters' you have on a typical day in the market? A psychologist would say roughly 200 interactions. Can you recollect who was the first person you saw in the morning, whom you talked to – the guard in your apartment, your neighbour, your wife and children, the taxi driver or the bus conductor, the dealers, the stockist, the distributor his accountant, their salesmen, their attendants or the van driver etc. Each contact is an encounter. In each of these encounters, you create positive or negative energy around you, which touches you and the person you have encountered. Creating positive energy initially takes effort, but later on becomes a part of your personality and is an integral attribute of a successful salesperson.

Creating positive energy initially takes effort, but later on becomes part of your personality and is an integral attribute of a successful salesperson.

Learn to Empathize

Many a time we react based on what the other person tells us. If we could step back and think, is there something bothering him or her? Why is he or she doing that? If you ask that question, you start empathizing. But the moment I say something rude and you respond with equal rudeness, it creates a negative attitude, which we do not realize. One should step back and ask what happened? Why did that person say that? Learning to let go is important. There is this one big thing in all of us called E-G-O. Learning to keep that under control is one of the biggest challenges that we as salespersons face, and it is the most important part of self-management.

There is this one big thing in all of us called E-G-O. Learning to keep that under control is one of the biggest challenges that we as salespersons face.

Keep Learning and Changing

Just because a person is intelligent does not mean that he knows everything. Often intelligence creates a disabling amount of ignorance, because such people are unable to

> If you think you have achieved a lot, look ahead and see how much others have achieved and when you feel that you have done nothing with your life, then look back and see how much better off you are than others. This is what will keep you going.

see merit in what others are doing or saying. If you think you have achieved a lot, look ahead and see how much others have achieved and when you feel that you have done nothing with your life, then look back and see how much better off you are than others. This is what will keep you going.

There is a great *shloka* in Sanskrit, which translates into: The sun rises and sets with the same copper colour. Similarly, a prudent person has the same demeanour in times of both affluence and hardship.

Stand up for Your Values

A value system, to put it simply, is what is acceptable to you and what is not. It is a belief system that has been repeatedly tried and tested in your mind. There is a difference between standing up for your values and being arrogant about your values. Learning to make that subtle distinction is where the success lies.

Being able to manage yourself is to understand what your values are. It is about warding off temptations and pursuing your goals with a dispassionate mind. In times of a value dilemma, follow the truth; take blessings of your parents and inspiration from God. In market, you have options; to work or postpone it, there are no immediate controls, and you are your own master and have to decide what you should do and what you should not! Your accountability towards the company, the customers and your commitment come in here. Your commitment as a value to these 'stakeholders' should be of prime importance to you.

Leverage Self-Confidence

There will be times when you need to leverage your self-confidence to your advantage. But let me caution you that you cannot make self-confidence a substitute for your ignorance all the time. Self-management does not mean that you can substitute ignorance with self-confidence.

Recognize your insecurities and talk about them with friends and loved ones. Each day you should chip away at them and wear them down. There is no quick fix. Get to the root of the problem; focus on it and understand that you need to resolve each issue before you can move on.

Be thankful for what you have. A lot of the time, the root of insecurity and lack of confidence is due to a feeling of not having enough of something, whether it is emotional validation, good luck, money, etc. By acknowledging and appreciating what you do have, you can combat the feeling of being incomplete. This works wonders for your confidence.

Be positive even if you do not feel positive. Avoid self-pity, or the pity and sympathy of others. Never allow others to make you feel inferior – they can only do so only if you let them. If you continue to loathe and belittle yourself, others are going to do likewise. Instead, speak positively about yourself, about your future, and about your progress. Do not be afraid to project your strengths and qualities to others. By doing so, you reinforce those ideas in your mind and encourage your growth in a positive direction.

Look at the Larger Picture

Does your behaviour reflect the degree of awareness that you have about yourself? For example, if you believe that you are emotionally mature, does it reflect in your behaviour? How do you take disappointment, success or conflict? Many of us do not know how to deal with conflict. How do you deal with conflict with your dealers, distributors or your office colleagues? Do you sulk or do you talk the matter over? Your behaviour should reflect your self-awareness.

Self-restraint

Self-restraint is the highest of virtues in the sales profession. Through self-restraint, a salesperson is able to acquire happiness and contentment and achieve his goals without distractions. Self-restraint means restraint can also be thought of as self-control. During a day's work a salesperson is faced with many distractions. These might include going to the market late, moving out of the market early or not going to the market at all and sending false reports. It might also mean inadequate coverage of the market, subjective handling of dealers/stockists or being influenced by a particular distributor which might be damaging to the interest of the company.

> There are four qualities i.e., anger, pride, deceit and greed that often entrap salespersons and deter them from pursuing their goals/targets. Such acts are damaging to the profession, and pride and credibility of salespersons and must be discarded.

A salesperson needs to exercise restraint, and be objective to achieve targets. There are four qualities, namely, anger, pride, deceit and greed that often entrap salespersons and deter them from pursuing their goals/targets. Such acts are damaging to the profession, and pride and credibility of salespersons and must be discarded.

SELF-DISCIPLINE

Self-discipline is the ability to take the necessary actions regardless of your emotional state. It is one of many personal development tools available to a salesperson. Though not a panacea, the problems which self-discipline can solve are significant. Self-discipline can empower you to overcome any distractions that have been discussed above. It can wipe out procrastination, disorder, and ignorance. Within the domain of problems it can solve, self-discipline is simply unmatched. Moreover, it becomes a powerful teammate when combined with other tools like passion, goal-setting, and planning.

The Five Pillars of Self-discipline

> The pinnacle of self-discipline is when you reach the point that when you make a conscious decision it is virtually guaranteed you will follow through on it.

The five pillars of self-discipline are: Acceptance, Willpower, Hard Work, Industry, and Persistence (A WHIP). This acronym is a convenient way to remember them, since many people associate self-discipline with whipping themselves into shape. Without self-discipline an intention will not become a fact, but with sufficient self-discipline, it is sure to. The pinnacle of self-discipline is when you reach the point that when you make a conscious decision it is virtually guaranteed that you will follow through on it.

Building Self-discipline

How to build self-discipline is best explained by an analogy. Self-discipline is like a muscle – the more you train it, the stronger you become. Just as everyone has different muscular strength, we all possess different levels of self-discipline. Everyone has some amount – if you can hold your breath a few seconds, you have some self-discipline. But not everyone has developed their discipline to the same degree. Just as it takes muscle to build muscle, it takes self-discipline to build self-discipline.

> You must start with weights/challenges that are slightly greater than your current ability.

The basic method to build self-discipline is to tackle challenges that you can successfully accomplish but which are within your limits. This does not mean trying something and failing at it every day, nor does it mean staying within your comfort zone. You will gain no strength trying to lift a weight that you cannot budge, nor will you gain strength lifting weights that are too light for you. You must start with weights/challenges that are slightly greater than those within your current ability.

Progressive training means that once you succeed, you increase the challenge. If you keep working out with the same challenges and problems, you will not get any stronger. Similarly, if you fail to challenge yourself in life, you will not gain any more self-discipline.

MANAGING TIME

The purpose of self management is to have the maximum time available for sales and spend as much time as possible with clients. This can only be achieved by organizing your time properly, taking into consideration your activities and constraints.

All salespersons want to call on as many customers as they can. At the same time, they want enough time for other activities like reporting and other paperwork. It is seen that as a lot of their time is spent in the market, by the time they return, they are too tired to do the necessary paperwork, and do it in a hurry. This dilutes the quality of their reports. Reporting is often considered as a routine task and takes the last priority in a salesperson's day. It is forgotten that sales strategy is made primarily on the basis of the reports received by marketing managers from the market.

> Reporting is often considered as a routine task and takes the last priority in a salesperson's day. It is forgotten that sales strategy is made primarily on the basis of the reports received by marketing managers from the market.

Ten Rules to Maintain Self-discipline

1. Be punctual: Reach the prospect on time.
2. Respect the value of customers' time: Be precise and productive in your discussions.
3. Set a call target everyday and stick to it: Achieve it at any cost.
4. Deliver what you commit to your customers even if it means hardships for you.
5. Cover the entire market, customers and also other outlets who do not deal with you.
6. Avoid distractions: Do not get trapped in attractions proposed by some channel members.
7. Be objective and rational in your approach: Do not bend rules to make someone happy.
8. Work hard: Stretch yourself to the maximum: It pays.
9. Be sincere and honest: It enhances your credibility.
10. Work as if there is no tomorrow.

SALES REPORTING

The vast majority of sales managers require their salespeople to compile a daily or weekly call report. There is no doubt that sales' reporting is a critical part of a salesperson's duties. This includes daily sales reports and monthly sales reports. However, salespersons also have to send reports on competitors' activities.

What is sales reporting?

By sales reporting is meant analysis and reporting of sales activities and performance against the set targets. It is a salesperson's detailed record of sales calls and results for a given period. Typically, a sales report will include information such as the sales volume per product or product line and the number of existing and new accounts called upon and the expenses incurred in making the calls. It is a written record of sales calls made by a representative for submission to a supervisor. For a salesperson, reporting includes conveying all possible information and data from the market to his superiors that could be used to take timely decisions to achieve marketing targets in his territory. Competitive markets are dynamic in nature and are continuously going through a process of change. The variables – supply and demand patterns, availability of products, competitive offerings etc. keep on changing. This calls for an urgent need to keep tabs on the changing dynamics of the market and redefine strategies to be ahead of competition. The input for such strategies comes from the reports that are received from the salespersons.

The input for such strategies comes from the reports that are received from the salespersons.

What are Sales Reports used for and how useful are they?

Most salespersons feel that sales reports are one of the most useless traditions that management clings to. Often the reports are filled with fictitious information, and the information which is true is often useless.

Most salespersons feel that sales reports are one of the most useless traditions that management clings to. Often the reports are filled with fictitious information, and the information which is true is often useless.

A typical sales report will identify whom the salesperson met, if and when the company plans to make a purchase, an estimate of the size of the purchase, and any information the buyer wants from the salesperson. The report may even give an idea of the likelihood of securing a contract.

Consider a sales report. Does it

- Indicate why there is a change in the number of units to be purchased?
- Discuss why the purchase decision will be made by the end of the quarter instead of now?
- Indicate the likelihood of closing the sale?
- Indicate what actions the salesperson plans on taking other than giving revised numbers?
- Indicate whom the salesperson is competing against?
- Indicate if there are other decision makers in the process?

Reasons for Imperfection in a Sales Report

- Usually sales reports lack sharpness for three major reasons:
- Salespeople have not been taught how to prepare a useful call report.
- Salespeople see no use in the reports. Although they are told the reports will be used to help them sell more, they believe their real purpose is to keep an eye on them.
- They believe management is only interested in how many appointments they have, so they often pad them with fictitious appointments.

Salespeople see call reports as a weapon – or potential weapon – in the hands of management instead of a training and coaching tool and often, that is what they are used for.

A typical sales report does not give the manager enough information to be able to help identify the areas in which a salesperson needs training and coaching. Consequently, the most frequent result of submitting a report is a response of, "You are not seeing enough people. You need to make more calls."

That response is worthless. It does not help the salesperson in the least. There is no guidance on how to 'see more people.' There is no identification of what the real root problems and issues are.

Sales Reports as Real Tools

Sales reports, however, can be real tools that managers can use for coaching, training, market and competitor analysis, and managing department assets.

The problem with call reports is not with the concept, but with the execution. Salespeople must be taught how to construct a meaningful call report and managers must be trained how to analyze the report for the purpose of coaching, training, and market analysis.

In addition, sales reporting can be used to motivate salespersons, because rewarding the best salespersons without accurate and reliable sales reports is not fair.

Sales reports are not made only for internal use or top management. If another division's compensation plan depends on final results it is necessary for the sales department to present the final results to that other department.

Finally, sales reports are required for investors, partners and the government, so the sales management system should have advanced reporting capabilities to satisfy the needs of different target audiences and help the sales force to be more effective and make more sales.

A Meaningful Sales Report

Sales reports do not have to be massive documents, but each call must be broken into three sections:

- **Synopsis of the call** – A brief summary of the sales call. This should include, who, what, when, bullet points of key information from the call, including the length of the call.
- **An analysis of the call** – A longer discussion that analyzes the call and the sale, indicating:
  - Who the decision makers are and where the sale stands with each one
  - What issues must be dealt with before the sale can be closed
  - Who the competition is
  - The salesperson's best estimate of the probability of closing the sale
  - The salesperson's rating of each potential prospect as to the long-term value of the account
- **Moving forward** – What specific steps the salesperson intends to take, and when, to move the sale forward.

A sales report that follows the format above can be used to help salespeople close more deals. It describes what happened, where the sale stands, what is expected to happen, and what the salesperson is going to do to make it happen.

Using the Report

Sales reports that summarize, analyze and outline how the salesperson will move the sale forward offer both the salesperson and their manager real information that can be used:

- To spot issues where the manager can step in to coach and train.
- Opportunities where the manager can offer specific help in identifying and addressing prospect needs.
- Spot accounts where the salesperson is investing too much – or not enough – time and energy.
- Spot buyer, competitor, and product trends within the local market.

Some sales performance management technology products and CRM programs make the call report generation process easier and more accurate. They can turn call reports into highly useful tools for helping the members of the sales team become better sellers, spotting and analyzing changes in your local market, and maximizing both the department's human and non-human resources.

Whether you are using hand written reports or using a system, you must turn the reports from a wasted effort into a real tool that can improve sales and your salespeople.

Key Performance Indicators

The sales reporting includes the Key Performance Indicators (KPI) of the sales force.

The KPI indicate whether or not the sales process achieves the results as set forth in the sales planning and enables the salespersons to take corrective action in time in case the indicators deviate from the projected targets.

Key performance indicators are financial and non-financial metrics used to help an organization define and measure progress toward organizational goals. KPIs can be delivered through business intelligence techniques to assess the present state of the business and to assist in prescribing a course of action. The act of monitoring KPIs in real-time is known as Business Activity Monitoring (BAM). KPIs are frequently used to "value" difficult to measure activities such as the benefits of leadership development, engagement, service, and satisfaction. KPIs are typically tied to an organization's strategy (as exemplified through techniques such as the balanced scorecard).

Categorization of Indicators

Key performance indicators define a set of values used as a measure. These raw sets of values fed to systems to summarize information against are called indicators. Indicators identifiable as possible candidates for KPIs can be summarized into the following sub-categories:

- Quantitative indicators which can be presented as a number.
- Practical indicators that interface with existing company processes.
- Directional indicators specifying whether an organization is getting better or not.
- Actionable indicators are sufficiently in an organization's control to effect change.

Key performance indicators in practical terms and strategy development means are objectives to be targeted that will add the most value to a business.

Analyzing KPIs

Among the sales KPIs top management analyses are:

- Customer related numbers:
  - New customers acquired
  - Status of existing customers
  - Customer attrition

- Turnover generated by segments of the customers – these could be demographic filters.
- Outstanding balances held by segments of customers and terms of payment – these could be demographic filters.
- Collection of bad debts within customer relationships.
- Demographic analysis of individuals (potential customers) applying to become customers, and the levels of approval, rejections and pending numbers.
- Delinquency analysis of customers behind on payments.
- Profitability of customers by demographic segments and segmentation of customers by profitability.

These customer KPIs are helpful in developing and improving relationship with customers.

KEY CONCEPTS

- Self-management is essential to excellence in sales; unless a salesperson regulates his emotional and physical self carefully, he may find it difficult to succeed in spite of all his knowledge about the market and skills of handling distributors/dealers or customers.
- Self management is one's ability to handle emotions, feelings, sentiments, thoughts and attitude with the single purpose of winning in the marketplace. Managing oneself means managing time, controlling emotions, avoiding distractions and focusing on the targets with one hundred percent attention.
- The first challenge of managing oneself is to understand oneself. It is important for us to ask "How do I learn better?" Do I learn better when I read something, when I listen to something or is there any other way that I learn better?"
- It is important to find out whether you enjoy sales and if the answer is yes, are you good at it? If the wrong person is put in sales there will be no output from him.
- An excellent salesperson must be honest, sincere, hardworking, have good communication and interpersonal skills and must have great adaptability. He must also be a great leader and at the same time an equally good team member.
- Radiate positive energy. Creating positive energy initially takes effort, but later on becomes part of your personality and is an integral attribute of a successful salesperson.
- Recognize your insecurities and talk about them with friends and loved ones. Each day you should chip away at them. Get to the root of the problem; focus on it and understand that you need to resolve each issue before you can move on.
- Remember that no one is perfect. Even the most confident people have insecurities. At some point in our lives, we may feel we lack something. That is reality. Learn that life is full of bumps along the way.
- Identify your successes. Discover the things at which you excel and then focus on your talents. Take pride in yourself. Give yourself credit for your successes. Inferiority is a state of mind where you believe yourself to be a victim. Express yourself and enjoy your profession.

- Have faith in yourself. Believe in your strengths and develop them.
- Be thankful for what you have. By acknowledging and appreciating what you do have, you can combat the feeling of being incomplete and unsatisfied. Finding that inner peace will do wonders for your confidence.
- Be positive even if you do not feel positive. Avoid self-pity, or the pity and sympathy of others. Never allow others to make you feel inferior - they can only do so if you let them.
- Do not be afraid to project your strengths and qualities to others. By doing so, you reinforce those ideas in your mind and encourage your growth in a positive direction.
- Self-restraint is the highest of virtues in the sales profession. Through self-restraint, a salesperson is able to acquire happiness and contentment and achieve his goals without distractions. It means self-control.

THE COURAGE TO CHANGE

Ajai Mathur was an ambitious young man. He hailed from Mumbai, studied in a good school and aspired to do something great in life. But he wanted everything good to happen to him here and now. He completed his graduation and decided to join a good company and start chasing his dreams. Ajai was handsome, smart and a good communicator; and as luck would have it, he was selected in the Indian arm of Zenex Pharma Ltd, a multinational corporation making pharmaceutical products with a worldwide presence. Ajai was sent for an extensive training of six months and then posted in Mumbai with southern Maharashtra as his territory. His task was to achieve sales targets, develop the market, contain outstanding payments and manage his stockists and C&F agents.

Ajai was thrilled to see his dreams coming true. During his training, he was told that his basic assignments would include making doctors' calls, maximizing collections, managing stocks at stockists' level, ensuring a steady flow of supplies from the factories, monitoring competitors' activities including prices and monitoring competition. However, after six months, once his initial euphoria was over, he could see the realities of selling. Ajai was assigned areas that were primarily rural markets. The difficulty of working in rural markets was becoming unbearable. The miserable travelling in local buses, awful food, difficult stockists, delays in payments and on top of that, long waiting times while calling on the doctors were all taking their toll. Also, administrative work like writing reports, and getting ready for sales conferences was becoming too much for him.

Ajai was totally disillusioned. He decided that he would talk to his branch manager, Mr. Dev Gaekwad. He was a very seasoned, matured sales professional who listened carefully. Then he smiled and said, "Ajai, behind every success is hard work, behind every achievement is a lot of toil and sweat! So don't be upset. Think that you have been given the opportunity to take the company to new heights with your brilliance and hard work. What you have to do is to organize yourself and your tasks and work to a plan. Prepare your plan and show it to me. I will help you to refine it, if needed. I am sure you will surmount all the problems that you are facing today."

Question

1. What plan should Ajai prepare and show to Mr. Gaekwad?

REFERENCES

1. Branson, Richard (2011), Smart Talk, *BRW*, Vol. 33 Issue 15, p. 16.
2. Cohen, Susan G., Ledford Jr, Gerald E., Spreitzer, Gretchen M. (1996), A Predictive Model of Self-managing Work Team Effectiveness, *Human Relations*, Vol. 49 Issue 5, pp. 643-676.
3. Friel, Brian (2007), Manage Yourself, *Government Executive*, Vol. 39 Issue 7, p. 66.
4. Freeman, Peter (2005), One Up for the Self-managed, *Money* (14446219), Issue 1, p. 24.
5. Gosling, Jonathan, Mintzberg, Henry (2003), The Five Minds of a Manager, *Harvard Business Review*, Vol. 81 Issue 11, pp. 54-63.
6. Hogg, Michael A. (2009), Managing Self-uncertainty Through Group Identification, *Psychological Inquiry*, Vol. 20 Issue 4, pp. 221-224.
7. Jamieson, David W., Auron, Matthew, Shechtman, David (2011), Managing 'Use of Self' For Masterful Facilitation, *T+D*, Vol. 65 Issue 7, pp. 58-61.
8. Jorgensen, Haley (2008), Cultivating Self-insured Group Best Practices, *Risk Management*, Vol. 55 Issue 2, pp. 28-31.
9. Kelley, Robert E. (1998), How to Manage Your Work Life (and Become a Star), *Training & Development*, Vol. 52 Issue 5, p. 56.
10. Laumenskaitu, Egidija (2003), Self-management in Times of Change, *Management of Organizations: Systematic Research*, Issue 27, p. 71.
11. Levy, Paul F. (2001), When Good Teams Go Wrong, *Harvard Business Review*, Vol. 79 Issue 3, pp. 51-59.
12. Lovelace, Kathi J., Manz, Charles, C., Alves, José C. (2007), Work Stress and Leadership Development: The Role of Self-leadership, Shared Leadership, Physical Fitness and Flow in Managing Demands and Increasing Job Control, *Human Resource Management Review*, Vol. 17 Issue 4, pp. 374-387.
13. Manz, Charles C., Sims Jr, Henry P. (1987), Leading Workers to Lead Themselves: The External Leadership of Self-Managing Work Teams, *Administrative Science Quarterly*, Vol. 32 Issue 1, pp. 106-129.
14. Manz, Charles C. (1992), Self-leading Work Teams: Moving Beyond Self-management Myths, *Human Relations*, Vol. 45 Issue 11, pp. 1119-1140.
15. Parikh, Jagdish (1991), Managing Your Self, Management by Detached Involvement, *Long Range Planning*, Vol. 24 Issue 3, p. 106.
16. Wageman, Ruth (1997), Critical Success Factors for Creating Superb Self-managing Teams, *Organizational Dynamics*, Vol. 26 Issue 1, pp. 49-61.

11 Selling and the Distribution System

"Managers who see channel functions merely as the physical transportation, storage and distribution of finished goods to the end-user fail to utilize the channel of distribution as a competitive weapon."

—Philip Kotler

CHAPTER OUTLINE

- Distribution: An introduction
- Need for distribution channels
- Kinds of channels
- Channel members
- Role of channel members
- Creating distribution channels
- Channel coordination issues
- Steps to create a powerful distribution channel
- Creating a sales support system
- Evaluating channel performance

OBJECTIVES

After studying this chapter, you will be able to:

- Understand the critical role of distribution as an integral part of sales
- Understand distribution as a strategic tool for gaining and sustaining a competitive advantage
- Understand the need for distribution channels
- Appreciate the issues involved in channel design
- Be able to create efficient distribution channels

Opening Case: Modern Adhesive Company (MAC)

Modern Adhesive Company produced a complete line of adhesives. It had a product for every use in both retail and manufacturing companies. The company had an annual turnover of Rs. 10 crore and a plan to grow by at least 40% in the next five years. Rohan Mishra, the new sales executive of Modern Adhesive Company in Chennai, had been told by his Area Sales Manager, Joy Fernandes that his territory was not giving the desired sales volume as most of the good dealers were held firmly by their competitors. As a result, MAC's market share was only 10%. Rohan was aware that his dealers were not active and reputed dealers were not dealing with his company. Fernandes told him to review the entire distribution set up so that he could achieve 17% of the market share. Accordingly, Rohan was advised to prepare a plan of action to increase the market share. Rohan realized that he had to do something that would get him a quick increase in sales. He thought that this could be done by working with smaller prospects where competition was not so intense.

In Rohan's territory, the distribution network consisted of small and medium category dealers. In the industrial segment, there were only two manufacturing set-ups where MAC was able to sell its products. Fernandes attributed this lag to the lack of aggression of the Area Sales Manager who manned this territory before Fernandes took charge. Rohan decided to analyze the profile of the market and nature of competition and ascertain the extent to which he could augment his offer to attract industrial customers and/or the retail market. Rohan was worried about the task as he had heard about the large ego of these big dealers and manufacturers, from his colleagues. Moreover, most of them were dealing with Johnson & Johnson, Permacel and Fixtape – all international brands and they hardly gave any orders to smaller companies like MAC. Considering their size of operation, they invariably asked for maximum discounts and payment terms, which were granted to them by the international companies.

Rohan felt that if he was to achieve his sales target, he had to convince the big dealers to accept his products, expand his retail base and also gradually tap a greater number of manufacturing companies. The task was very challenging and he had submitted a new distribution plan to Mr. Fernandes.

Question

1. What should Rohan do to revamp MAC's distribution policy to achieve the new sales target?

SELLING AND THE DISTRIBUTION SYSTEM

Integral Design for Programmed Learning

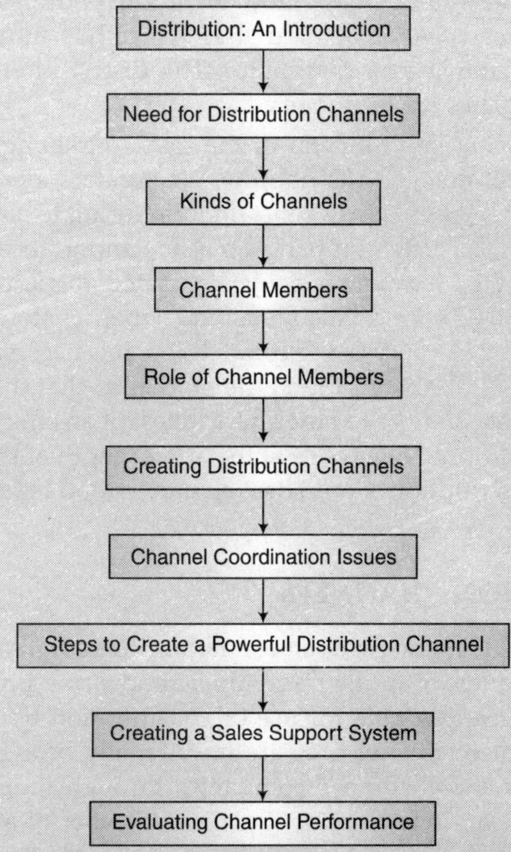

"How many marketing channels should a company use to distribute its products and services? The higher the number of channels, the greater the company's market coverage and rate of growth of its sales. This principle is well illustrated by Starbucks Coffee Company. Starbucks started with only one channel, namely company-owned stores that were staffed carefully and operated profitably. Later Starbucks franchised operations in other venues: airports, bookstores, and college campuses. The company recently signed a licensing agreement with Albertson's food chain to open coffee bars in its supermarkets. Not only is Starbucks coffee served in these venues, but other Starbucks products are sold along with coffee. A comedian quipped about Starbucks: "I don't know how fast they are growing but they just opened one in my living room."

–Peter Drucker

DISTRIBUTION: AN INTRODUCTION

Distribution is one of the four significant arms of marketing, the other three arms being product management, pricing, and promotion. Distributors, wholesalers, dealers, retailers, etc. all act as channels to ensure a steady flow of products from the manufacturer to the customers. After a product is manufactured it is typically handed over (or sold) to an intermediary, commonly known as a distributor. The distribution channel tries to ensure that the product finally reaches the customers.

A distribution system is a key function of the total marketing chain. It takes years to create a marketing channel, develop distributors, wholesalers, dealers and retailers and it requires constant monitoring to achieve the sales targets of the company. Thus, the importance of distribution channels cannot be under estimated. It is known that products should be available as and when customers require them. With increasing competition, it is necessary that products should be visible in the market so that they draw the attention of customers and thereby create an urge to buy. The acid test of an effective distribution channel is to ensure that "products should always be at the arm's length of the customers." To do this the following aspects of distribution should be well understood before designing an effective channel.

> The aim of distribution is to ensure that the customer gets the product at the right form, the right place and time.

NEED FOR DISTRIBUTION CHANNELS

Distribution channels are independent avenues that facilitate the sale of your products and services. In other words, they comprise individuals and firms involved in the process of making a product or service available for use or consumption by consumers or industrial users. Think about how merchant services are traditionally brought to the market; banks operate through branches and insurance companies through independent sales agents to sell their wares. In essence an independent agent is a member of a distribution channel for the bank or insurance company. Another example of an industry that relies on multiple distribution partners is software companies; they use Value Added Resellers (VARs) to sell, install, train and maintain their product offerings. The majority of Business to Business (B2B) companies utilize multiple distribution or indirect sales channels. In the consumer sector, there are similar channels to ensure that durables or Fast Moving Consumer Goods (FMCGs) reach the sales points in the fastest possible time.

Frequently there may be a chain of intermediaries; each passing the product down the chain to the next organization, before it finally reaches the consumer or end-user. This process is known as the 'distribution chain' or the 'channel.' Each of the elements in these chains will have their own specific needs, which the producer must take into account, along with those of the all-important end-user.

Hotels, for example, may sell their services (typically rooms) directly or through travel agents, tour operators, airlines, tourist boards, centralized reservation systems, etc. There

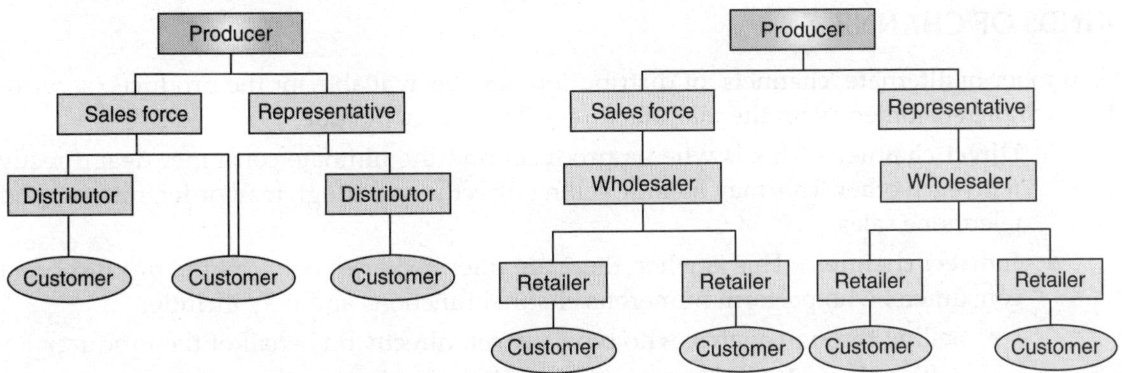

Fig. 11.1 *Typical Distribution Channel*

have also been some innovations in the distribution of services. For example, there has been an increase in franchising and in rental services – the latter offering anything from televisions to tools. There has also been some evidence of service integration, with services being linked together, particularly in the travel and tourism sectors. For example, links now exist between airlines, hotels and car rental services. In addition, there has been a significant increase in retail outlets for the service sector. Outlets such as estate agencies and building society offices are crowding out traditional grocers from major shopping areas.

> Distribution channels may not be limited to physical products alone. They may be just as important for moving a service from producer to consumer in certain sectors, since both direct and indirect channels may be used.

Traditionally, distribution has been seen as dealing with logistics i.e. how to get the product or service to the customer. As such, it must answer questions such as:

- Should the product be sold through a dealer/retailer?
- Should the product be supplied only to wholesale outlets from where it will be further distributed to retail outlets?
- Should multi-level marketing channels be used to market products?
- What should be the length of a channel (how many intermediaries)?
- At what locations should the product or service be available?
- When should the product or service be available?
- Should distribution be exclusive, selective or intensive?
- What should be the system to monitor and control the channel?
- What should be the contractual aspects of channel relationships?
- Should channel members share advertising (referred to as co-op ads)?
- Should electronic methods of distribution be used?
- Are there physical distribution and logistical issues to deal with?
- What will it cost to keep an inventory of products on store shelves and in channel warehouses (referred to as filling the pipeline)?

KINDS OF CHANNELS

A number of alternate 'channels' of distribution may be available for the products/services to reach the customers from the manufacturers. These may include:

- **Direct channel** – This is when a producer and the ultimate consumer deal directly with each other. This may include selling directly, or through mail order, Internet and telephone sales.
- **Indirect channel** – This is when there are intermediaries between the producer and consumers, who perform numerous channel functions and may include:
  - Selling through agents, who typically sell directly on behalf of the producer
  - Selling through distributors and/or wholesaler, who sell to retailers
  - Retailers (also called dealers or resellers), who sell products to the end customers

CHANNEL MEMBERS

The term channel membership refers to the number of intermediaries that a channel has, to effectively discharge the function of dispatching the products to the end customers. Accordingly, the following methods of distribution are normally adopted by companies.

1. **Intensive distribution** – Where the majority of resellers stock the 'product' (with convenience products, for example, and particularly the brand leaders in consumer goods markets). In such a situation there is a high possibility of competitive pricing.
2. **Selective distribution** – This is a carefully decided pattern of setting up a distribution network (in both consumer and industrial markets) where selection of 'suitable' resellers is more judicious and their stocking the product does not lead to competitive pricing.
3. **Exclusive distribution** – Where only specially selected resellers or authorized dealers (typically only one per geographical area) are allowed to sell the 'product'.

The simplest level, that of direct contact with customers, i.e. where no intermediaries are involved, is called the 'zero-level' channel. The 'one-level' channel, uses just one intermediary. They are known by different titles. For instance, in consumer goods they are called retailers and in industrial goods, they are referred to as distributors. In the telecom industry, levels are named as "tiers". A one tier channel means that vendors and product manufacturers (or software companies) work directly with the dealers. In a two tier channel vendors work with dealers and distributors.

ROLE OF CHANNEL MEMBERS

Some of the important functions performed by middlemen are as follows:

- Members of a distribution channel are the company's face in the market and the customer's spokesperson to the company.

> Members of the distribution channel play a crucial role in the entire value-chain of marketing. While they ensure a smooth flow of goods and services from the manufacturer to the end consumer, they also perform a number of important functions that help in consummating the sales effectively.

- As it is not possible for the company to reach the end consumers, middlemen perform this task and ensure a smooth flow of goods and services.
- Many manufacturers lack financial resources to market their products directly to the consumers.
- At times the credibility of middlemen is a deciding factor to purchase goods.
- Members of the distribution channel help in providing vital market information that helps companies to plan sales.
- Channel members act as an important source of promoting the product by communicating the product attributes and convincing customers about the services attached to it.
- Channel members help in looking out for and communicating with prospective customers.
- They contribute in assessing the exact needs of customers and try to fit products and services to match their needs.
- Channel members facilitate the transportation and storage of goods.
- They help by arranging loan facilities for purchase of goods.
- Channel members take the risk of buying and promoting goods of companies.

All these functions are mutually exclusive and are performed to create a win-win situation. The manufacturers and the channel members work in tandem only if both benefit from the transaction and are certain of short-term or long-term gains.

CREATING DISTRIBUTION CHANNELS

Several issues are to be considered while creating channels of distribution. In a nutshell these issues can be categorized into the following two groups:

1. Channel design issues
2. Channel coordination issues

Channel Design Issues

Channel design issues generally relate to setting up of effective channels that ensure timely availability of products to customers, promote the company and its products and ensure a positive experience in customer's minds.

The distribution channel must therefore be designed in the light of the following factors:

- Reach
- Efficacy

- Vulnerability
- Adaptability
- Strength

Reach

The first task of salespersons is to decide the kind of distribution channel that they want to distribute the products. Generally, this decision depends upon the kind of products and resources available with the company, and the target population. Salespersons should identify the service outputs that matter in their markets. Efforts should be made to segment the market for effective distribution channel design and target the highest-potential channel segments in the market.

> The primary function of a distribution channel is to ensure timely availability of goods to the customers. To make it happen, salespeople must set up a channel that covers the target market adequately and is able to reach the targeted customers most effectively.

Efficacy

The value of a distribution channel rests on its efficacy to convert the customer enquiry into actual sale. A good channel member even generates a need and then fulfils the need by selling the products. To be able to handle the channel members requires very careful strategy. It has been observed that due to competitive pressure, channel members are generally swayed by attractions offered by competitors, thereby reducing the efficacy of channel distributors in the market. This leads to low sales, delays in payments, non-movement of stocks and loss of market share.

To offset such a situation, the primary task of salespersons is to ensure "new attractions" in the market at regular intervals and involve channel members so as to ensure their maximum contribution in meeting sales objectives. These promotional efforts could be organizing in-shop promotions, display contests, seasonal discount schemes, quantity based discount schemes, organizing business meetings at exotic locations, offering lucrative prizes for achieving pre-determined targets and making them members of exclusive clubs like the Chairman's club etc. Companies may also think of offering timely payment schemes, product tagging and new market development awards.

Vulnerability

The degree of commitment is an important determining factor for the appointment of a good channel member. As stated earlier, channel members are prone to lucrative offers of competitors, without looking to long-term gains. Though counter offers may help in retaining their interest in your company, they may not lead to long term market stability.

> In selecting channel members, salespersons must give due credence to their reputation, status of other companies they are dealing with and the quality of response to their business proposal.

Adaptability

One of the preferred features of a good marketing channel is its ability to adapt to varying business conditions. It is known, that markets fluctuate as per changes in supply and demand. Accordingly, the pressure on the product in terms of storing it, sales pitch, pricing and promotion also have to change in order to ensure a grip on the market. Normally, in times of market stress, the channel members either tend to lose their confidence in their manufacturers or in the future of the business, leading to de-stabilizing the channel. Such weakening of the channel has a direct impact on loss of market share.

Strength

As with all chains, a marketing channel is only as strong as its weakest link. That weak link can be anywhere in the chain from a disinterested distributor to a damaging wholesaler to an inefficient retail outlet.

CHANNEL COORDINATION ISSUES

An important issue in managing channels is the coordination of activities between the company and the channel members. This coordination encompasses resolution of pending matters like non-settlement of financial claims, replacement of defective products or on-time information about status of orders and delivery of goods.

Channel Management

The channel decision is very important. In theory at least, there is a form of trade-off: the cost of using intermediaries to achieve wider distribution is supposedly lower. Indeed, most manufacturers of consumer goods could never justify the cost of selling directly to their consumers, except by mail order. A small company has no alternative but to use intermediaries, often several layers of them, but large companies do have a choice. However, many suppliers seem to assume that once their product has been sold into the channel (the beginning of the distribution chain), their job is over. However, the distribution chain merely assumes a part of the supplier's responsibility. If the supplier has any aspirations to be market-oriented, his job should really extend to managing, albeit very indirectly, all the processes involved in that chain, until the product or service reaches the end-user. This may involve a number of decisions on the part of the supplier.

> In practice, if the producer is large enough, the use of intermediaries can sometimes cost more than going direct. Many of the theoretical arguments about channels therefore revolve around cost. On the other hand, most of the practical decisions are concerned with control of the consumer.

1. Channel membership
2. Channel motivation
3. Monitoring and managing channels

Channel Motivation

It is difficult, though very important to motivate direct employees to provide the necessary sales and service support. Motivating the owners and employees of independent organizations in a distribution chain requires even greater effort. There are many devices for achieving such motivation. Perhaps the most usual is offering incentives: the supplier offers a better margin, to tempt the owners in the channel to push his product rather than his competitors' products; or a reward is offered to the distributors' sales personnel, so that they have the incentive to push the product. At the other end of the spectrum is the almost symbiotic relationship that the all too rare supplier in the computer field develops with its agents; where the agent's personnel, support as well as sales, are trained to almost the same standard as the supplier's own staff.

Issues of Distribution

Many managers are baffled by the extent of the problems that arise when managing their supply or distribution channels. These worries are generally the result of the unpredictability of responses of the channel members – distributors, wholesalers, dealers or retailers. Normally, the problems encompass all areas of channel management i.e. setting up distribution channels, managing the channel members, revitalizing them and strengthening the channels for achieving the sales targets.

The problems relating to creation of distribution channels (or setting up a network of distributors/wholesalers/dealers and retailers could include lack of interest shown by the channel members, availability of the prime channel members and convincing them to invest sufficiently in your products.

Management of distribution channels includes generating targeted sales orders from them, making them move in the market and contacting their retailers, ensuring timely supply of stocks, maintenance of stocks, servicing the market and customers in their areas, taking responsibility of local advertisements, organizing local sales promotion campaigns and ensuring timely payments.

> In case of selling to small-scale customers or geographically scattered markets, many manufacturers use either distributors/dealers, or agents/representatives, which also help in minimizing the cost of marketing.

Perhaps an equally important task before sales people is to continuously ensure the interest of the channel members towards their company and products. The extent to which channel members will invest will depend upon the interest that they have in you, your products and company.

Most channel problems fall into one of two categories: coordination issues or incentive issues. We use a series of case studies, to familiarize the reader with these issues, anticipate when they will occur and learn how to solve them.

Inventory or stock control is a very important factor in business organizations. In industrial marketing, distribution channels have to be directly from the manufacturer to the customer. There are some channel alternatives, which are feasible in the industrial market rather than the consumer market.

Often, manufacturers use their own sales/marketing personnel to sell the products directly to major customers. In case of selling to small-scale customers or geographically scattered markets, many manufacturers use either distributors/dealers, or agents/representatives, which also helps in minimizing the cost of marketing. In case of consumer marketing, the channel of distribution is longer with multiple levels of intermediaries/middlemen, since household consumers are geographically dispersed all over the country. Implemented correctly, a powerful distribution channel can be a potent sales driver for the company.

STEPS TO CREATE A POWERFUL DISTRIBUTION CHANNEL

There are five steps to launching and empowering a new distribution channel:

- Identify natural partners
- Develop their role in the process
- Set clear expectations
- Develop and deliver training
- Create a sales support system

Identify Natural Partners

The most important step in this process is identifying the best potential partners. They should be financially strong, enjoy high reliability and looked upon as dependable outlets. These channel partners can be distributors, wholesalers or retailers. While identifying channel partners, the focus must be on creating a partnership for a win-win situation.

> Ideally, salespersons must aim to select the best counters in the market. These channel partners should have a very high credibility and should be looked upon by customers as the most trustworthy outlets.

Develop their Role in the Process

Depending on the type of distribution partner, they would naturally have different roles in the sales process. One has to determine the scope of their work by specifying a definite territory, fixing sales targets and ensuring that they have adequate resources to implement the company's sales plan successfully. Considering the intensive sales pitch in the market, the channel members are susceptible to shifting from one company to another, if there is the slightest additional monetary attraction. One has to use a common sense approach. If the distribution partners are currently not meeting your key targets, face to face, and do not have a large sales force it may be better for you to rework the entire sales process. One should keep this in mind when developing a compensation program. A good rule of thumb is: the more they do – the more they make.

Set Clear Expectations

To ensure a successful relationship both parties must have a clear understanding of what is expected, a clear definition of the terms of the agreement, what the company expects from them and what they can expect from the company. Setting clearly defined sales goals and targets, will give you a yard stick to gauge the success of the arrangement.

Develop and Deliver Training

The roles assigned to each participant will drive training and development. A key factor that will determine your success is whether your new distribution partner and their team are trained thoroughly. Make sure you develop a comprehensive program that meets all their needs and is easy to implement. Training is vital, many new partnerships look good on paper but if you cannot mobilize the sales force it will never take off. Partners need to have confidence in their ability to explain and sell your products.

CREATING A SALES SUPPORT SYSTEM

Transporters have to ensure speedy delivery of goods, the finance department has to resolve financial matters quickly, stores have to have stocks to be dispatched and salespersons have to have continuous communication with the distribution channels and reinforce them to serve better. If the organization is small, and does not have the resources to support a large sales network appropriate training of key employees might be necessary before sending them out to the field. One must give them the tools to be successful, if it is done correctly the first time, it will result in fewer support calls and increased sales.

> A strong distribution channel must have the support of a number of agencies like transporters, finance department, stores and sales functions of the company. They have to work in perfect tandem to ensure efficacy to the distribution channel.

Distribution channels are an attractive and flexible way for companies to develop new markets and garner additional revenue. Synergistic relationships come in all shapes and sizes, but the best relationships and partnerships are the ones that benefit everyone. One should focus on creating win/win distribution programs to increase your merchant portfolio.

Monitoring and Managing Channels

In much the same way that the organization's own sales and distribution activities need to be monitored and managed, so do those of the distribution chain. In practice, many organizations use a mix of different channels; in particular, they may complement a direct sales force, calling on the larger accounts, with agents, covering the smaller customers and prospects.

Vertical Marketing

This relatively recent development integrates the channel with the original supplier – producer, wholesalers and retailers working in one unified system. This may arise because one member of the chain owns the other elements (often called 'corporate systems integration'); a supplier owning its own retail outlets, is called 'forward' integration. It is perhaps more likely that a retailer will own its own suppliers, this being 'backward' integration. (For example, MFI, the furniture retailer, owns Hygena which makes its kitchen and bedroom units.) The integration can also be by franchise (such as that offered by McDonald's and Benetton) or simple co-operation (in the way that Marks & Spencer co-operates with its suppliers). Alternative approaches are 'contractual systems', often led by a wholesale or retail co-operative, and 'administered marketing systems' where one (dominant) member of the distribution chain uses its position to co-ordinate the other members' activities. This has traditionally been the form followed by manufacturers. The intention of vertical marketing is to give all those involved (and particularly the supplier at one end, and the retailer at the other) 'control' over the distribution chain. This removes one set of variables from the marketing equations. Other research indicates that vertical integration is a strategy which is best pursued at the mature stage of the market (or product). At earlier stages it can actually reduce profits. It is arguable that it also diverts attention from the real business of the organization. Suppliers rarely excel in retail operations and, in theory, retailers should focus on their sales outlets rather than on manufacturing facilities (Marks & Spencer, for example, very deliberately provides considerable amounts of technical assistance to its suppliers, but does not own them).

Horizontal Marketing

A less frequent example of new approaches to channels is where two or more non-competing organizations agree on a joint venture – a joint marketing operation – because it is beyond the capacity of each individual organization alone. In general, this is less likely to revolve around marketing synergy.

Managing Channel Conflicts

Although a well designed distribution channel has several benefits as mentioned, it is not the ultimate answer for the manufacturers. There are several differences and problems that still exist between manufacturers and distributors due to the various reasons given below.

Dissimilar objectives – If the objective of the manufacturer is to offer good customer service to develop long-term relationships while that of the distributor is to somehow make short-term profits, it gives rise to a conflict between them.

Less interest on certain products by the distributors – If distributors concentrate on a particular manufacturer's products which earn them greater profits or which are fast moving in the market, then it creates a conflict between this manufacturer and the other manufacturers whose products the distributors do not focus on.

Customer dealings – This is another common source of conflict that generally happens when the manufacturer tries to cater to large customers directly and makes the distributors serve small customers, leading to the distributors earning less profits and hampering their business growth.

Dissimilar views – If the manufacturer is of the view that a promotional scheme would increase the business while the distributor feels that it would decrease their margins as it involves extra costs, then conflict arises.

Commission to distributor – If the distributor demands a higher commission while the manufacturer feels that even the existing commission is too high, it leads to conflict.

Territorial Problems

A dispute in the channel network can seriously affect the performance of channel members. It is necessary for the industrial marketers to assess the areas of conflict and take corrective measures. There are different ways in which channel conflict can be controlled.

> When the areas among the distributors are not properly demarcated then it leads to conflict as one tries to enter the other's territory to get business.

Creating an effective communication set-up – There should be effective communication between the manufacturer and other members of the channel network. This can only happen through frequent interaction with the channel members where common issues can be discussed and sorted out.

Setting joint goals – All the channel members should jointly set the goals they wish to achieve through common agreement. The goals can be customer satisfaction, increasing the market share, increasing profits, reducing costs, improving quality of service etc.

Involving mediators – A third party in the form of an arbitrator or mediator can help in solving conflicts that arise between the two parties.

EVALUATING CHANNEL PERFORMANCE

The performance of the channel is said to be effective if the channel members are able to reach the overall objectives smoothly. This calls for periodic evaluation of their performance where various parameters like meeting the sales target, maintaining the required inventory levels, timely delivery to customers, their cooperation and service levels, generation of new customers, etc., are taken into consideration. The aspects where the middlemen do not do well during the evaluation process are analyzed. The reasons are discussed and they are motivated to improve in such areas. Sometimes, manufacturers terminate their services with middlemen if they are unable to meet their expectations or shape up as required.

> An inefficient and untimely delivery can cause customers to terminate their relationship with the manufacturer and go in search of a new supplier.

Logistics

This means that products must be delivered to the customers as and when required by them, at their place of choice, while maintaining the quality. Hence, there should be proper Supply Chain Management (SCM) systems in any channel network, which requires substantial investment of resources in the entire process. An efficient SCM helps the channel network to reduce the average cost per customer, minimize wastage, prevent duplication, cut down on delivery time, and provide better customer service.

The entire network is well connected, with the organizations in the chain being dependent on each other and mutually cooperating to work together. This helps in the systematic flow of products, services and information from the manufacturer to the intermediaries and finally to the customers.

> Supply chain management deals with all the activities in the channel network. It begins with the manufacturer procuring the raw material and ends with the delivery of the goods to the end user.

While logistics management helps to optimize the flow of material within the organization, supply chain management goes beyond the boundaries of the organization extending material flow integration upwards to suppliers and also downwards to customers. Logistics basically represents two primary product movements: (i) Physical supply, concerned with the supply of raw materials, component parts, and other related supplies necessary for the manufacturing process. This comes under the purchase function (materials management). (ii) Physical distribution, concerned with delivering the finished product to customers and the middlemen. This comes under marketing management, also called marketing logistics. Our focus in this chapter is on the physical distribution (marketing logistics), which is a very important part of industrial marketing strategy.

Physical Distribution (Marketing Logistics)

Marketing logistics is the process of delivering the finished goods to the intermediaries as well as customers. An efficient delivery system helps to reduce the costs, improve customer service, and minimize delivery time, which helps to gain customer loyalty. A physical distribution system involves various related tasks (see Table 11.1), that play an important role in the overall performance of the logistics system. A particular logistics activity cannot be performed without evaluating its impact on other areas. For instance, the objective of maximized customer service may develop into a conflict with the objective of minimized distribution cost. Hence, the total cost has to be considered to manage such inconsistencies.

Table 11.1

Tasks	*Key Aspects*
1. Transportation	This is an important activity that involves movement of goods from the manufacturer to the customer.
2. Warehousing	A place where goods are stored till they are made available in the market as and when they are required.

3. Inventory	This ensures that the right mix of products is available at the right place/time in sufficient quantity.
4. Packaging	Protects the products, maximizes use of warehouse space, and maintains product identity.
5. Materials handling	Maximizes speed, minimizes the cost of orders, moving the goods to and from storage, loading and unloading operations.
6. Order processing	Communicates requirements to appropriate locations through inventory management. Starts the physical distribution process.
7. Production planning	Goods are made available for inventory. Planning of warehouse facility utilization, transportation requirements.
8. Customer service	Establishes customer service levels with marketing objectives as well as cost limitations.
9. Plant location	Facilities planning (factory and warehouse location) to ensure maximum capacity and reduce transportation costs.

Total Cost Approach (Trade-off Approach)

The total cost approach focuses on balancing two essential variables:

1. Total distribution costs
2. The level of logistical service provided to customers.

The total cost approach is designed to achieve a combination of cost and service levels that maximize the profits to the company and the channel members. In this approach, the total cost of distribution is considered instead of the individual cost of the elements of physical distribution as the decision made for one logistical variable affects all, or some of the other logistics variables. For example, if inventory is reduced below the required quantity in order to reduce inventory costs, it may result in stockout and an increase in order backlogs. This may necessitate extra production to provide the stockout items and air-freight them at high cost to customers whose production was held up due to non-delivery of products. All this would finally lead to reduction in future orders from the unsatisfied customers due to poor delivery performance. Thus, to save a small individual cost, the total cost substantially increased. The interactions among logistics activities (i.e. transportation, inventory, warehousing) involves a cost trade off as these cost elements are sometimes in economic conflict with one another. Thus, a manager must be willing to trade-off a cost increase in one activity for a larger cost decrease in another activity that will finally result in reduced total logistics costs.

Service cost trade-off – The service aspect is the other half of the total cost approach. It is to be understood that all customers or products do not require the same level of service. Each element of service has different levels of importance that the industrial marketer should recognize. The cost involved in providing the level of service must be evaluated in light of the revenue generated. Once the important elements of customer service are determined by the industrial marketer, he should set goals of customer service levels for each service element, compare the actual levels achieved with the goals and finally take corrective actions to minimize the difference.

Physical Distribution: Impact on Middlemen

In any mode of distribution, the factors impacting the physical distribution on middlemen are given below. While configuring a strategically well placed distribution system, they have to be taken into consideration.

- **Advising** – This involves a very important function of advising the right course of action to channel members in order to reap the best gains.
- **Technical** – A specialized service that is often termed as value-added service. This is necessary for products that are technical in nature and which channel members are not fully competent to confidently handle.
- **Ease of ordering** – Sales persons have to ensure that while the product is always available on the shelf, there is no unnecessary blocking of stocks at the channel points.
- **Excellence awards** – It is the duty of the sales force to see that the channel members are always motivated. To ensure this, the channel members must be given due recognition for any extra effort that they put in to increase sales.
- **Maintaining inventory** – Salespersons must always ensure that their products are always available at all points of the distribution channel and that at the same time there should also be some material in the pipeline so that there is a continuous flow of material.
- **Speedy and accurate delivery of goods** – This is one of the most important sales functions, as it has a tremendous impact on the motivation of the dealers to sell a company's products. Dealers never want a customer to go back empty handed and if a particular product is unavailable, he will definitely try to sell a competitor's products.
- **Warranty** – This is one of the very important aspects that customers look for; salespersons must ensure that the warranty terms are well executed in practice or they will lose their significance.
- **Annual maintenance** – In the case of technical products like photocopying machines and computers, there is a need for an annual maintenance contract. While this should instil confidence in the minds of channel members and customers, it is also an effective source of profitability for the company.
- **Installations/Repairs** – These are important services that salespersons should follow up with the channel members as they fulfil the implicit needs of the customers.
- **Training** – Training is necessary for all products and services as it helps dealers to explain the product and service attributes clearly and instils confidence in the minds of customers.

If followed meticulously, the above factors will have a noticeable impact on the level of enthusiasm and motivation of the channel members. So while formulating a distribution system, salespersons must consider the above points to gain an advantage in the market.

KEY CONCEPTS

- Distribution is one of the four aspects of marketing, the other three aspects being product management, pricing, and promotion. A distributor, wholesaler, dealer and retailer are all part of the distribution channel. They ensure a steady flow of products from the manufacturer to the customers.
- It takes years to create a marketing channel, develop distributors, wholesalers, dealers and retailers and requires constant effort to monitor them all the time so that they achieve the sales targets of the company.
- Distribution channels are independent avenues that facilitate the sale of your products and services. In other words, they consist of individuals and firms involved in the process of making a product or service available for use or consumption by consumers or industrial users.
- Distribution channels are not restricted to physical products alone. They are just as important for moving a service from the producer to consumer in certain sectors, since both direct and indirect channels may be used.
- Members of a distribution channel are the company's face in the market and the customers' spokesperson to the company. As it is not possible for the company to reach the end consumers, middlemen perform this task and ensure the smooth flow of goods and services
- Members of the distribution channel perform a number of functions for the company that include providing vital market information, communicating product attributes to customers, storage of goods, assessing the exact need of customers and matching products and services to their needs.
- The major tasks performed by distribution channels include ensuring timely availability of products to the customers, promoting the company and its products and ensuring a positive experience in customers' minds.
- The distribution channel must be designed on the basis of its reach, efficacy, vulnerability, adaptability and strength
- Channel coordination issues encompass resolution of pending matters like non-settlement of financial claims, replacement of defective products and timely information about the status of orders, deliveries etc.
- Salespersons must ensure periodic evaluation of channel performance vis-a-vis parameters like sales targets, inventory levels, on time delivery to customers, their cooperation and service levels, generation of new customers

Case Study

THE PRESSURE OF SALES

21st Century Electronics was a consumer electronic company. The company dealt in a wide range of products like television sets, DVD players, tape recorders through an extensive network of dealers all over India. The sales people called on dealers and other small retailers who dealt with the company's products. Since there was cut-throat competition in the industry, the dealers operated on high volumes and very low margins. To maintain their profitability, they depended, to a large extent, on the credit terms offered by different manufacturers. At times by design and on other occasions by default, many of the dealers in this trade resorted to delaying the payments much beyond the prescribed limit on different pretexts – defective quality, poor service, non-settlement of claims etc. placing the producers in a lot of difficulty. As the sales force of most of these companies were always under tremendous pressure to meet their sales targets, they often underplayed the collection of outstanding payments and pushed more and more material to the dealers, often without orders. 21st Century Electronics also faced similar problems.

To take care of such a major problem, a commercial department was set up in the company to monitor and control the credit part of the company's sales operations. As the pressure on sales and the company's thrust on selling were both very high, the sales people of the company were not specifically asked about delays in giving reports, delayed payments and recovery of the same. This was done by the credit manager who had been following a procedure that did not call for participation of the company's sales force.

As the credit sales was increasing alarmingly, the credit manager proposed an innovation – the sales people should also submit a credit report when sending in orders from customers. The credit manager, Mr. Ramaswamy felt very strongly that the sales people should represent the entire company, not just the sales department, and that they should be concerned with the net profit and not just the sales volume. Mr. Ramaswamy was of the opinion that new orders could be approved or disapproved more quickly if accompanied by a credit report submitted by the salesperson. Moreover, he hated to see a salesperson spend time working on a prospective customer who would later be denied supply because of his non-payments of old bills. Accordingly the company fixed credit limits for each of their dealers and sales executives had to meet their sales target without crossing the credit limits of their existing dealers.

The sales manager, Mr. Shetty knew very well that the new dictum would cause problems for his sales team. The company had a moderate chain of 83 dealers in a market of over 450 dealers in the entire territory where company was operating. Competition was tough, product supply exceeded demand and in order to push their products, dealers were resorting to undercutting. As such, payments were delayed. He wondered how a new strategy could be formulated that would create more avenues for sales. He organized a workshop for his entire sales team to resolve the matter and find alternative options.

Question

1. As part of the sales team, what would you suggest to Mr. Ramaswamy?

REFERENCES

1. Anderson, James C., Narus, James A., van Rossum, Wouter (2006), Customer Value Propositions in Business Markets, *Harvard Business Review*, Vol. 84 Issue 3, pp. 90-99.
2. Arora, Ashok Pratap, Kapil, Kanwal, Sundarajan, M. (2010), Case Diagnoses: Distributor Sales Force Performance Management, *Vision*, Vol. 14 Issue 4, pp. 323-326.
3. Beukenkamp, Pieter (1975), Consumerism and Distribution: A Management View, *European Journal of Marketing*, Vol. 9 Issue 3, p. 224.
4. Bloomsbury Business Library (2007), Distribution Management, *Business & Management Dictionary*, p. 2480.
5. Chipalkatti, Niranjan (Chips), Chatterji, Sanjoy, Bee, Sarah (2007), Effective Controls for Sales Through Distribution Channels, *CPA Journal*, Vol. 77 Issue 9, pp. 60-66.
6. Gatignon, Hubert, Anderson, Erin, Lajos, Joseph (2007), New Product Distribution and Inter-Channel Competition: Market-Making, Market-Taking, and Competitive Effects in Several European Countries, *INSEAD Working Papers Collection*, Issue 64, pp. 1-31.
7. Hsu, Hubert, Jap, Waldemar, Liao, Carol, Lui, Vincent (2010), Build a Winning Sales and Distribution System, *China Business Review*, Vol. 37 Issue 4, pp. 16-19.
8. Jones, Ross E. (1961), Three Keys to Distribution Management, *Transportation Journal*, Vol. 1 Issue 2, pp. 9-13.
9. Kotler, Philip (1967), Operations Research in Marketing, *Harvard Business Review*, Vol. 45 Issue 1, pp. 30-188.
10. Michael, David C. (2007), The Sales and Distribution Revolution, *China Business Review*, Vol. 34 Issue 5, pp. 20-23.
11. Purohit, Devavrat, Staelin, Richard (1994), Rentals, Sales, and Buybacks: Managing Secondary Distribution Channels, *Journal of Marketing Research (JMR)*, Vol. 31 Issue 3, pp. 325-338.
12. Steinert-Threlkeld, Tom (2006), Nestlé Pieces it Together, *Baseline*, Issue 54, pp. 36-52.
13. Stewart, Wendell M. (1965), Physical Distribution: Key to Improved Volume and Profits, *Journal of Marketing*, Vol. 29 Issue 1, pp. 65-70.
14. Young, Ian (2011), Distribution: A Steady Upturn, *Chemical Week*, Vol. 173 Issue 14, pp. 21-25.

Glossary of Sales and Selling Terms

The glossary of sales and selling terms is given to provide readers with a quick understanding of the meaning of the basic terms in the field of selling. This list, however, is not exhaustive, and is not meant to be an endorsement of any of these techniques or terms.

Account/Client	Another name for a customer; generally used in advertising companies.
Account/Client	A customer, usually a business-to-business organization; a major account is a large organization; a national account is a customer with branches or sites that constitute a nationwide coverage, which typically requires special pricing and senior sales attention.
Advertising	A non-personal communication of information usually paid for and usually persuasive in nature, about products (goods and services) or ideas an identified sponsor through various media.
Appointment	A personal sales visit to a prospect, usually arranged through the telephone or email.
Business markets	Specialized markets where business goods and services are sold, often to well-informed professional buyers who are skilled in evaluating competitive offerings.
Buyer	A person who purchases goods or services for his own or someone else's consumption.
C&F	C&F stands for carrying and forwarding agency. Many manufacturing or marketing companies, instead of having their own godowns, keep their goods in the warehouse of a third party and distribute them through these parties when the dealers or wholesalers or customers require them. The activities involved in further dispatch like invoicing, loading, unloading maintaining records etc. is done by the C&F agent, on behalf of the manufacturer/marketer against a certain commission.
Challenge	A difficult proposition that is to be surmounted successfully.
Channel membership	The term refers to the number of intermediaries that a channel has to effectively discharge the function of seeing that the products reach the end customers.
Competitive analysis	It involves an in-depth examination and study of the market competition and helps to review the competitor's strengths and weaknesses in the market and to choose and implement effective sales strategies for enhancing your competitive advantage.
Consumer	A person or group who buys products or services for personal use and not for manufacture or resale.
Consumer 'black box'	The customers/consumers/prospects' mind.
Consumer behaviour	It is the study of when, why, how, and where people do or do not buy a product. It attempts to understand the buyer's decision making process, both individually and in groups.

Consumer markets	Mass markets where typically goods and services of mass consumption such as soft drinks, cosmetics, air travel, and athletic shoes and equipment are sold.
Customer	Someone who buys goods or services, or purchases goods or services from a buyer. A customer may or may not consume the product or service that he buys. Prior to the sale he is usually referred to as a prospect. A customer can be an individual or group of people.
Customerrelationship management (CRM)	CRM is a commonly used term to describe the process of managing the entire selling process within a department or organization.
Customer satisfaction	Whenever the gain from the purchase of goods or services exceeds the cost of procuring it, the customer is satisfied, otherwise he is not.
Customer service	A series of activities designed to enhance the level of customer satisfaction – that is, the feeling that a product or service has met the customer's expectation.
Customer value	Value is a bundle of benefits that a customer expects to maximize and consists of all elements that a product consists of i.e. its core, formal and augmented elements – all at a minimum possible delivery price.
Customer Value Added (CVA)	The CVA approach is based on providing products and services to customers that have a greater value than purchases from competitive companies in similar markets.
Customer value chain	A chain of activities in the total marketing process to add value to the final product/service that reaches the customer.
Customer value management	A strategy to attract and retain customers by building on the value they assign to goods and services.
Deal	Common business parlance for the sale or purchase (agreement or arrangement). It is rather a colloquial term so one should avoid using it in serious company as it can sound flippant and unprofessional.
Decision-maker	A person in the prospect organization who has the power and budgetary authority to agree to a sales proposal.
Deliverable(s)	An aspect of a proposal that the provider commits to do or supply, usually and preferably clearly measurable.
Demographics	The study of, or information about, people's lifestyles, habits, population movements, spending, age, social grade, employment, etc., in terms of the consuming and buying public; anyone selling to the consumer sector will do better through understanding relevant demographic information.
Demonstration	The physical presentation by the salesperson to the prospect of how a product works. Generally done with no charge to the prospect, and normally conducted at the prospect's premises, but can be at another suitable venue, e.g. an exhibition, or at the supplier's premises.
Direct channel	When a producer and ultimate consumer deal directly with each other. This may include selling directly, or through mail order, the Internet and telephone sales.
Distribution	The channel of intermediaries through which products and services are taken to the market for sales.
Distribution	One of the four significant arms of marketing, the other three parts of the marketing mix being product management, pricing, and promotion.
Distribution channels	These are independent avenues that facilitate the sale of your products and services. In other words, they consist of individuals and firms involved in the process of making a product or service available for use or consumption by consumers or industrial users.

Empathy	Looking an event from the other person's viewpoint; understanding how another person feels, and typically reflecting this back to the other person. The ability to feel and show empathy is central to modern selling methods.
Esteem needs	This includes a need to be respected, to have self-esteem, self-respect, and to respect others.
Exclusive distribution	Where only specially selected resellers or authorized dealers (typically only one per geographical area) are allowed to sell the 'product'.
Feature	An aspect of a product or service, e.g. colour, speed, size, weight, type of technology, buttons and knobs, gizmos and gadgets, technical support, delivery, etc.
Function	In the context of an organization, this means the job role or discipline, e.g. sales, marketing, production, accounting, customer service, delivery, installation, technical service, general management, etc.
Gestation period	It typically refers to the time from enquiry to sale. It is also called the sales cycle. Awareness and monitoring of sale gestation period/sales cycle times are crucial in sales planning, forecasting and management, for individuals, sales teams and sales organizations.
Indirect channel	When intermediaries are inserted between the producer and consumers and perform numerous channel functions.
Intangible	It is that aspect of the product or service offering that has a value but is difficult to see or quantify (for instance, peace-of-mind, reliability, consistency).
Intensive distribution	Where the majority of resellers stock the 'product' (such as convenience products, for example, and particularly the brand leaders in consumer goods markets). In such a situation there is a great possibility of a price competition.
Introductory letter	A letter from the head of the selling organization (branch manager, area sales manager etc.) introducing the company and products to the prospective buyer. This is especially useful for selling to large organizations.
Lead-time	The time between order and delivery, installation or commencement of a product or service.
Margin/Profit margin	The difference between cost (including or excluding operating overheads) and selling price of a product or service. Percentage margin is generally deemed to be the difference between the cost and selling price, divided by the selling price ex tax (e.g. something that costs Rs. 100 and is sold for Rs. 200 plus tax produces a 50% margin - gross margin that is - net margin is after over heads are deducted).
Market segment	A homogenous subset of the market having customers/prospects with similar needs.
Market segmentation	This is breaking down larger markets into smaller ones requiring different marketing mixes. It is a significant vehicle available to you in attempting to limit and control the competition.
Marketing	It is a set of all the activities involved in identification of customer needs and fulfilling them profitably.
Mark-up	This is the amount of money that a selling company adds to the cost of a product or service in order to produce a required level of profit. Strictly speaking, percentage mark-up refers to the difference between cost and selling price as a factor of the cost, not of the selling price. So a product costing Re.1 and selling for Rs.2 has been given a mark-up of 100%; (at the same time it produces a margin of 50%).

Maslow's Hierarchy of Needs	Abraham Maslow proposed this theory in his paper *A Theory of Human Motivation* in 1943. It is depicted as a pyramid consisting of five levels: physiological needs, safety needs, social needs, esteem needs and self actualization. This theory states that the deficiency needs must be met first and once these are met, seeking to satisfy growth needs drives personal growth. In other words, the higher needs in this hierarchy only come into focus when the lower needs in the pyramid are satisfied.
Negotiation	The trading of concessions including price reductions, between supplier and customer, in an attempt to shape a supply contract (sale in other words) so that it is acceptable to both supplier and customer.
Objection	A point of resistance raised by a prospect, usually price but it can be anything at any stage of the selling process.
Open/Opening	The first stage of the actual sales call. Also called the introduction.
Persuasion	It is the act of influencing of beliefs, attitudes, intentions, motivations, or behaviours.
Physiological needs	Basic human needs for such things as food, warmth, water, and other body needs. These are the primary needs of human beings and precede any other kind of need.
Positioning	Positioning refers to how a product/service/proposition is presented or described or marketed in relation to the market place - with reference to customers, competition, image, pricing, quality, etc. Positioning basically refers to whether a proposition is being sold appropriately - in the right way, to the right people, at the right time, in the right place, and at the right price.
Preparation	In the context of the selling process this is the work done by the salesperson to research and plan the sales approach and/or sales call to a particular prospect or customer.
Presentation	The art of presenting yourself and your knowledge in simple language and words, easily understood by the recipient.
Presentation/Sales presentation	The process by which a salesperson explains the product or service to the prospect (to a single contact or a group), ideally including the product's features, advantages and benefits, especially those which are relevant to the prospect. Presentations can be only verbal, but more usually involve the use of visuals, commonly bullet-point text slides and images on a computer display or projected onto a screen. It can incorporate a video and/or physical demonstration of product(s) too.
Price	In normal terms, price is the amount of payment or compensation given by one party to another in return for goods or services.
Product	Anything that is capable of satisfying a want or a need. It can be a physical entity, a place, a person and event etc.
Publicity	A non-personal stimulation of demand for a product or service or business unit by planting commercially significant news about it in a published medium or obtaining a favorable presentation of it on television, radio, Internet or stage that is not paid for by the sponsor.
Retail	The sale of goods or merchandise from a fixed location in small quantities for direct consumption by the purchaser.
Retailer	A person or entity engaged in retail sales is called a retailer.
Retention/Customer retention	This simply means keeping customers and not losing them to competitors. Modern companies realize that it is far more expensive to find new customers than keep existing ones, and so put sufficient investment into looking after and growing existing accounts. Less sensible companies find themselves spending a fortune winning new customers, while they lose more business than they gain because of poor retention activity.

Safety needs	These include the need for protection of any kind of physical, psychological, economic or social insecurity.
Sales	The transaction between the buyer and the seller wherein the seller transfers the title of goods or services to the buyer in return for money or some other benefit.
Sales call	A personal face-to-face visit or telephone call by a salesperson to a prospect or customer. Usually, it is made without any prior intimation.
Sales cycle	It generally describes the time and/or process between the first contact with the customer to when the sale is made. It varies enormously depending on the company, type of business, the effectiveness of the sales process, the market and the particular situation applying to the customer at the time of the enquiry.
Sales forecast	A prediction of the quantum of sales that will be achieved over a given period, which could be anything from a week to a year.
Sales funnel	It describes the pattern, plan or actual achievement of conversion of prospects into sales, pre-enquiry and then through the sales cycle. So-called because it includes the conversion ratio at each stage of the sales cycle, which has a funneling effect. Prospects are said to be fed into the top of the funnel, and converted sales drop out at the bottom. The sales funnel is a very powerful sales planning and sales management tool.
Sales pipeline	A linear equivalent of the sales funnel principle. Prospects need to be fed into the pipeline in order to drop out of the other end as sales. The length of the pipeline is the sales cycle time, which depends on business type, market situation, and the effectiveness of the sales process.
Sales planning	It is the process of preparing for effective sales and service interactions with members. It requires thinking about activities and interactions in a systematic way, and it helps bridge the gap between current staff ability and desired staff ability.
Sales promotion	It is any initiative undertaken by an organization to promote an increase in sales, usage or trail of a product or service. Examples include contests, coupons, freebies, loss leaders, point of purchase displays, premiums, prizes, product samples, and rebates.
Sales proposal	Usually a written offer, with specifications, prices, outline terms and conditions, and warranty arrangements, from a sales person or selling organization to a prospect.
Sales report	A business report of sales results, activities, trends, etc. traditionally completed by a sales manager, but increasingly now the responsibility of sales people too. A sales report can be required weekly, monthly, quarterly and annually, and often includes the need to provide sales forecasts.
Sales target	The quantum of products/services that management sets for sales to be achieved within a specific time frame.
Sales territory	The geographical area wherein the sales professional operates to achieve his sales and other related targets.
Salesmanship	It is that unique quality of a salesperson that enables him to accomplish pre-conceived sales objectives. It is a fine blend of attributes that are essential for anyone to succeed in selling.
Selective distribution	This is a carefully decided pattern of setting up a distribution network (in both consumer and industrial markets) where selection of 'suitable' resellers is more judicious and their stocking of the product does not lead to price competition.

Self management	It is a unique ability to handle emotions, feelings, sentiments, thoughts and attitude with the single purpose of winning in the market.
Self-actualization	In Maslow's scheme, the final stage of psychological development comes when an individual either feels assured that his physiological, security, affiliation and affection, self-respect, and recognition needs have been satisfied or goes beyond these materialistic needs and seeks to realize all of his potential for being an effective, creative, mature human being.
Seller	Anyone who sells any product or service is a seller.
Selling	The art of accomplishing the transaction of exchange profitably.
Selling process	It is a set of activities undertaken to successfully obtain an order, supply it as per the requirement of the customers and begin building long-term customer relations.
Service	A type of economic activity that is intangible; is not stored and does not result in ownership. A service is consumed at the point of sale.
Service contract	A formal document usually drawn up by the supplier by which the trading arrangement is agreed with the customer. Also known as trading agreements, supply agreements, and other variations.
Signposting	It is a method by which you try to make a conscious effort to keep the attention of your audience with you all through the presentation.
Social needs	This involves emotionally-based relationships in general, such as friendship, intimacy and having a supportive and communicative family.
Stockist/Distributor	These terminologies are at times synonymous and at other times represent a hierarchy in the distribution channel. A stockist stocks the goods of the company and channelizes them further down the line to distributors/wholesalers and retailers to the customers. Distributors generally operate like stockists but at a lower scale. In many companies stockist and distributor are the same. Generally, these levels of distribution are kept in companies which have mass market products.
SWOT analysis	It is a general technique, which can be applied across diverse functions and activities, but it is particularly appropriate to the early stages of planning for sales. SWOT is the acronym for Strengths, Weaknesses, Opportunities and Threats. It is a simple, much-used technique, which can help to prepare or amend plans in problem solving and decision-making. SWOT analysis involves the generation and recording of the strengths, weaknesses, opportunities, and threats in relation to a particular task or objective.
Tangible	This is an aspect of the product or service offering that can readily be seen and measured in terms of cost and value (e.g. any physical feature of the product; spare parts; delivery or installation; a regular service visit; a warranty agreement).
Targeting	Focusing on a specific sub-group of a larger market as the focal point for a marketing or advertising campaign.
Telemarketing	Any pre-sales activity conducted by telephone, usually by specially trained telemarketing personnel - for instance, research, making an appointment, product promotion.
Tender	A very structured formal proposal in response to the issue of an invitation to tender for the supply of a product or service to a large organization or government department. Tenders require certain qualifying criteria to be met first by the tendering organization, which in itself can take several weeks or months by lots of different staff. Tenders must adhere to strict submission deadlines, contract terms, specifications and even the presentation of the tender itself, and usually only suppliers experienced in winning and fulfilling this type of highly controlled supply ever win the business.

Territory	The geographical area of responsibility of a salesperson or a team or a sales organization.
Territory planning	The process of planning optimum and most cost-effective coverage (particularly for making appointments or personal calling) of a sales territory by the available sales resources, given prospect numbers, density, buying patterns, etc. even one territory by one sales person; for one person this used to be called journey planning, and was often based on a four or six day cycle, so as to avoid always missing prospects who might never be available on one particular day of the week.
Unique selling proposition (USP)	USP, invented by Rosser Reeves of Ted Bates & Company is a marketing concept that was first proposed as a theory to understand a pattern among successful advertising campaigns of the early 1940s. Today the term is used in other fields or just casually to refer to any aspect of an object that differentiates it from similar objects.
Wholesale	Sale of goods or merchandise to retailers, industrial, commercial, institutional, or other professional business users, or wholesalers and related subordinated services. In general, it is the sale of goods to anyone other than a standard consumer.
Wholesaler	An entity in the distribution channel that buys a company's goods in bulk from and re-sells it to retailers. A wholesaler may buy directly from the company or from the stockists/ distributors.

Index